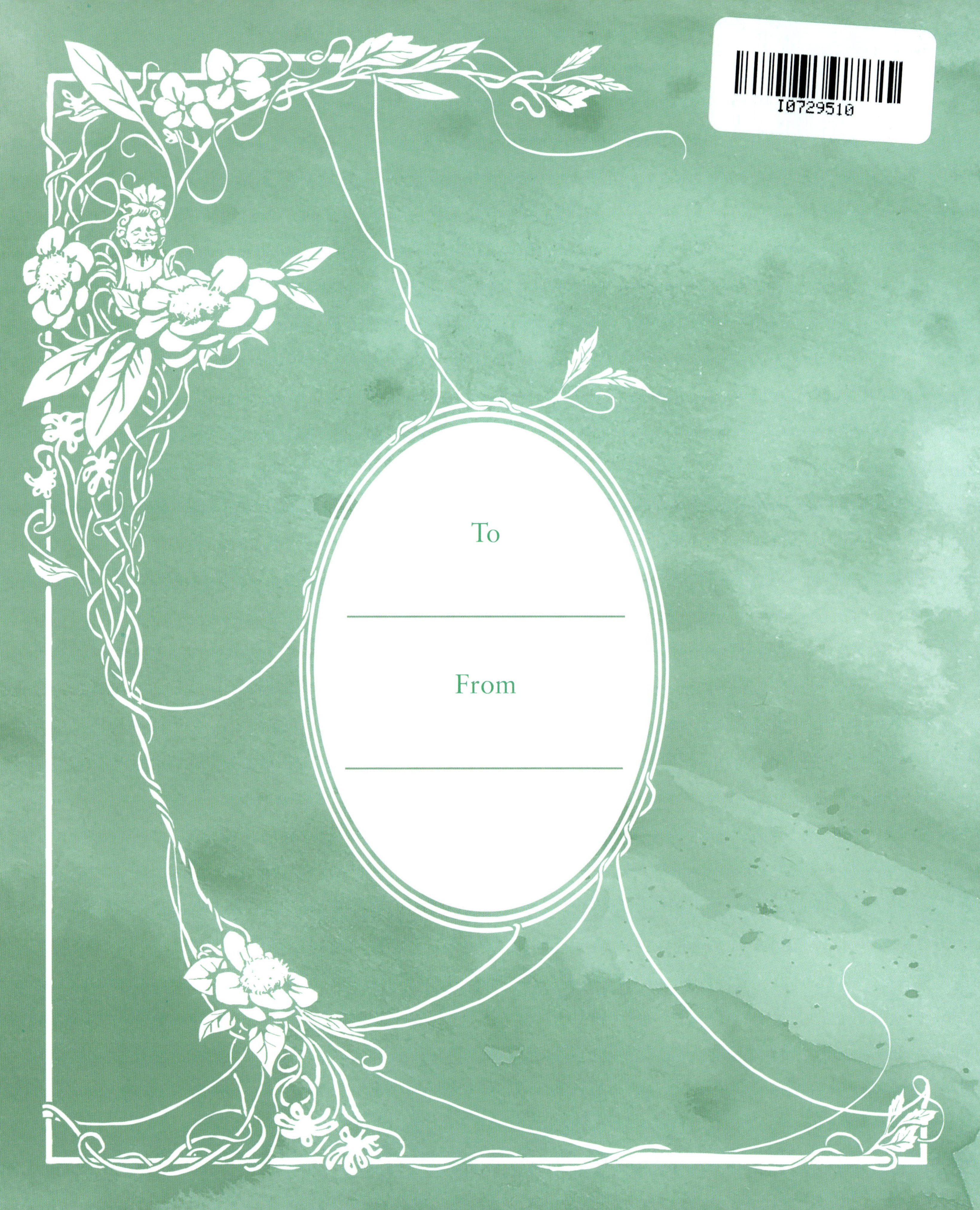

To
From

"Where do you get your inspiration from?"

This is the question I get the most about my books and artwork. I have an unconventional approach to writing. The stories in my own books all start with a piece of art I've made. Some illustrations pique my curiosity and I want to find out what happened to this person, how they ended up here.

As an example, I once made a painting of a bald man with a hen brooding on his head. After a lot of twists and turns it ended up as the children's picture book *Odd is an Egg* about a timid boy with an egg for a head. I rarely have a clear plan when creating, I just go with the flow and see if it takes me somewhere fun and interesting.

So, where do I get the inspiration for my artwork? That's harder to answer. I have a vivid imagination and my brain works visually, even when I'm doing other things than drawing or painting. Sometimes, ideas and pictures come to me almost unconsciously. When I'm in a good bubble, I just let my hand do the work without thinking. Well, that's if I'm lucky. Most times it takes more hard work than that. And a lot of trying and failing.

My imagination and ideas are deeply rooted in my childhood. As a child, my mother read aloud to me and my sister for hours on end and I was constantly drawing while listening to her making the universes of Tolkien, Roald Dahl, and Astrid Lindgren come alive. In fact, that's kind of what I still do most days. Sitting in my studio, drawing and listening to audiobooks.

I've always preferred drawing people and faces. Inanimate objects and landscapes haven't really interested me that much. Since a young age, I've been fascinated by and had loads of fun depicting quirky, imperfect characters. I draw inspiration from people I see on the bus or street—an interesting nose or a beautiful weathered old face. I find these imperfections interesting and beautiful. Perfection is boring in my opinion. I liked playing around with different facial expressions as a child. Small changes to eyebrows and the mouth can completely change a face! Also, I liked drawing scenes and characters from the stories my mother read to me.

When it comes to my technique, how I create art, that's also the result of not having a clear plan (and to a degree, not having any money). I use a lot of techniques now, and I almost always do the finishing touches with a digital pen on my computer and drawing board. But as a student, I developed my own technique out of necessity because I didn't have enough money for prepared canvases and proper equipment. So for a long time I made my pictures on unprepared cotton canvas and used a pen quill and ink, gouache paint, acrylic, worked with brushes and my fingers, still using the color box I got from my parents as a child. Just experimenting and using what I had on hand. That resulted in a distinct expression, and people to this day say they can see right away that a picture is by me.

There are pictures in this book you're holding that I created with ink-stained fingers in my sister's laundry room years ago. And there are others more recent, made in my studio on my computer and drawing board. I've had fun making them. I hope you like the book.

Lisa Aisato

LISA AISATO

ALL THE COLORS OF LIFE

Translated by Olivia Lasky

This translation has been published with the financial support of NORLA,
Norwegian Literature Abroad.

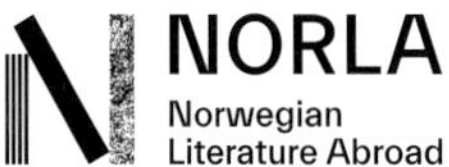

W1-Media, Inc.
Arctis Books USA
Stamford, CT, USA

Visit our website at www.arctis-books.com
Author website at www.aisato.no

2 3 4 5 6 7 8 9 10

Library of Congress Control Number: 2021940238

ISBN 978-1-64690-053-4

Printed in Latvia by Livonia Print, Riga, 2026.

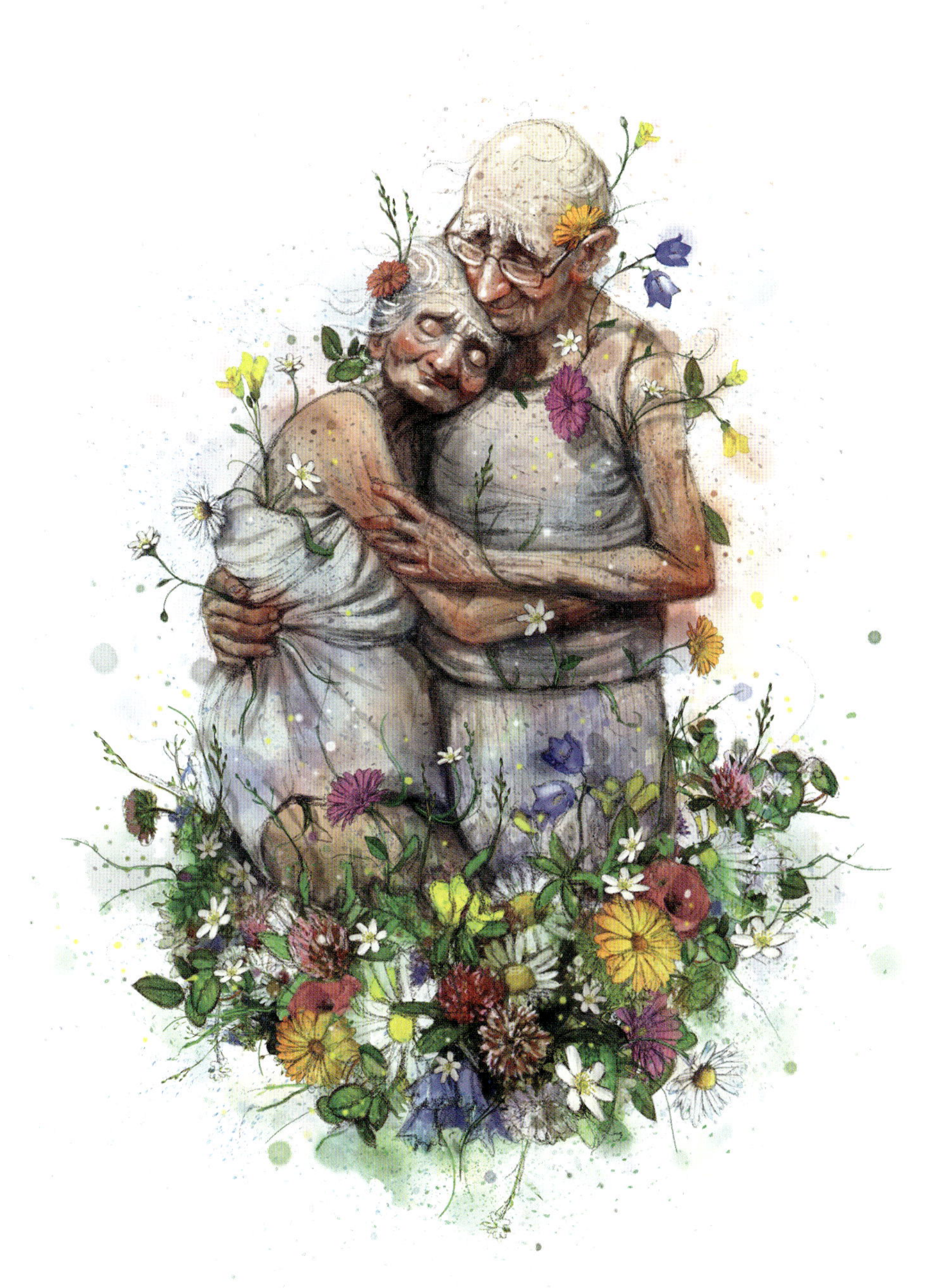

A Child's Life

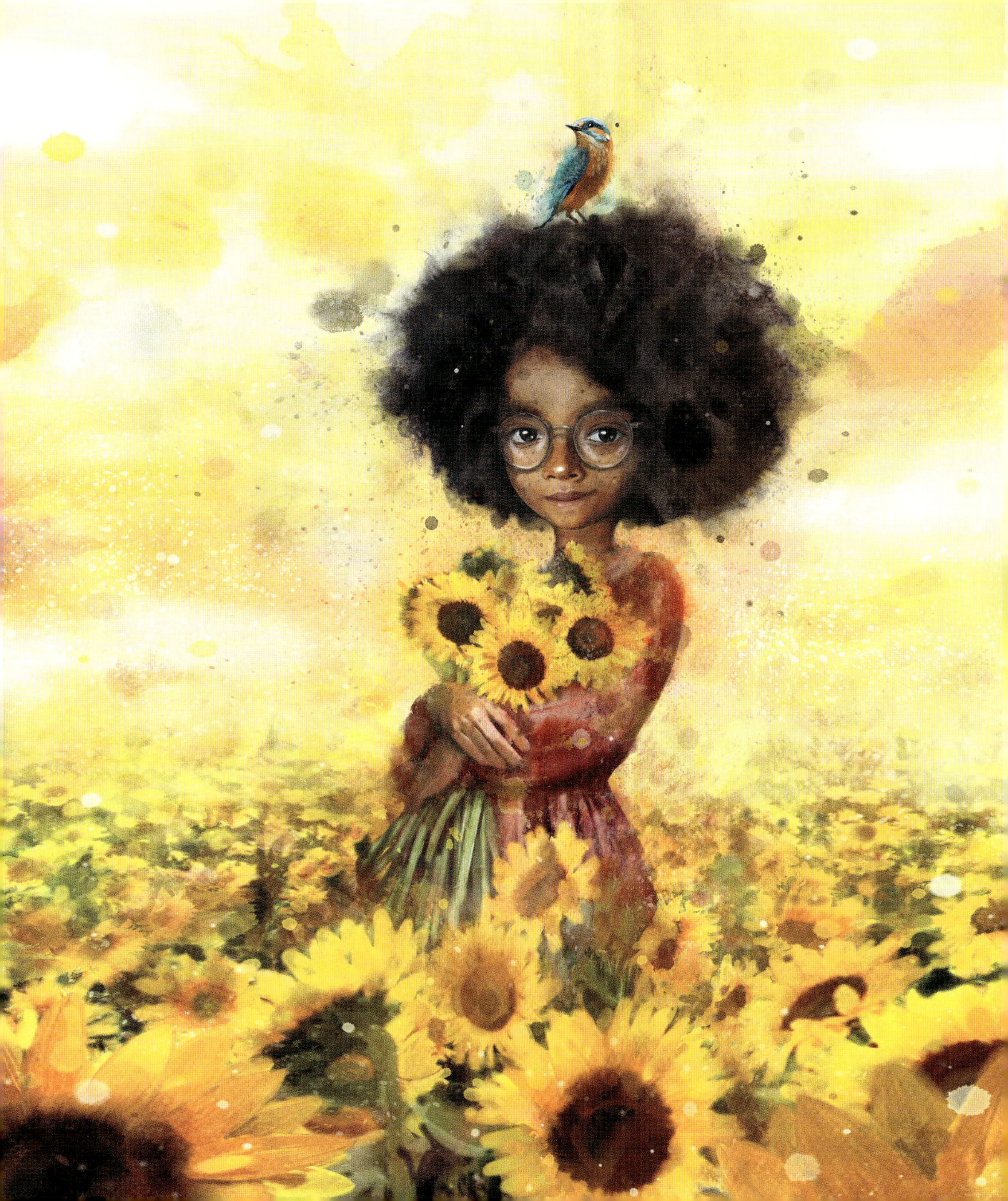

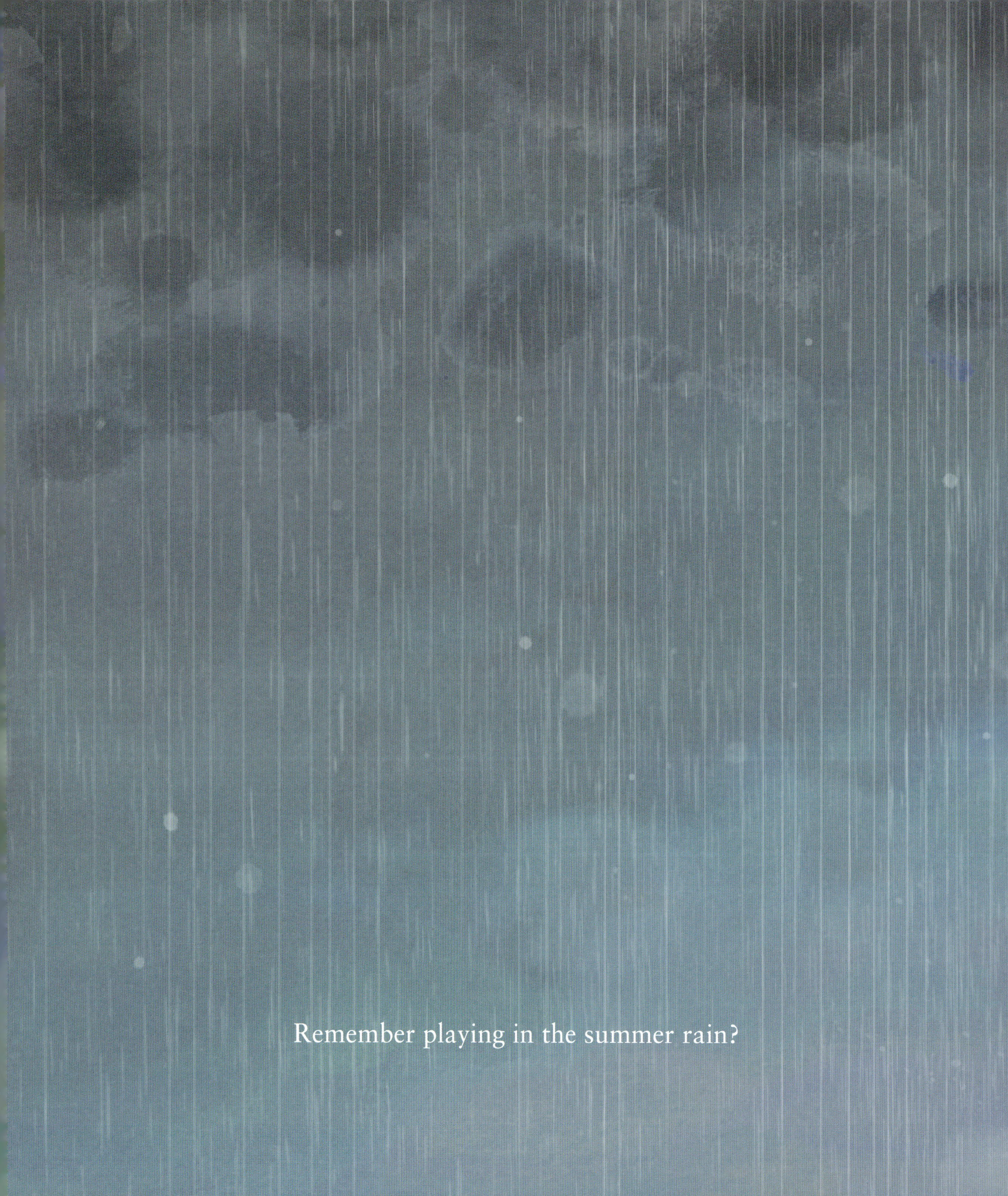

Remember playing in the summer rain?

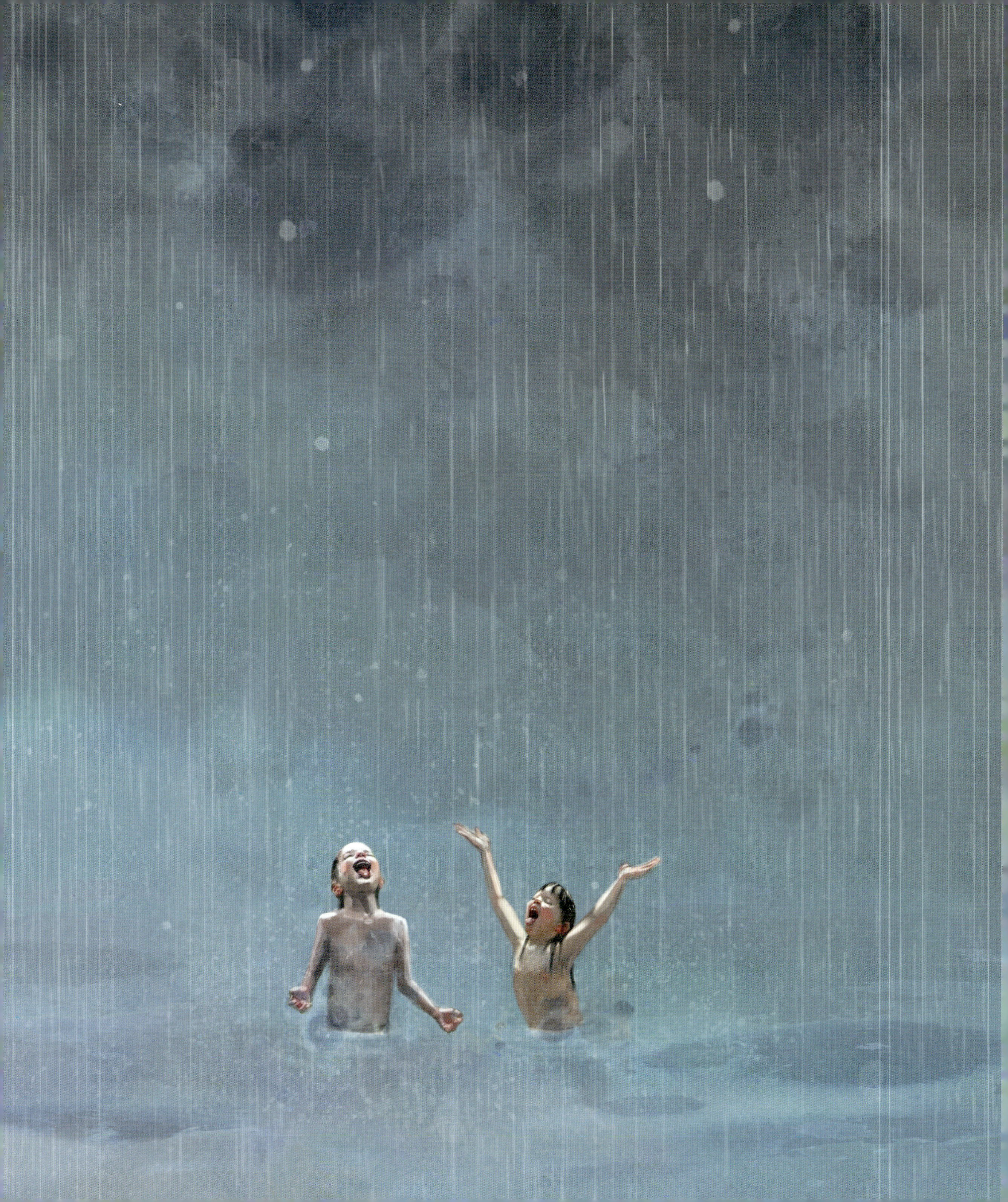

Remember bright summer evenings
and the scent of dandelions on your fingertips?

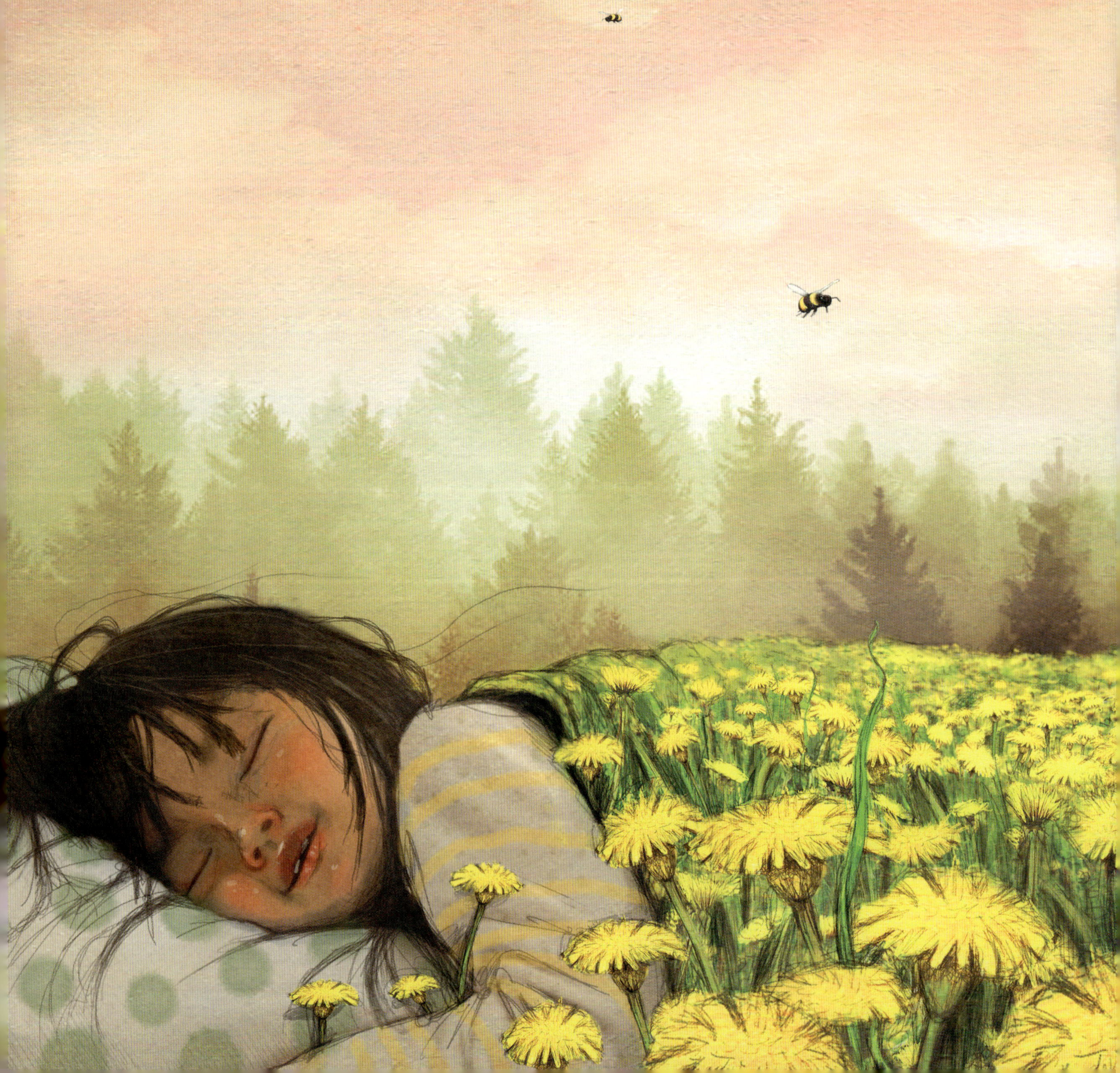

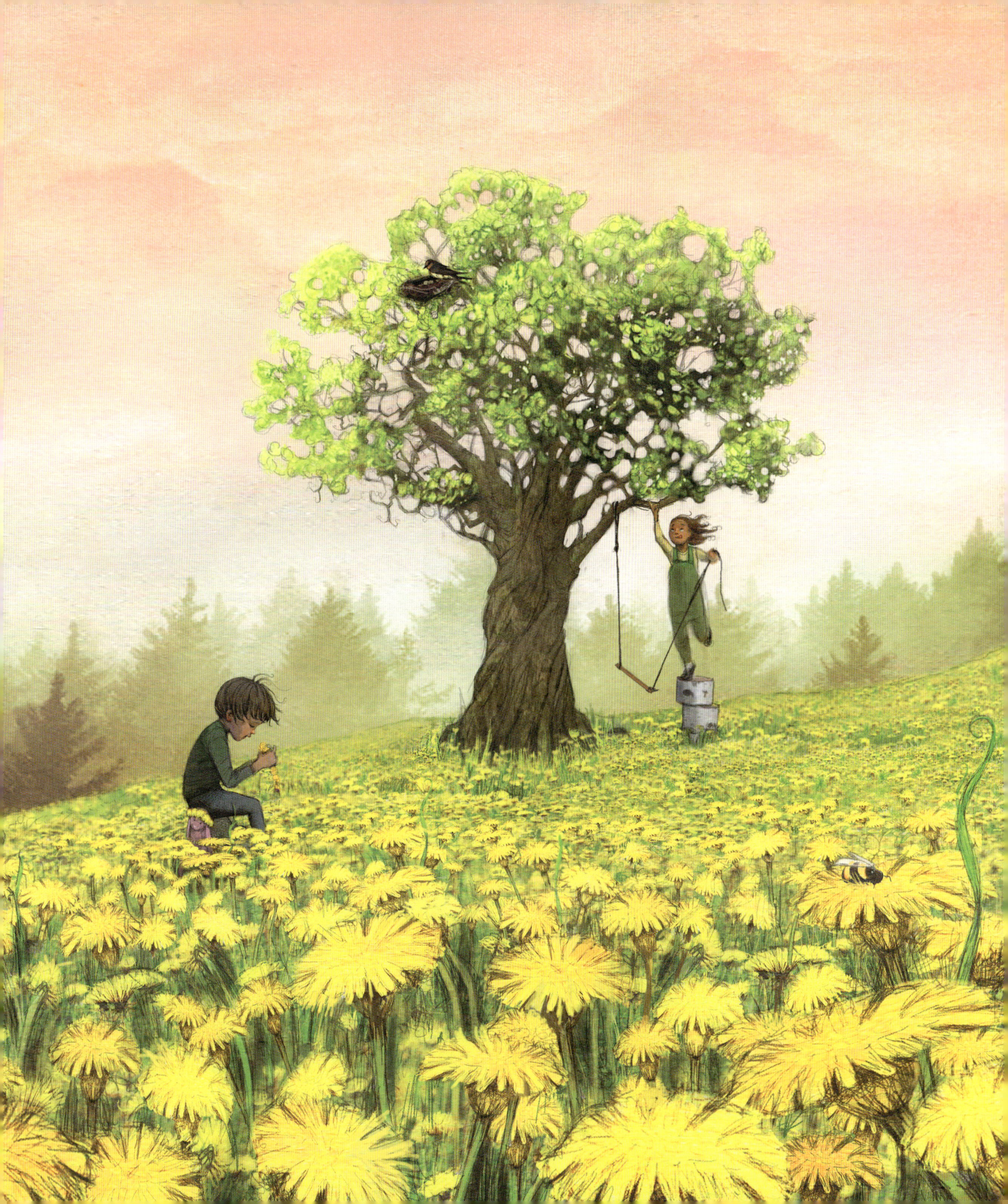

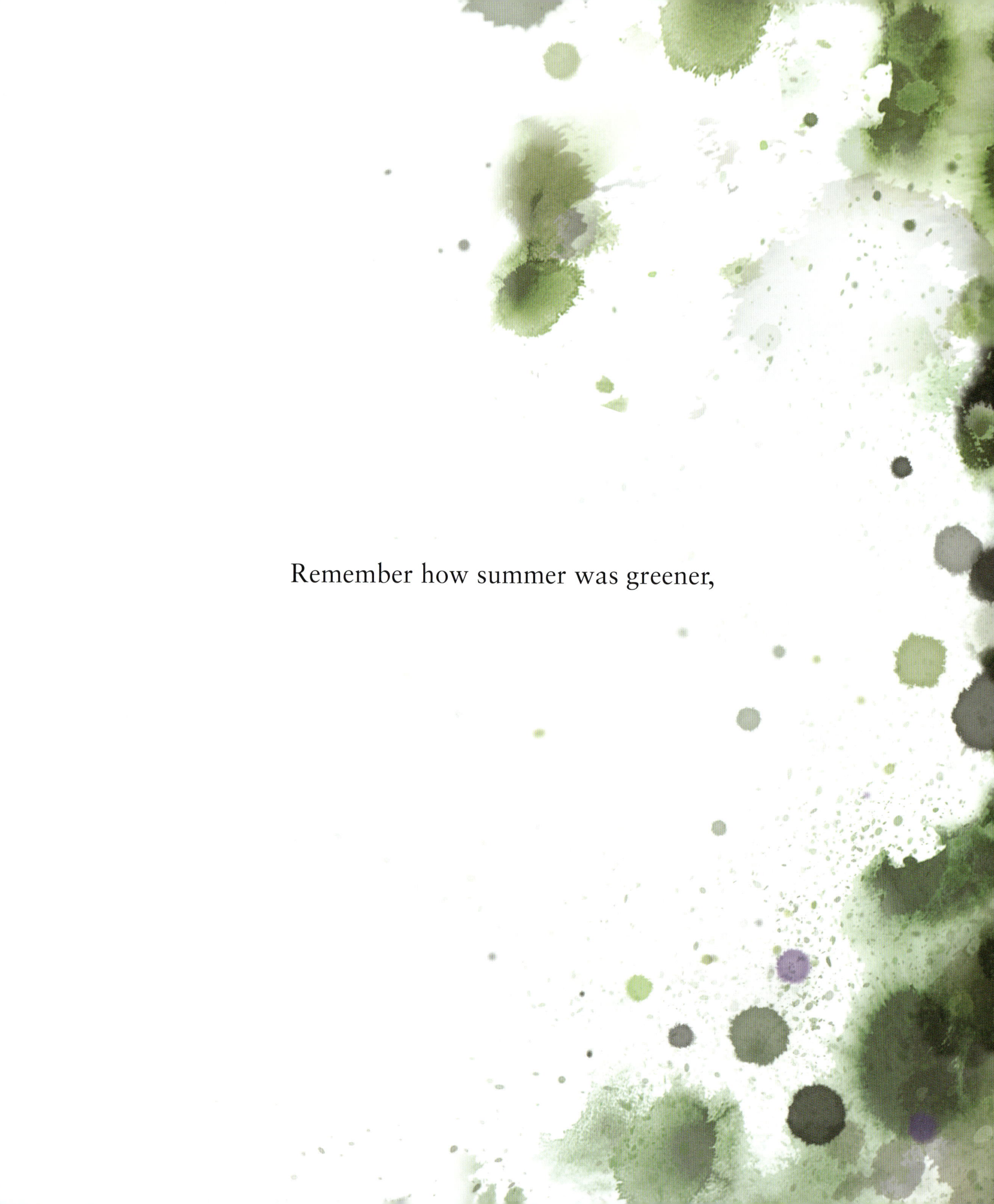

Remember how summer was greener,

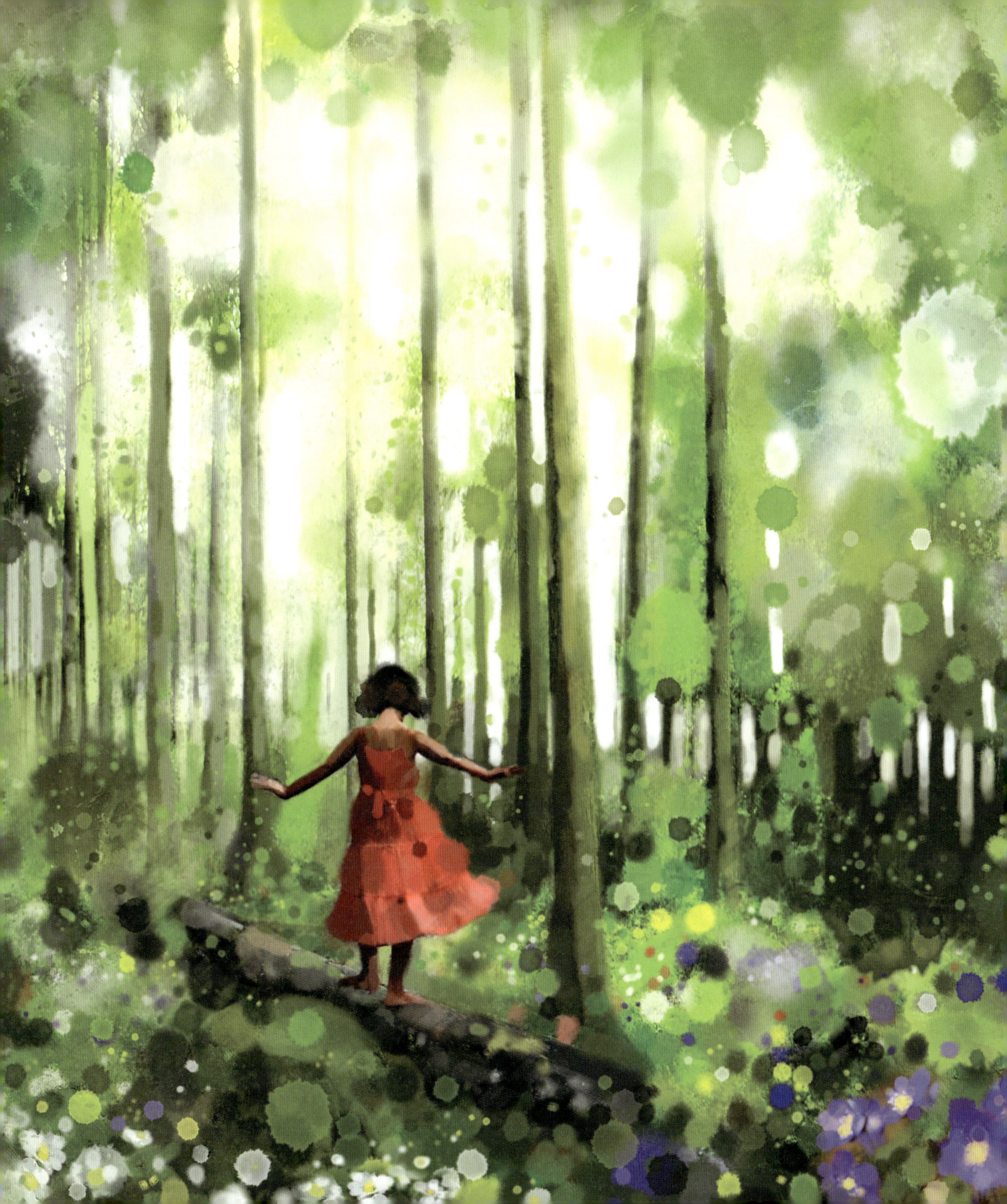

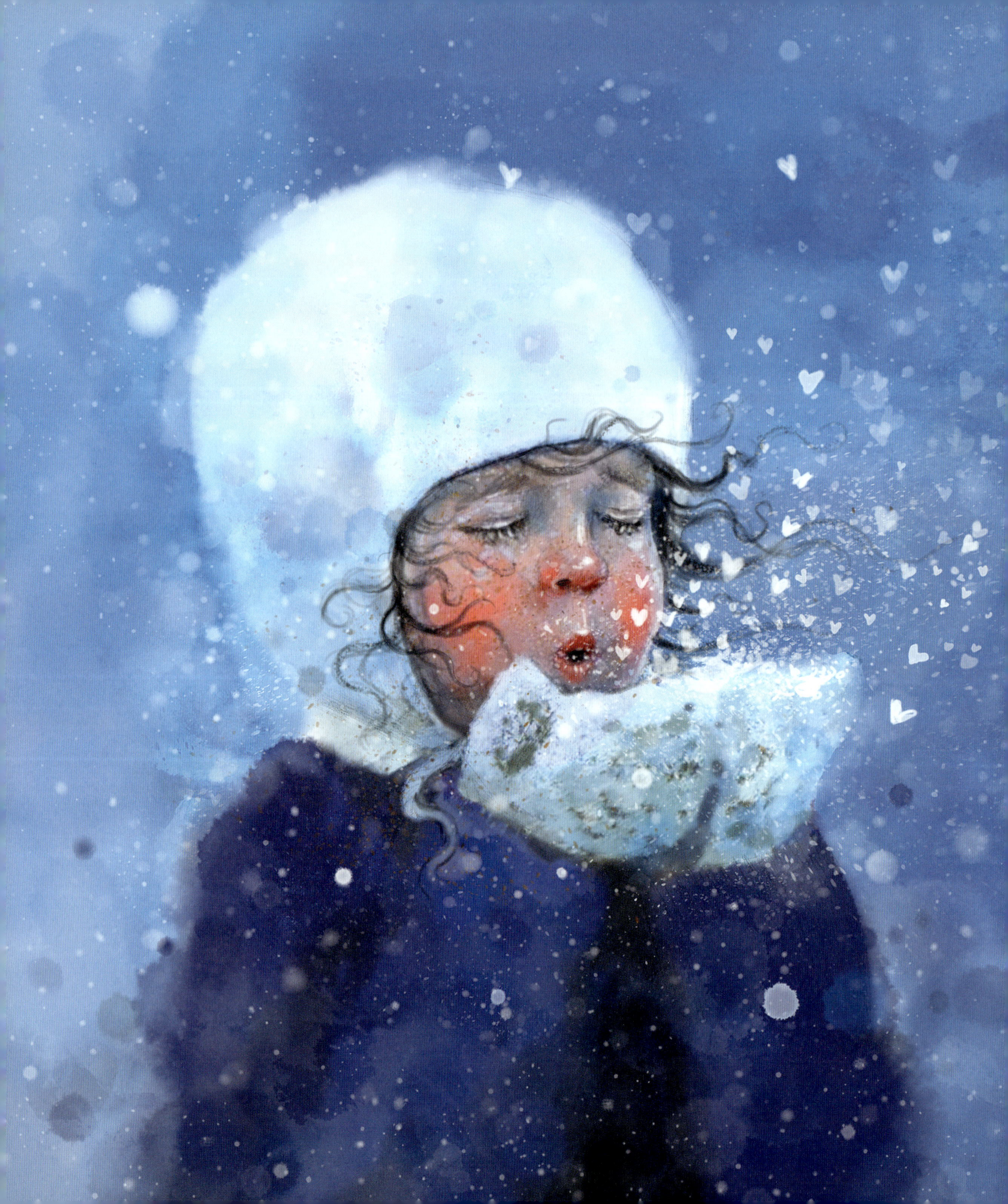

winter was whiter,

and Christmas was simply magical?

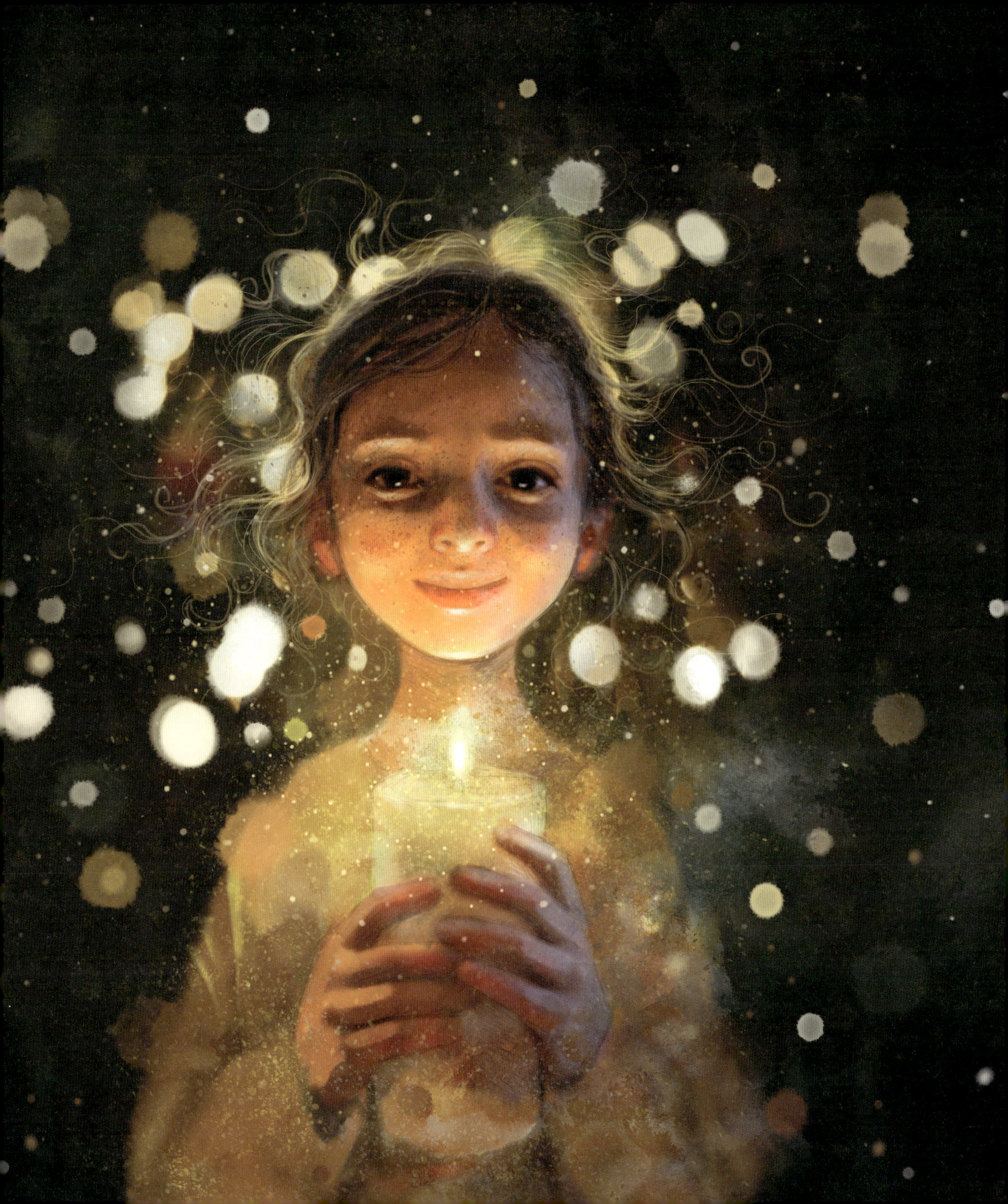

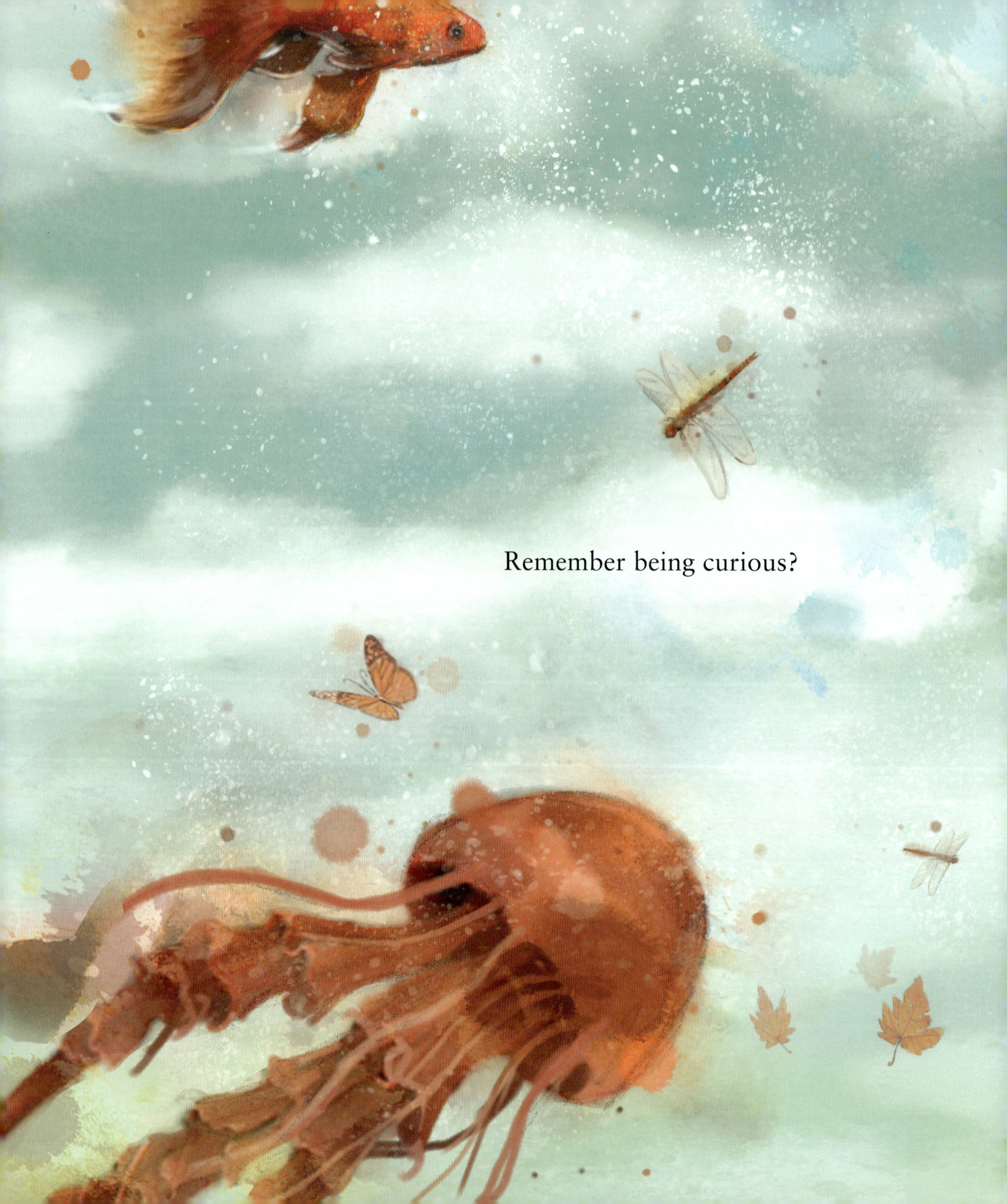

Remember being curious?

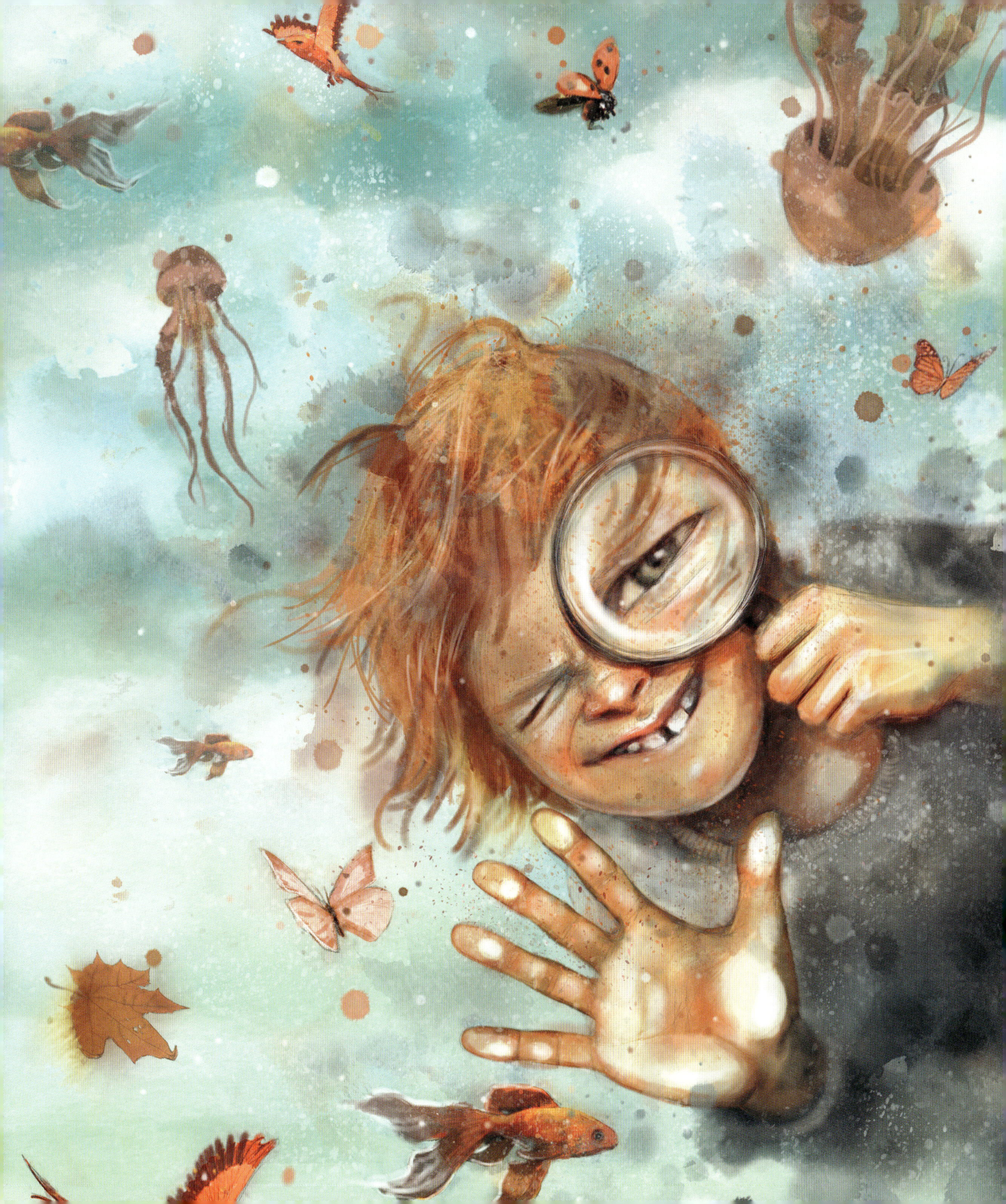

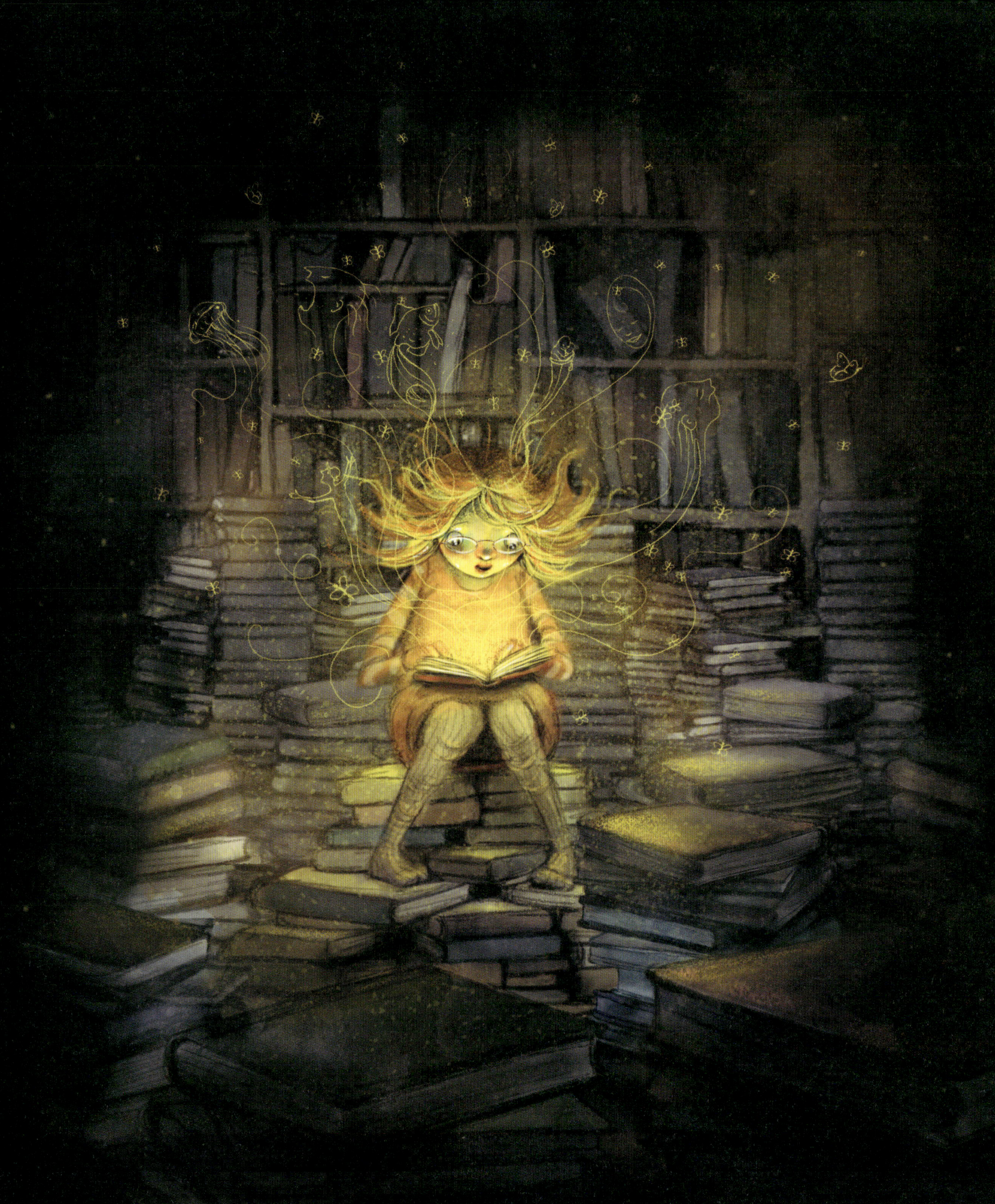

And how we discovered new worlds …

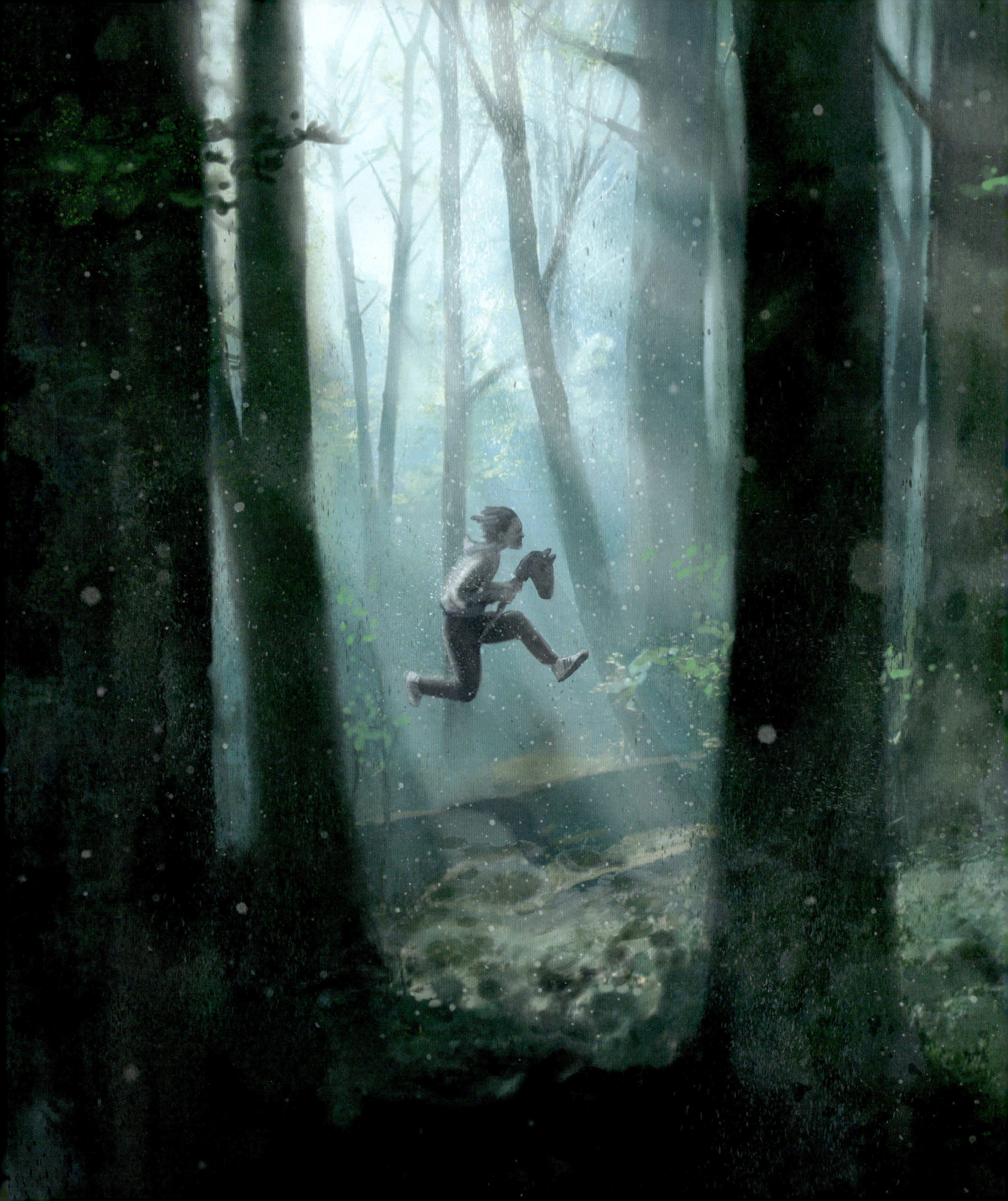

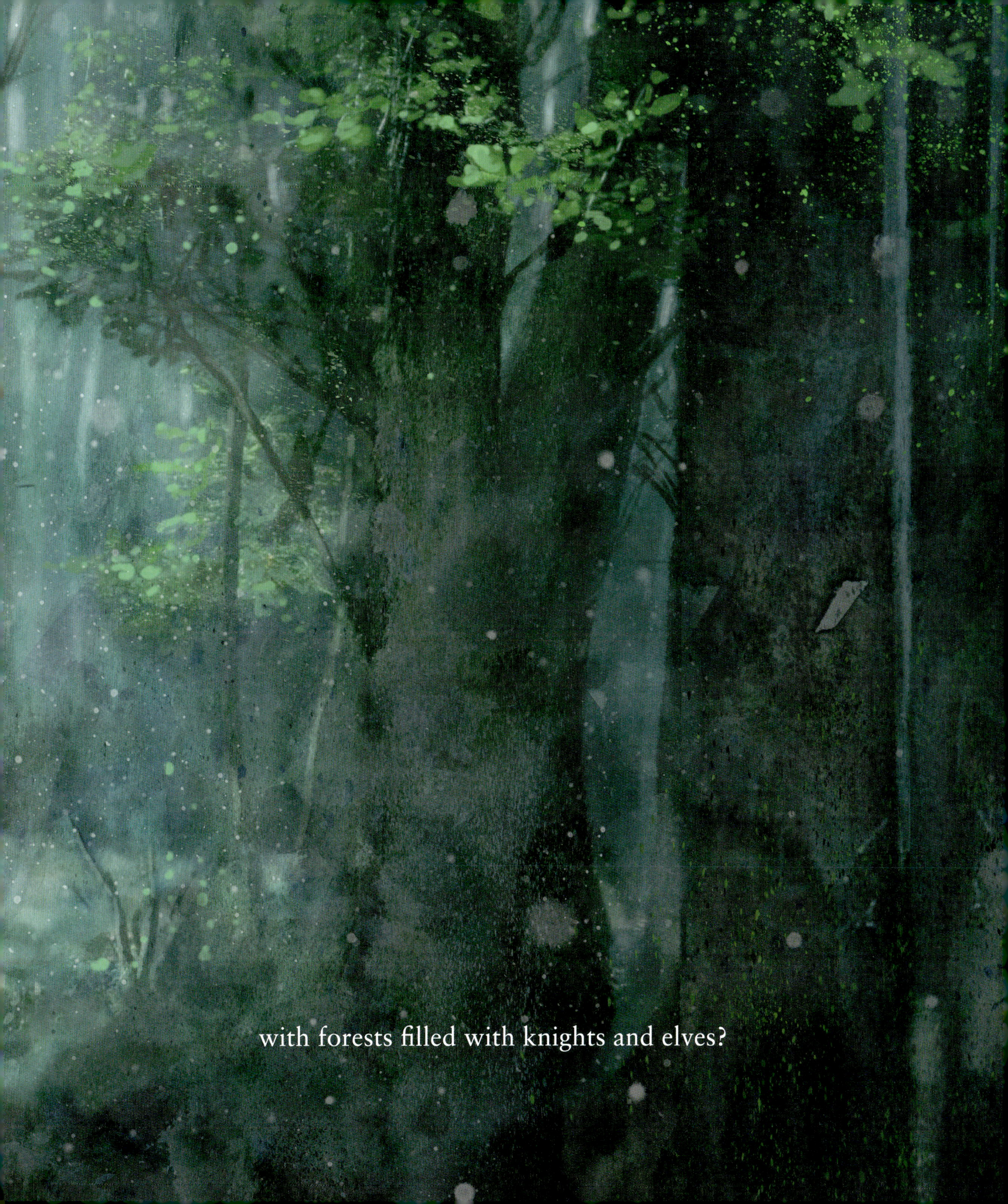
with forests filled with knights and elves?

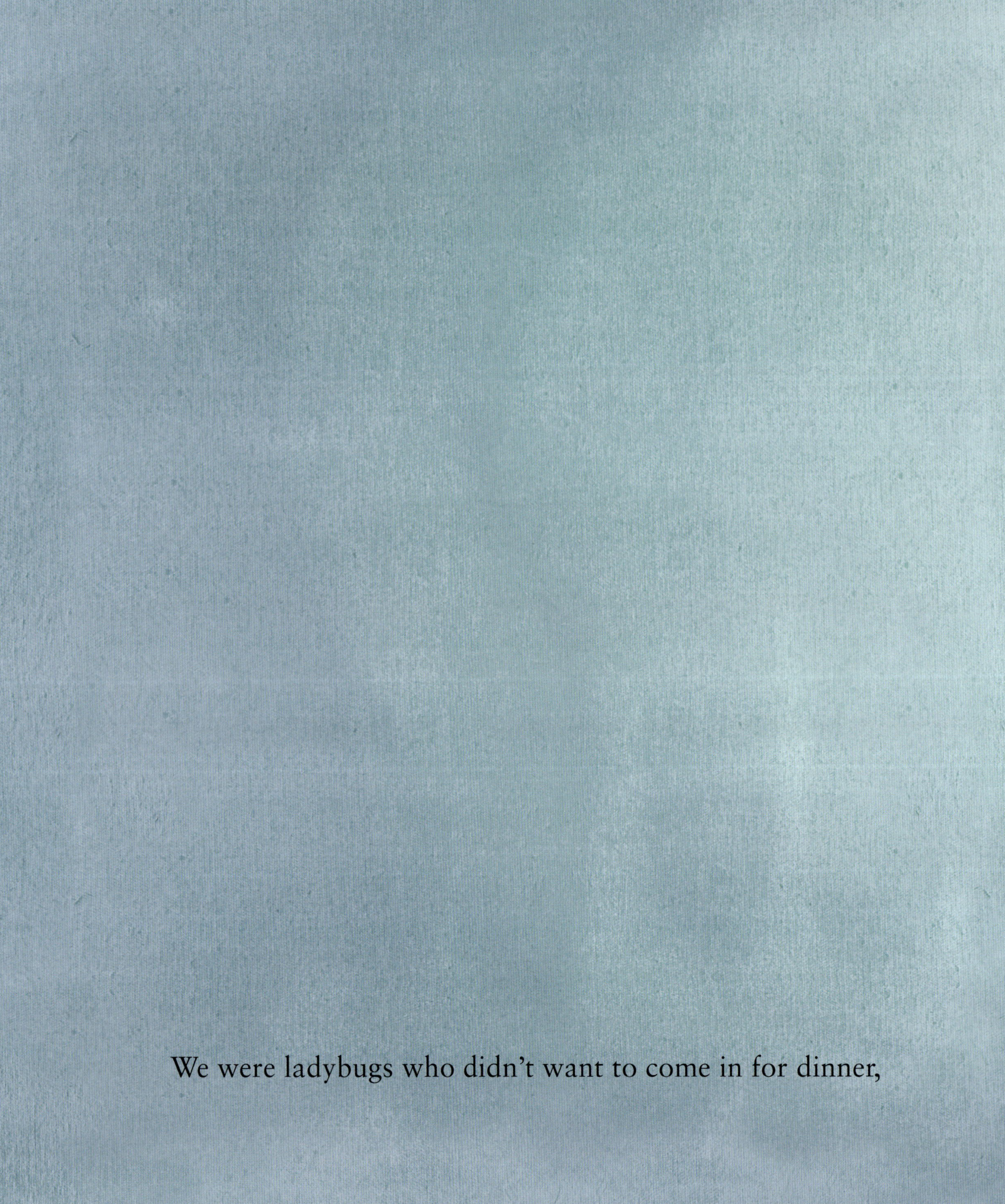

We were ladybugs who didn't want to come in for dinner,

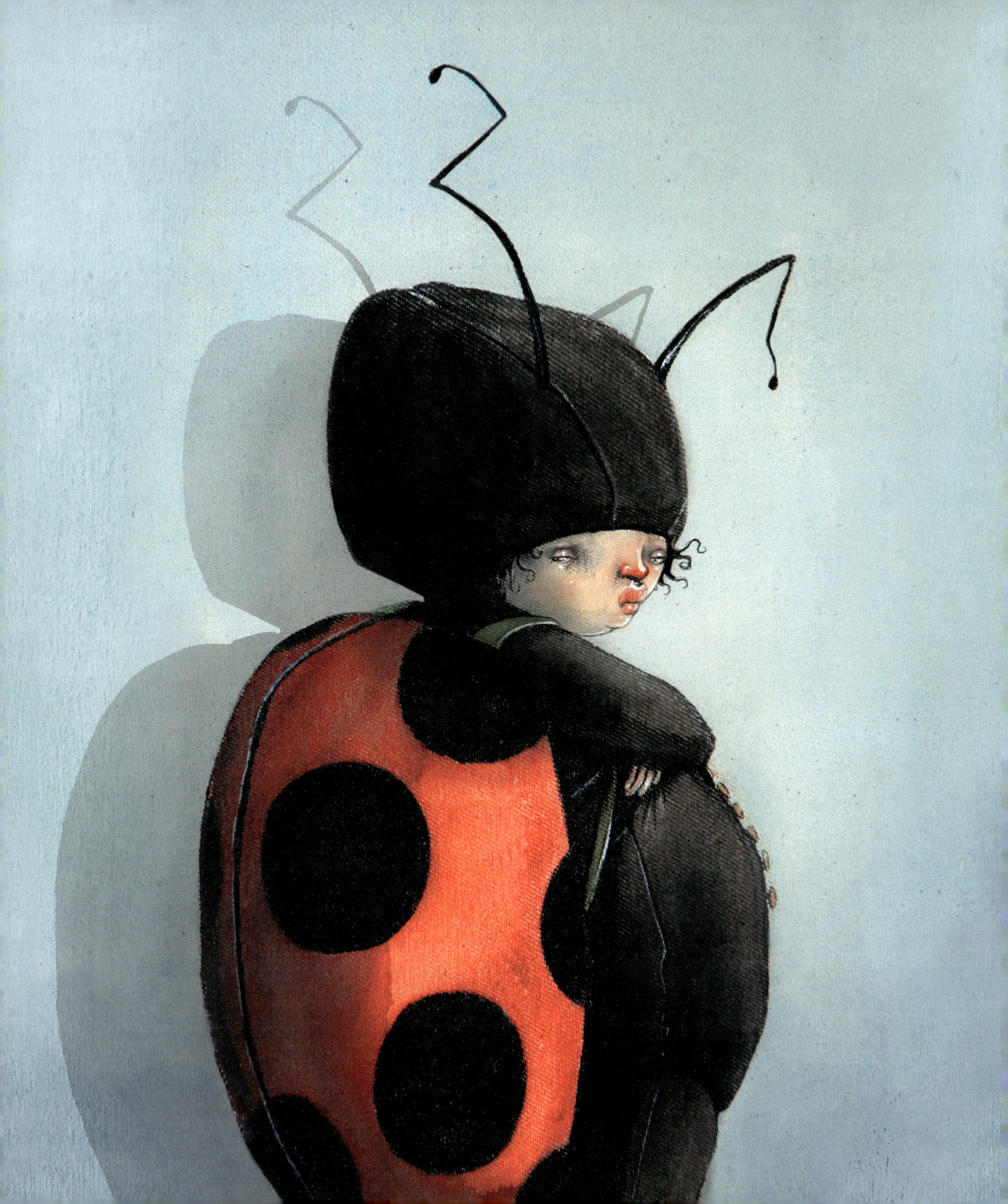

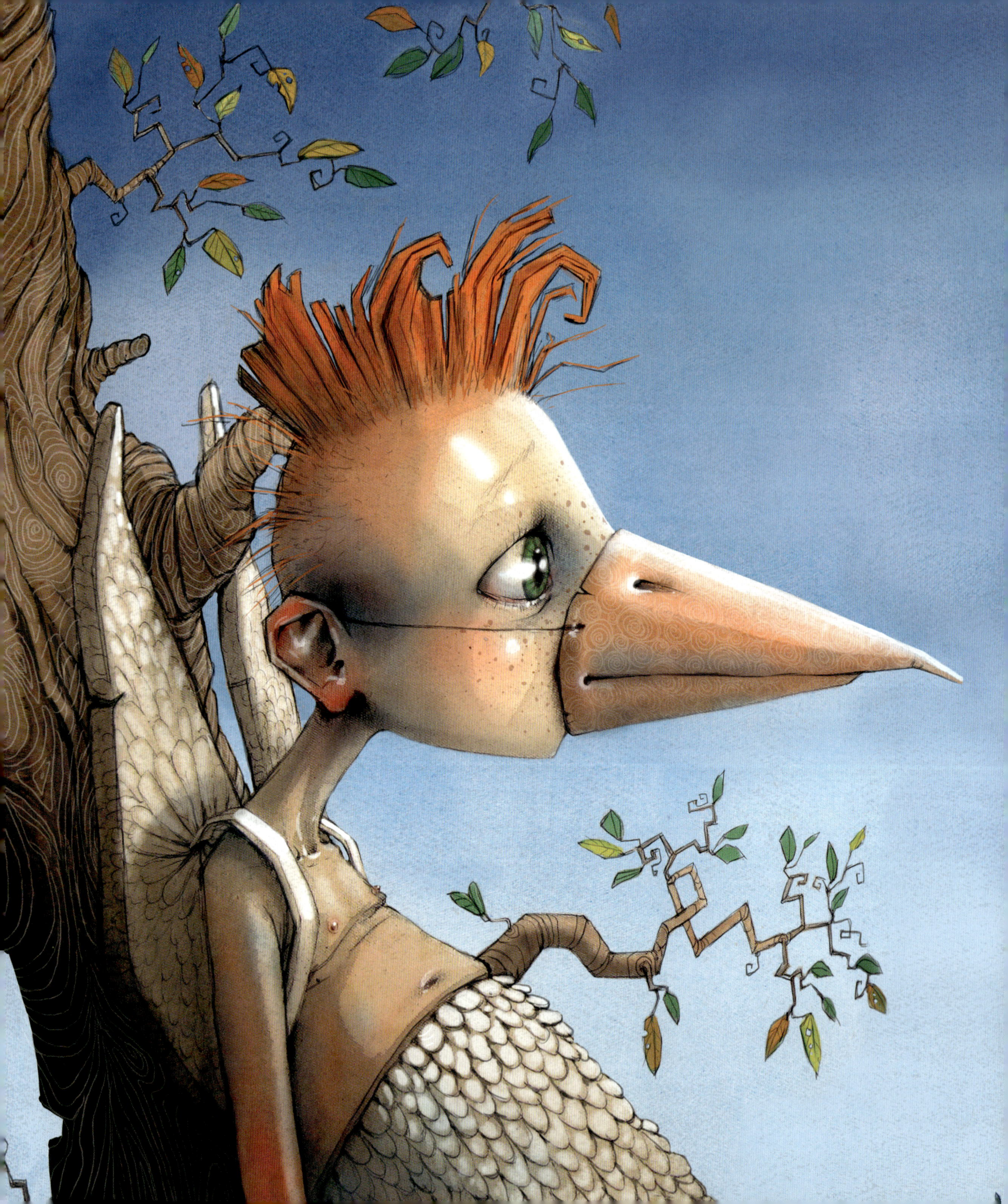

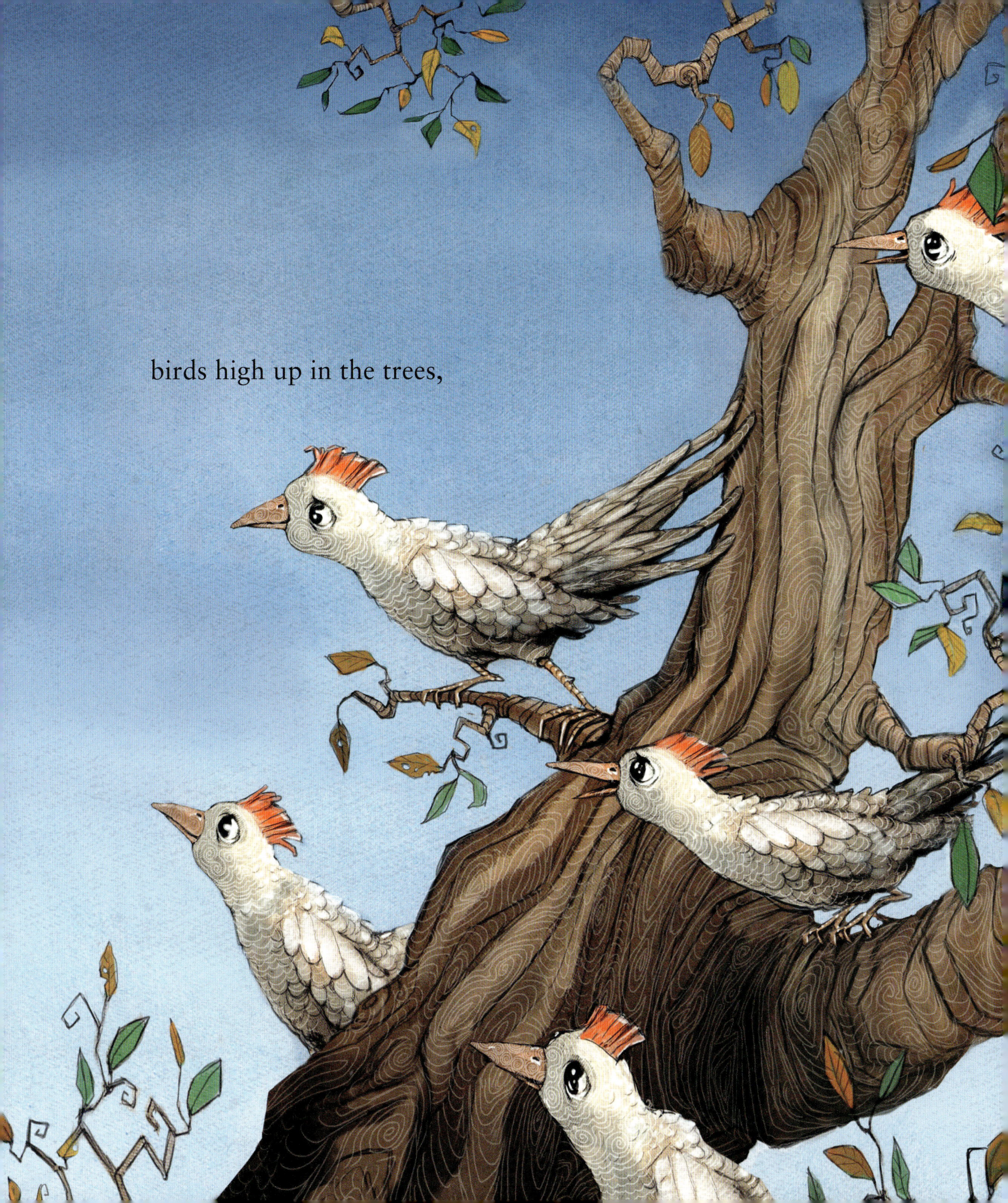
birds high up in the trees,

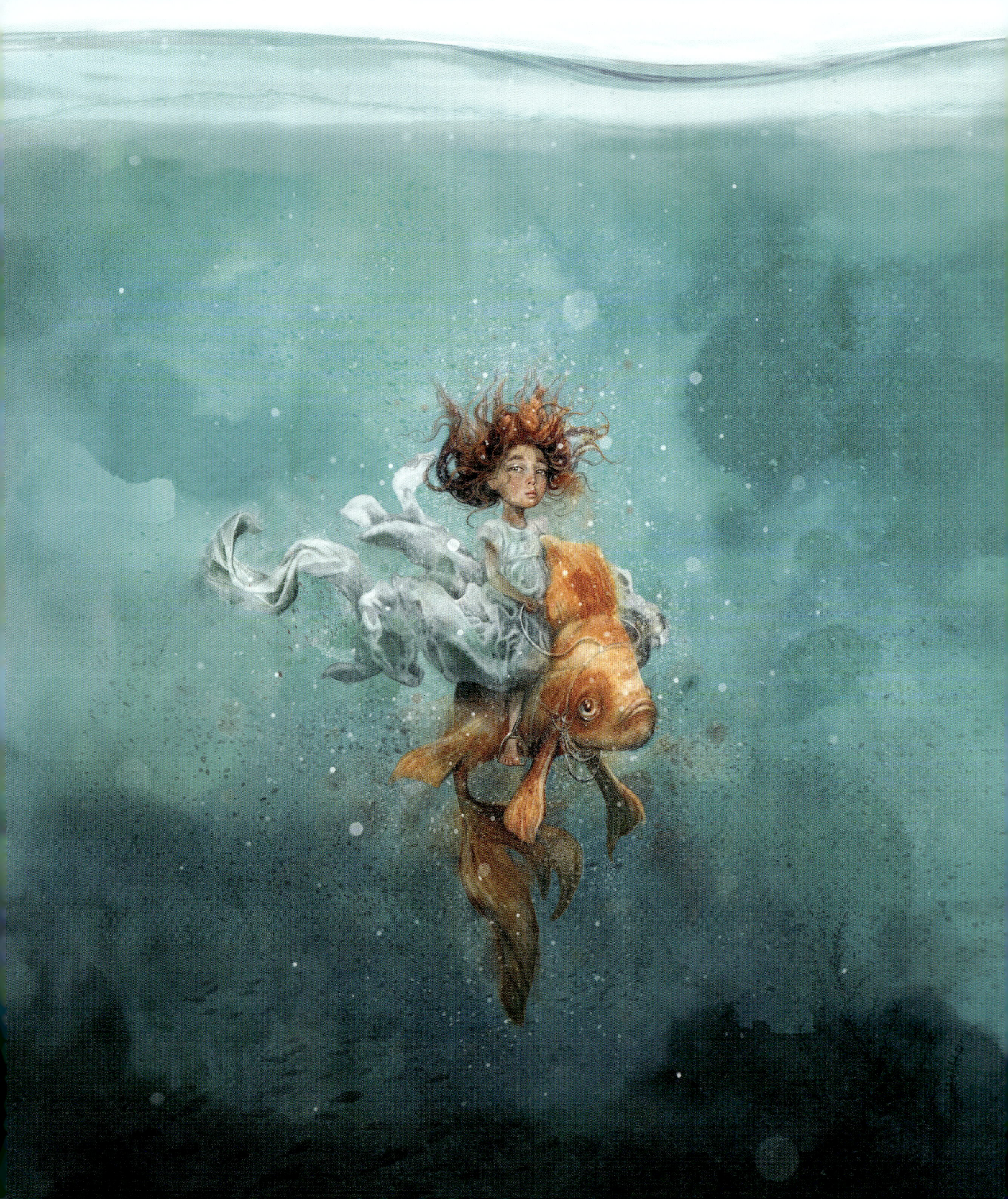

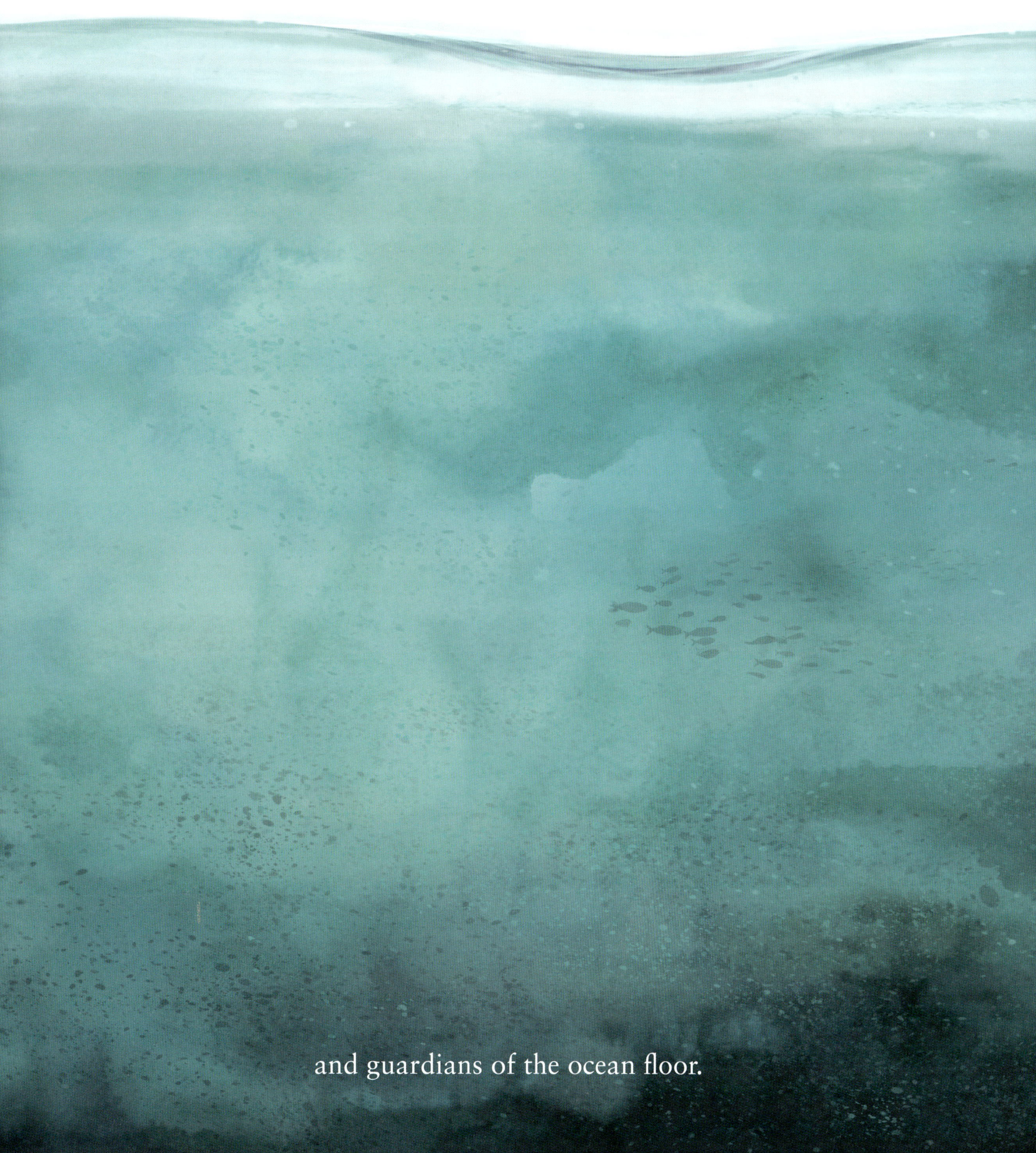
and guardians of the ocean floor.

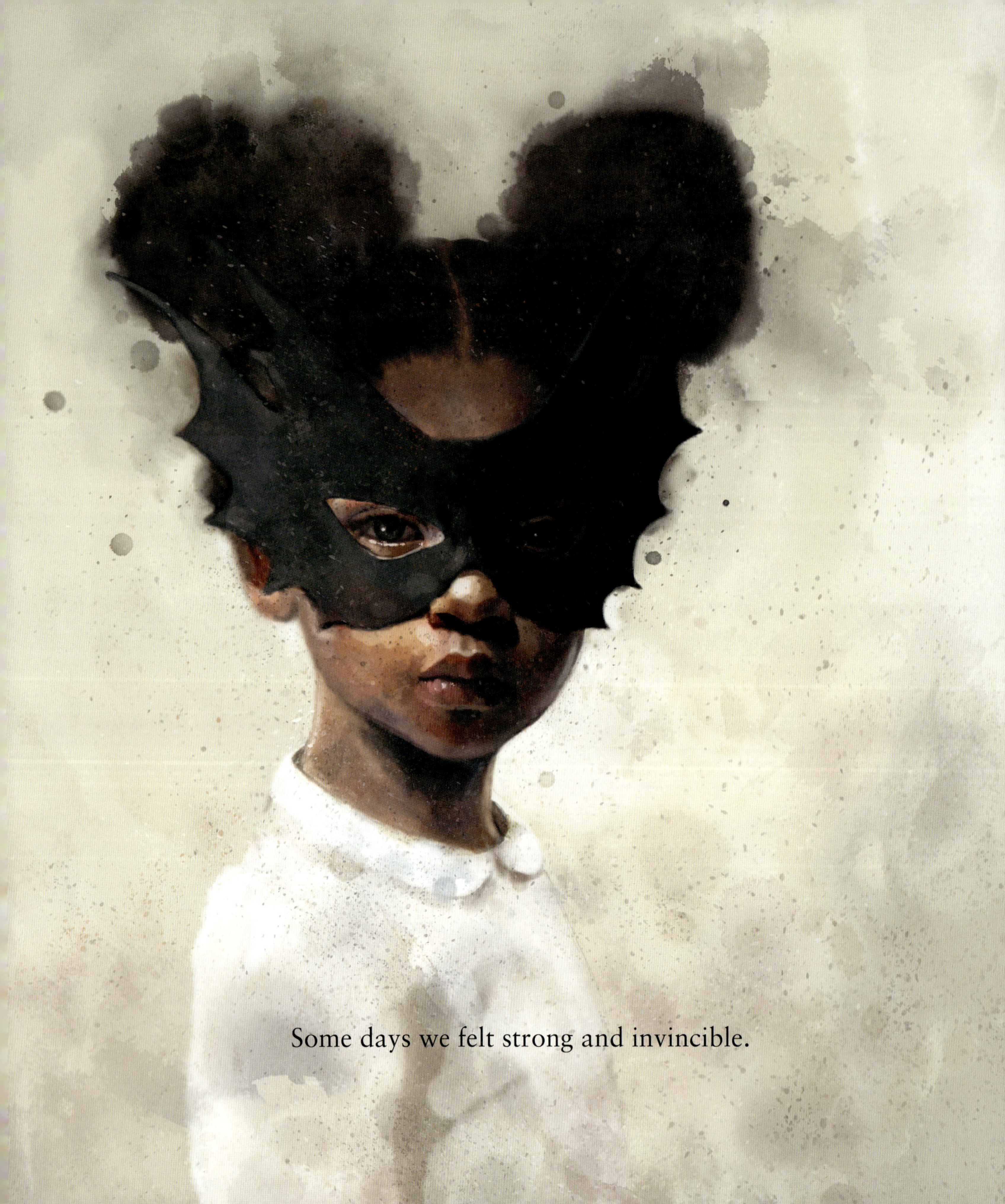

Some days we felt strong and invincible.

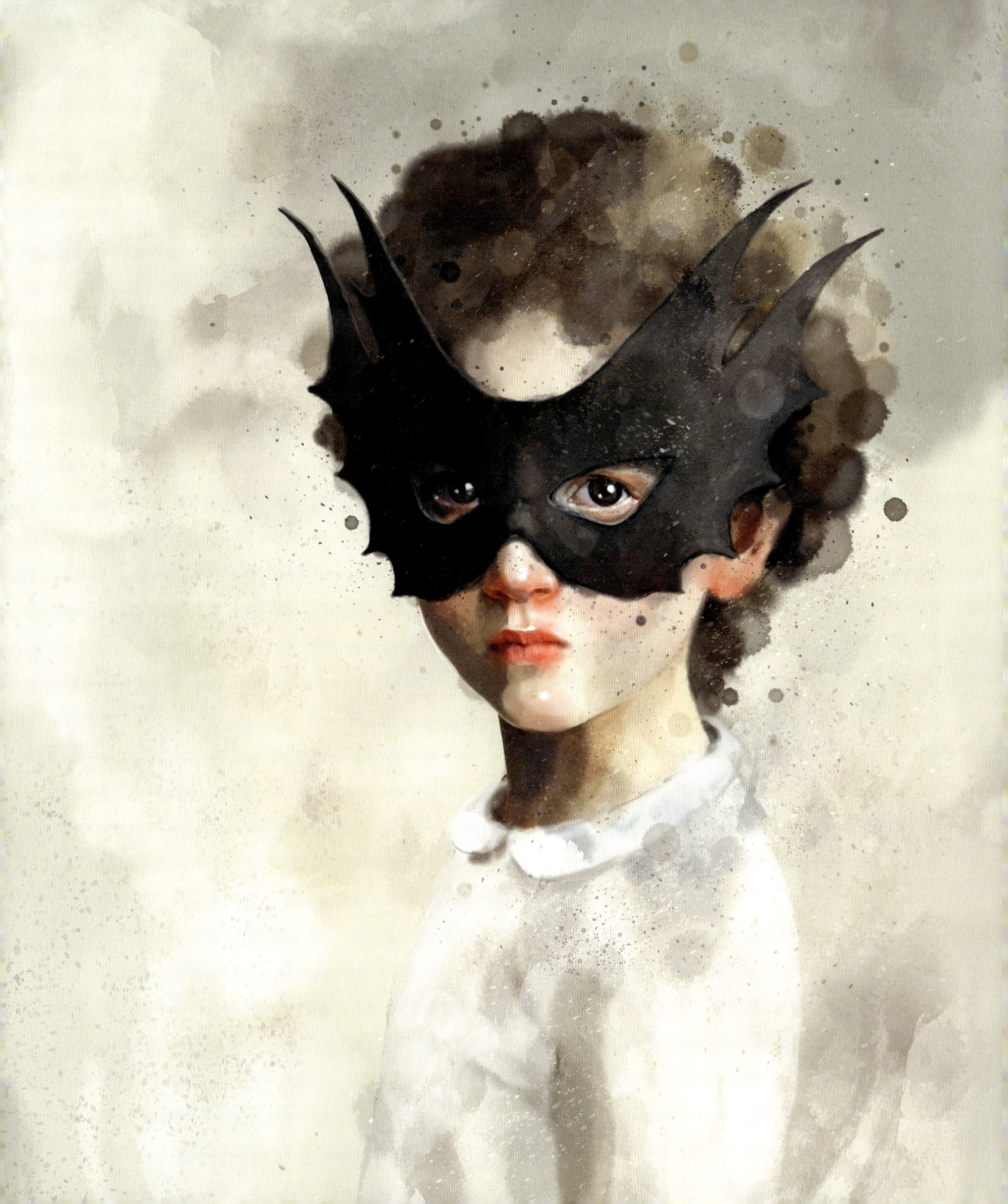

Other days we got scrapes and scars.

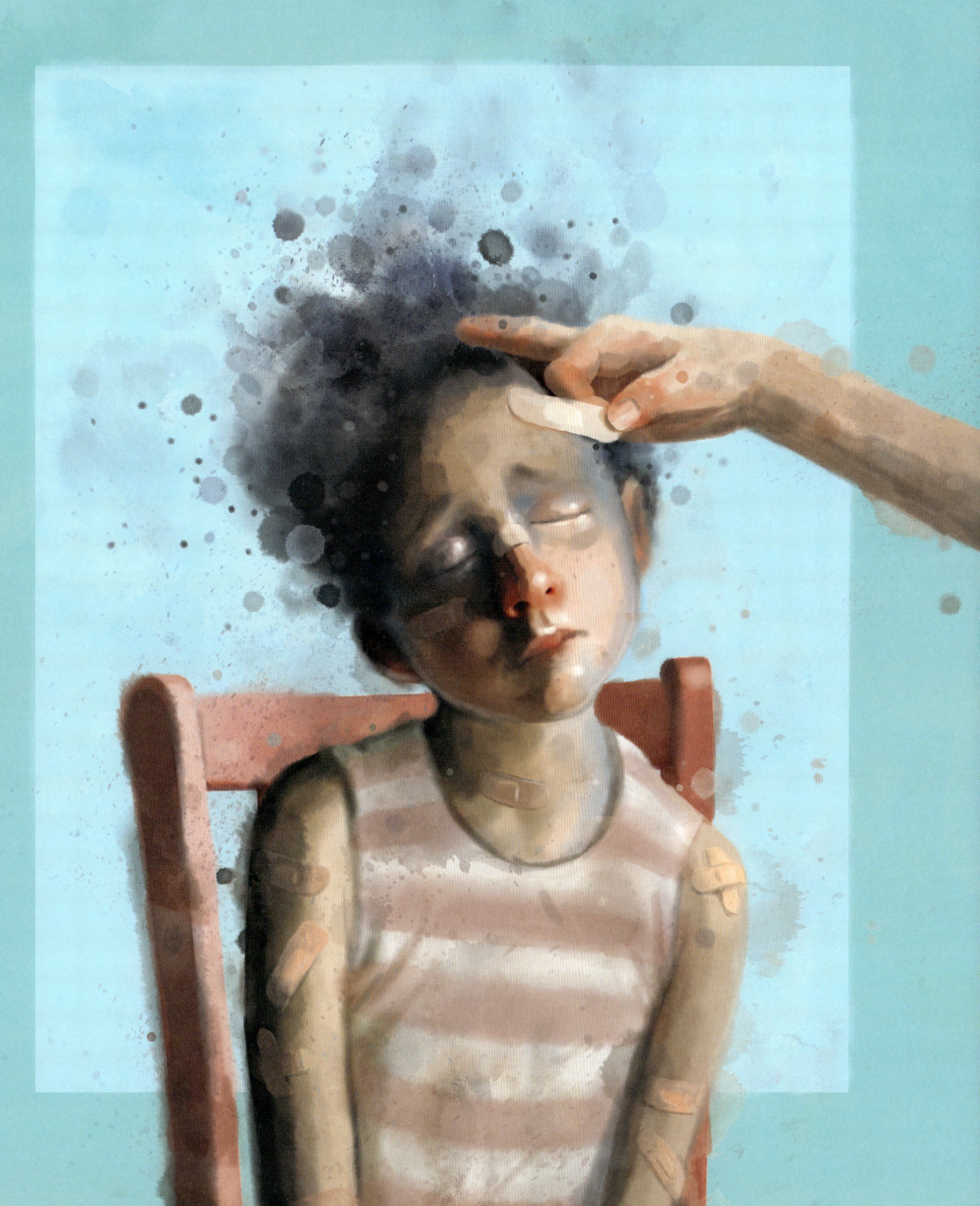

Sometimes the world was unfair,

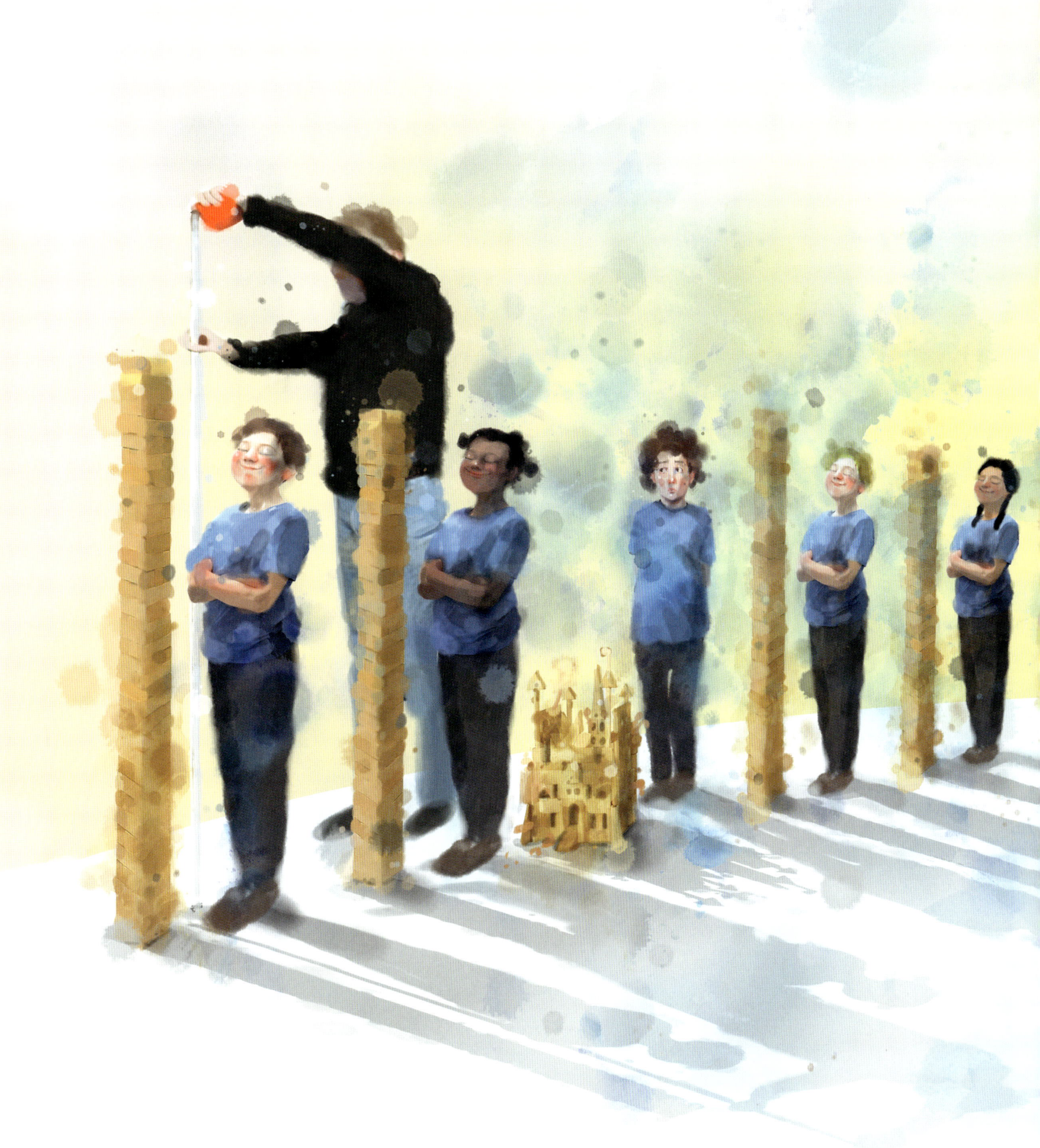

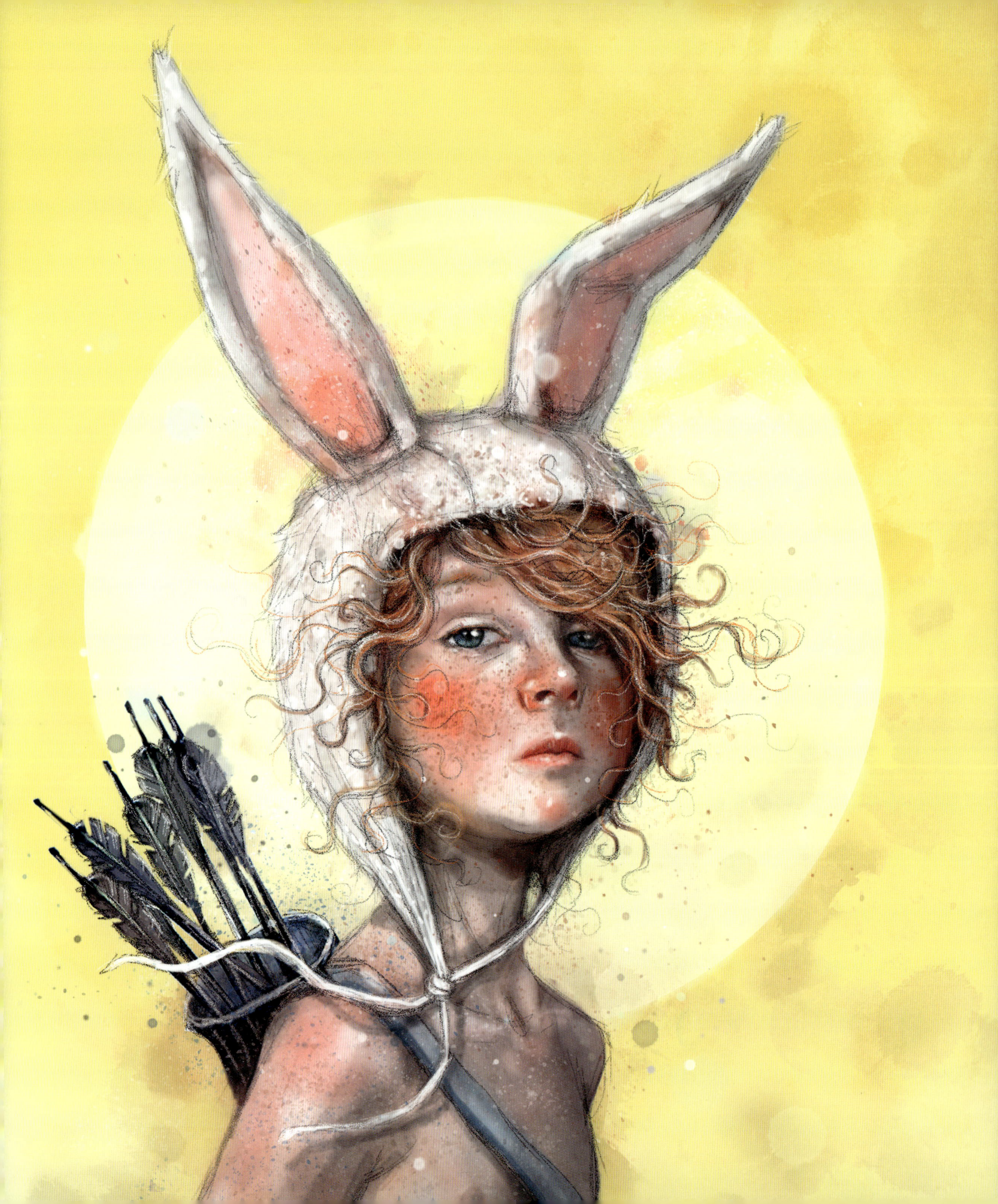

and you had to fight.

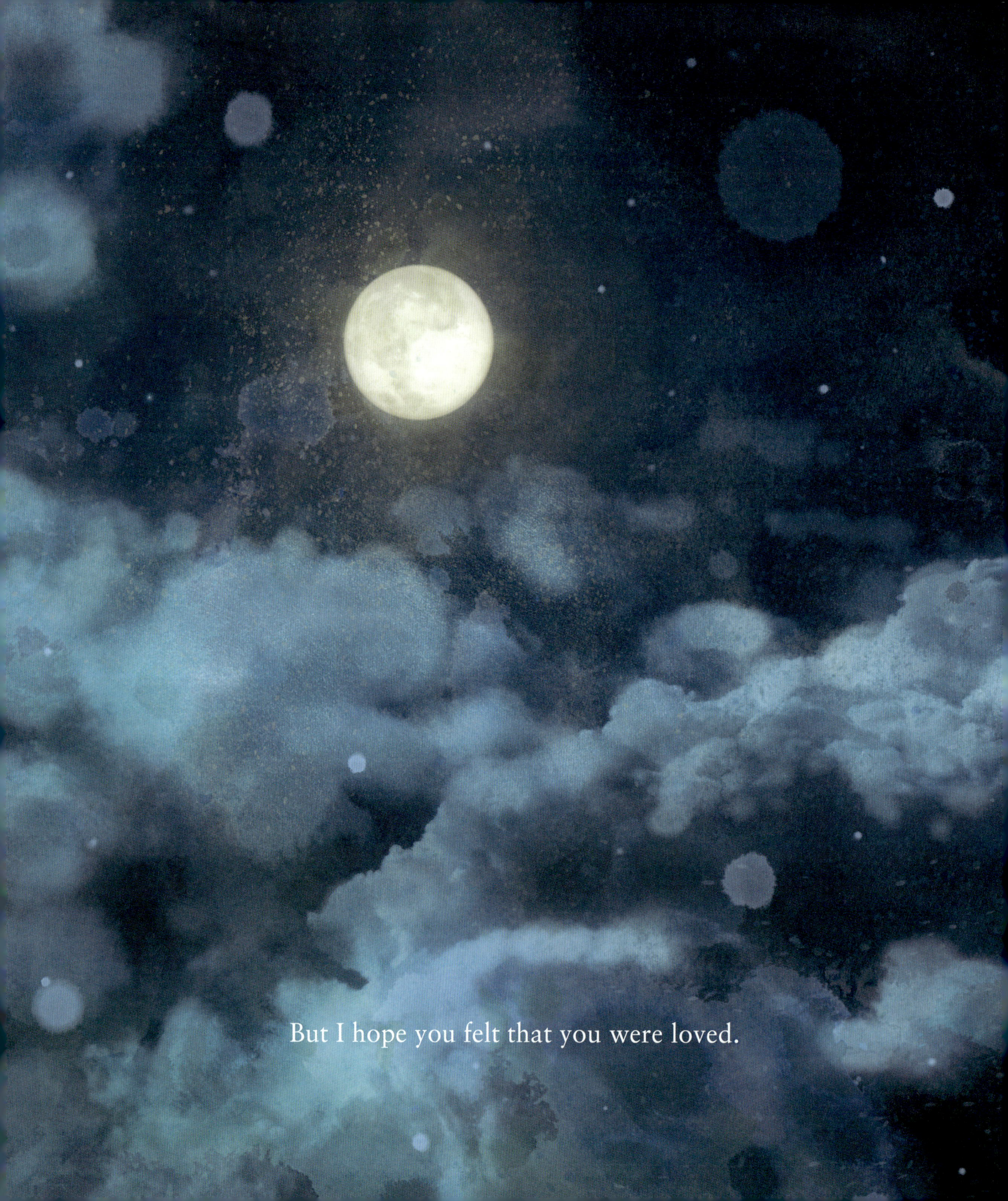

But I hope you felt that you were loved.

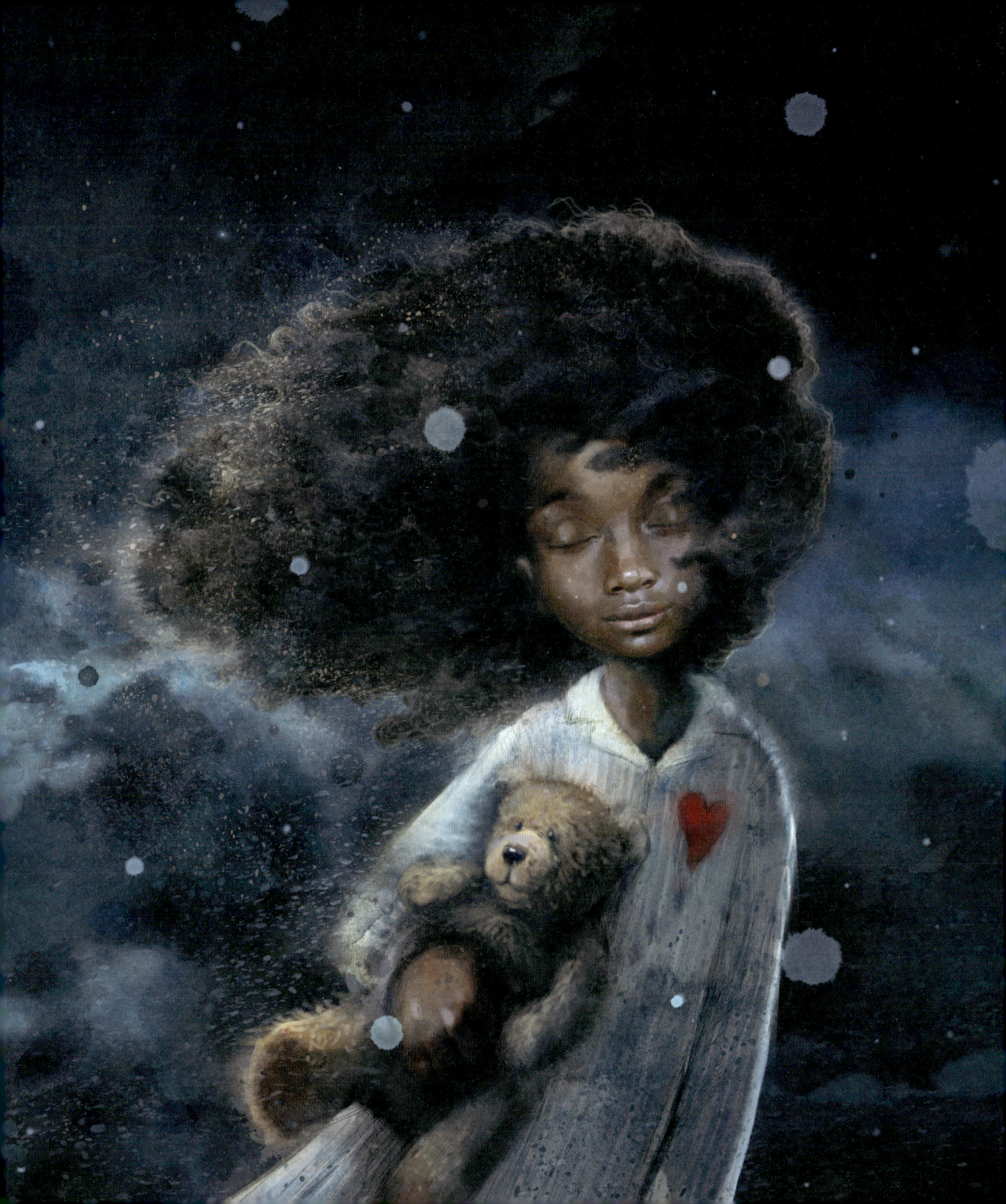

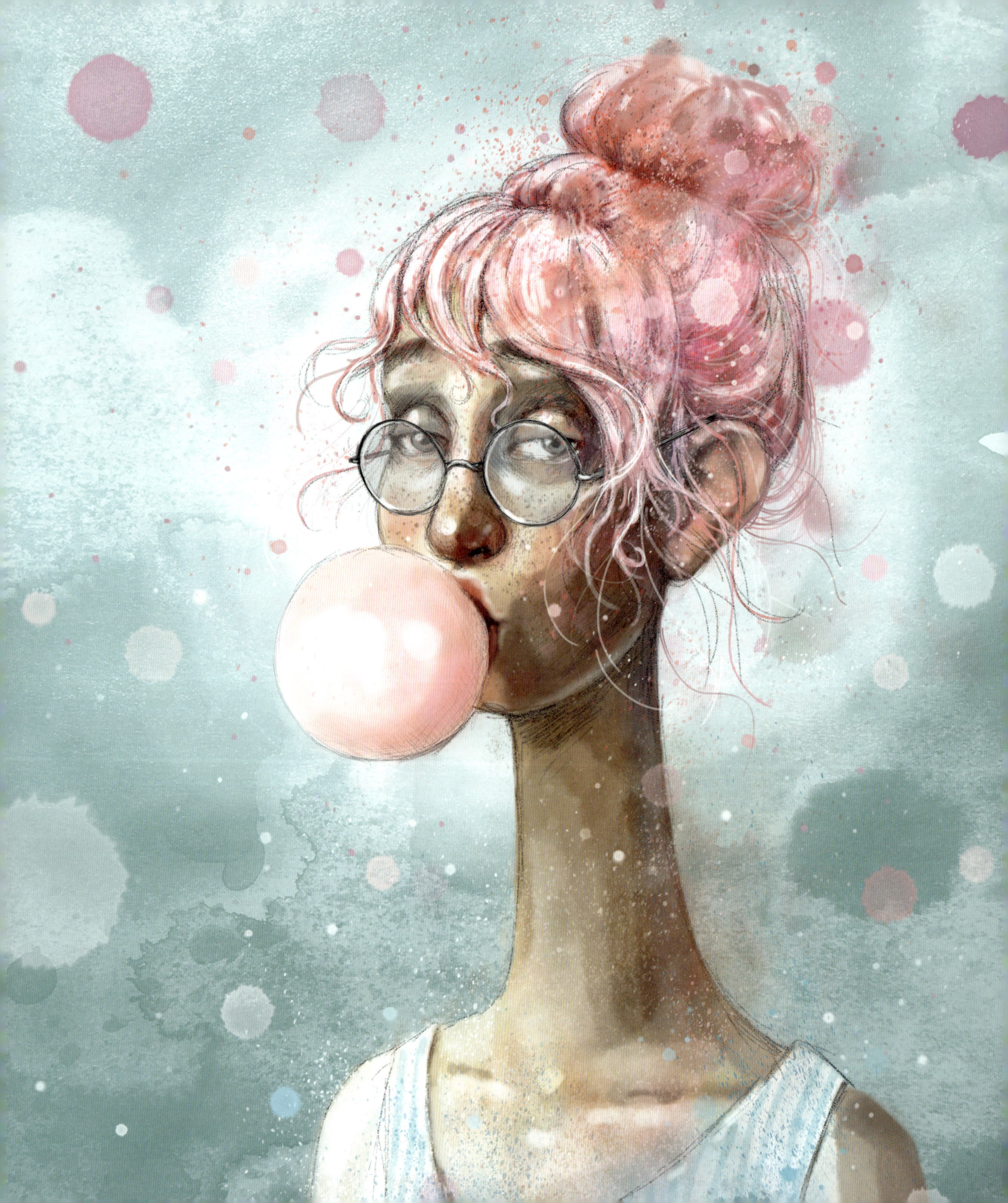

A Teenager's Life

We stopped playing.

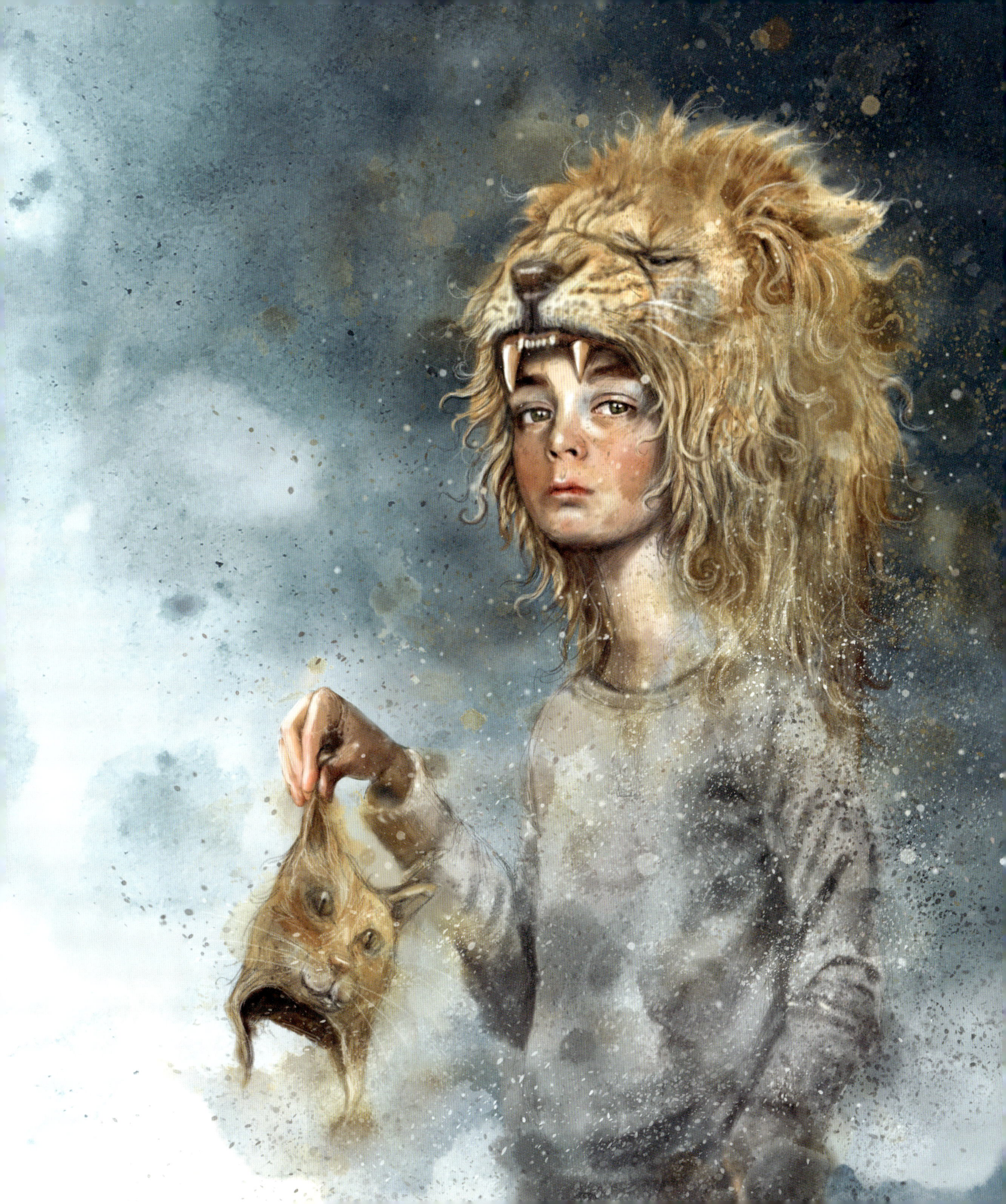

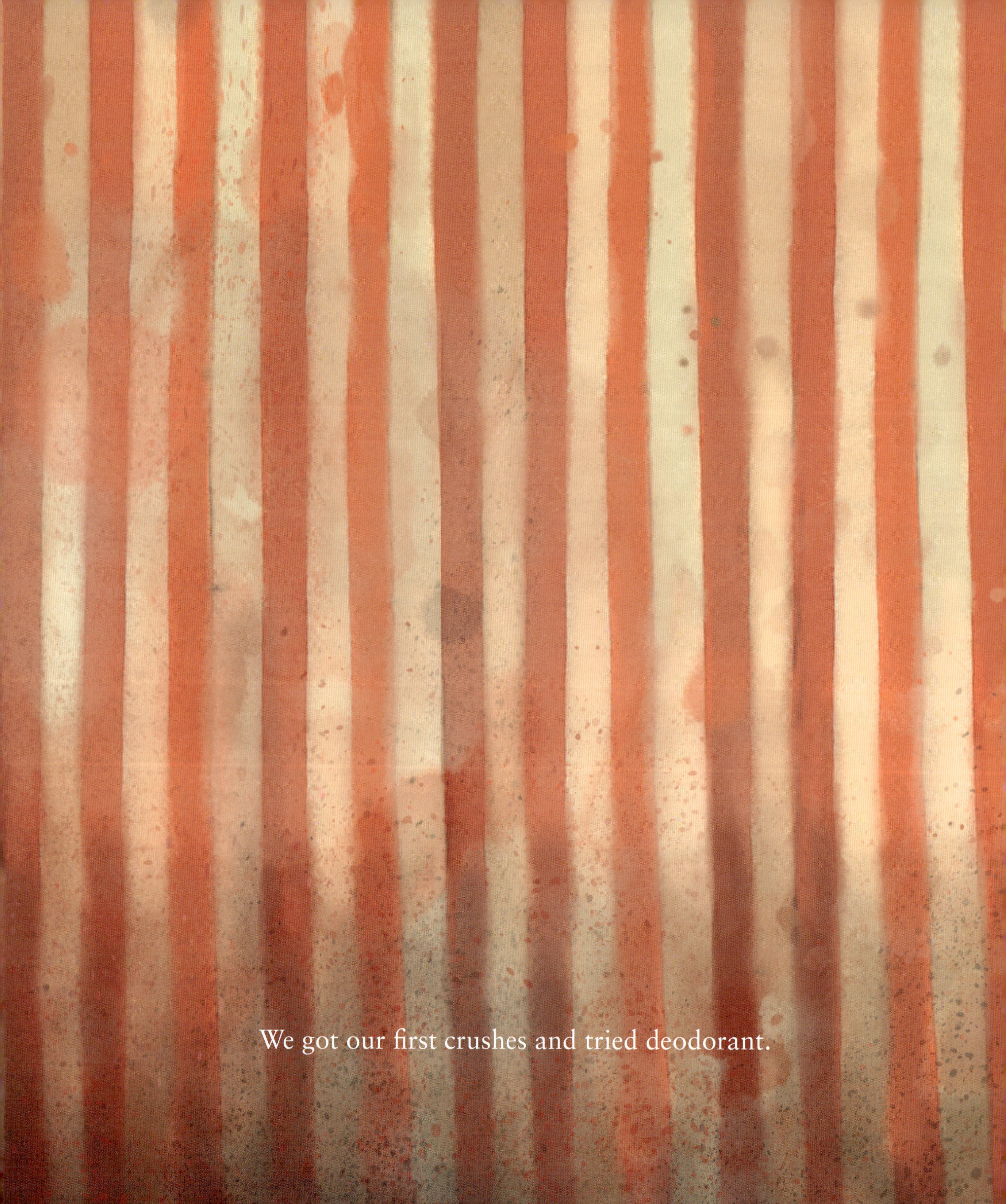

We got our first crushes and tried deodorant.

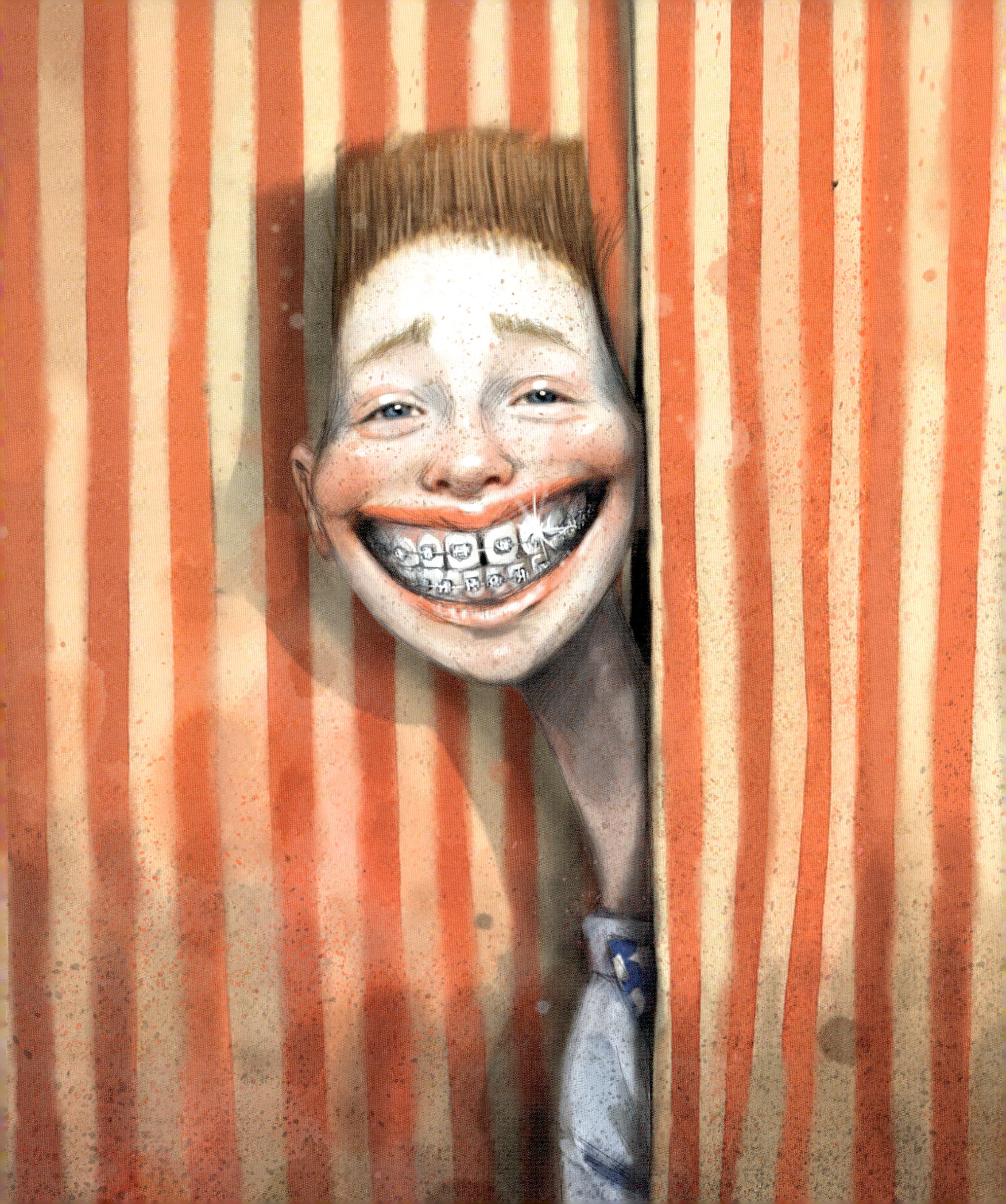

Maybe you loved school.

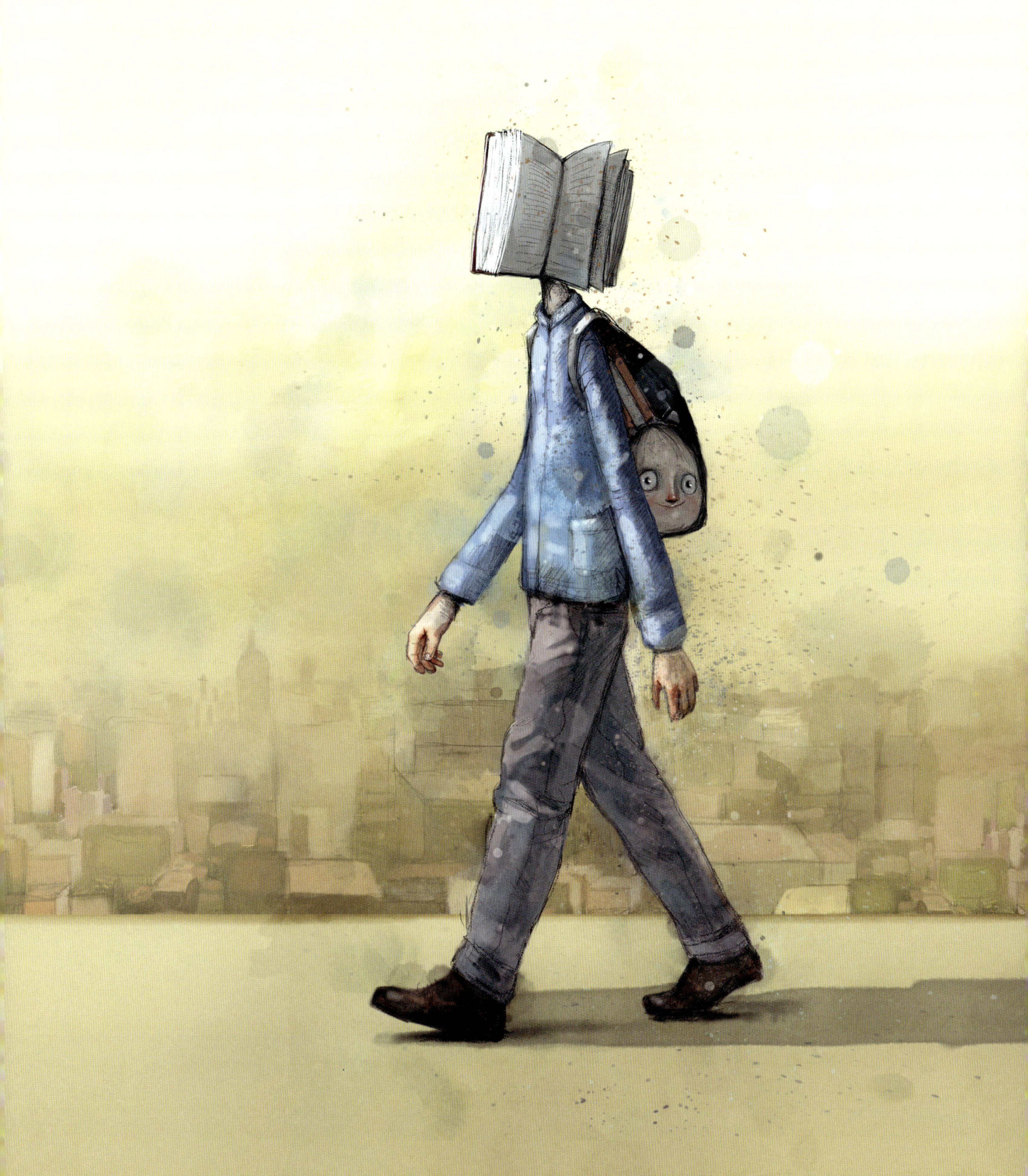

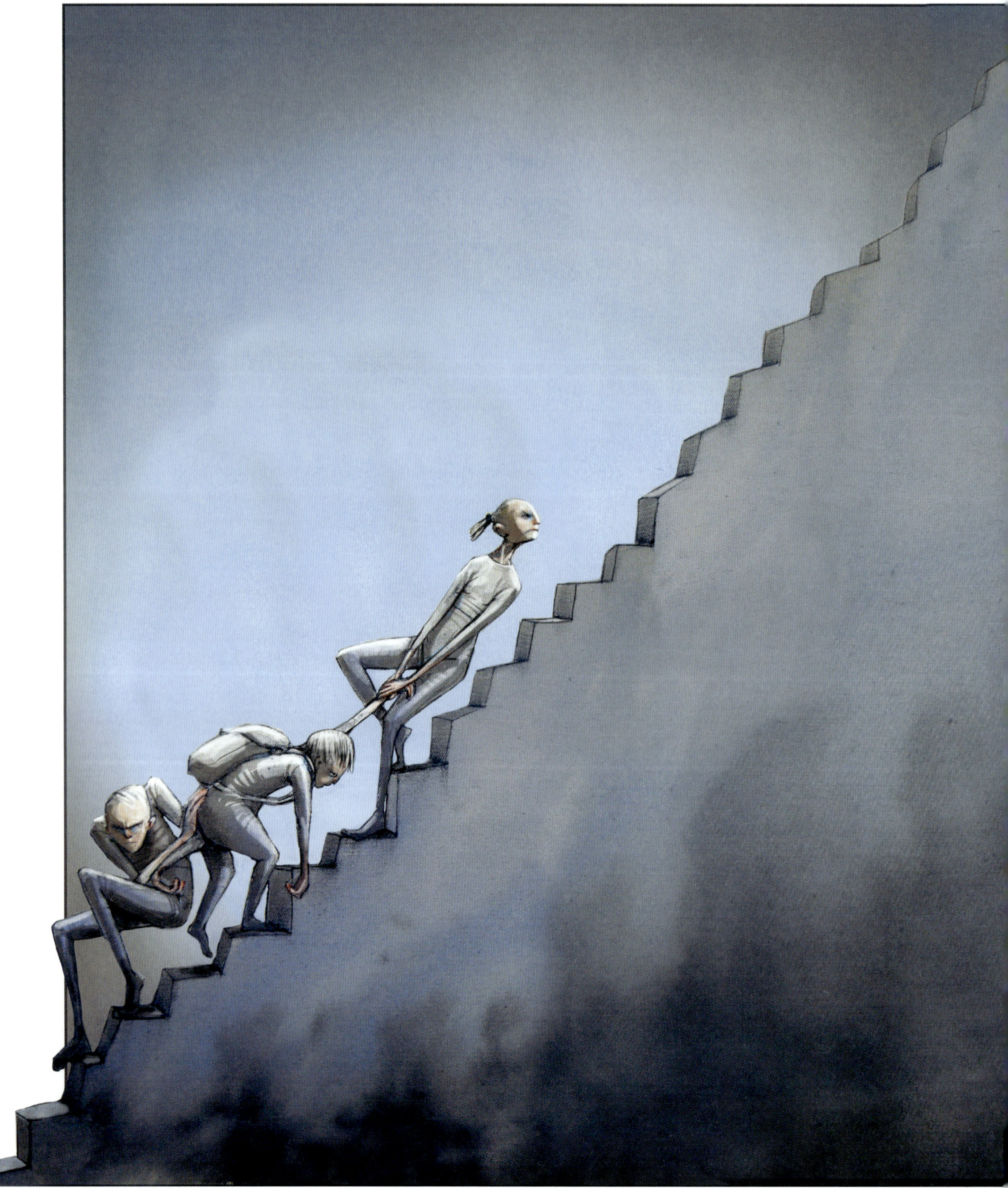

Maybe you struggled through it.

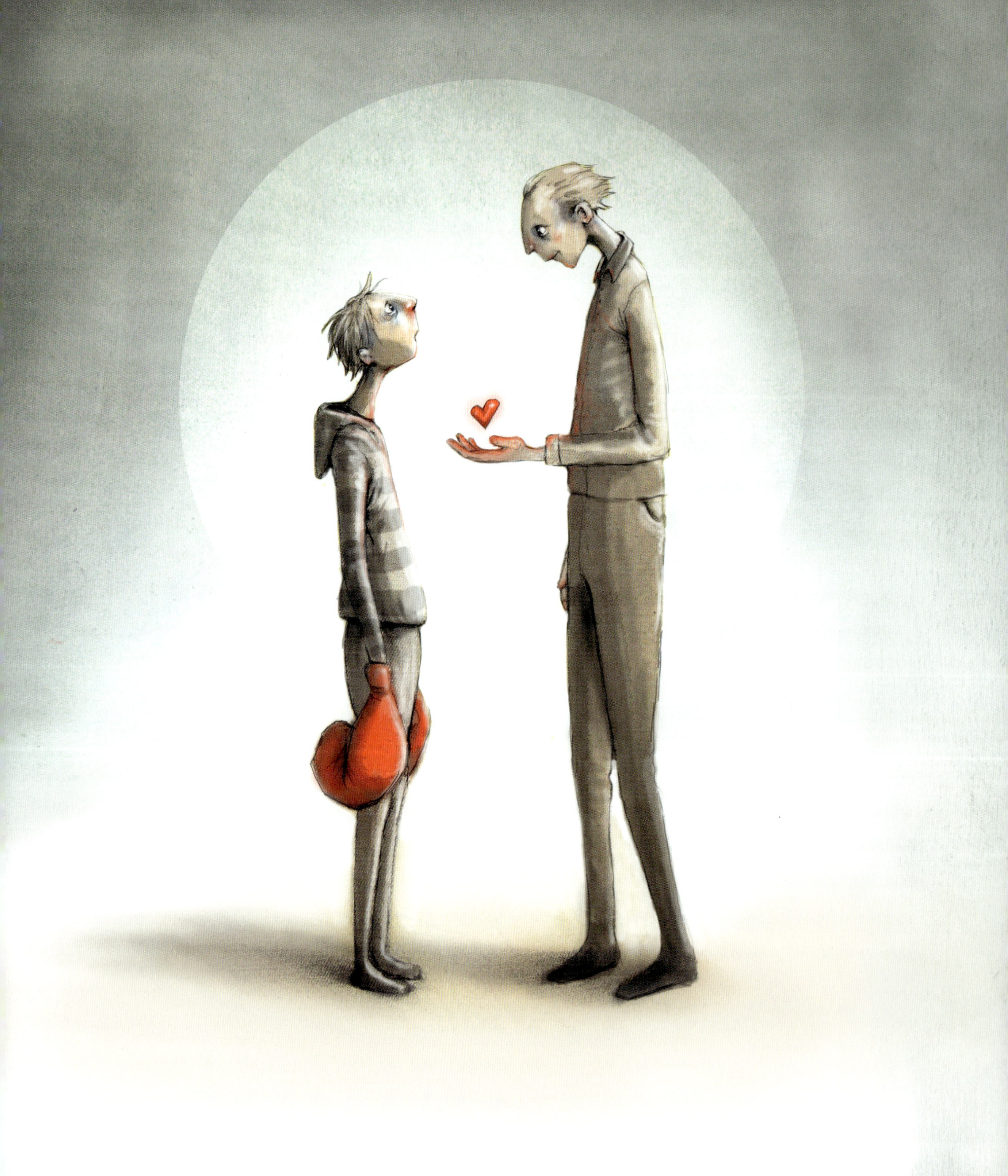

Maybe you had a teacher you've never forgotten.

We changed,

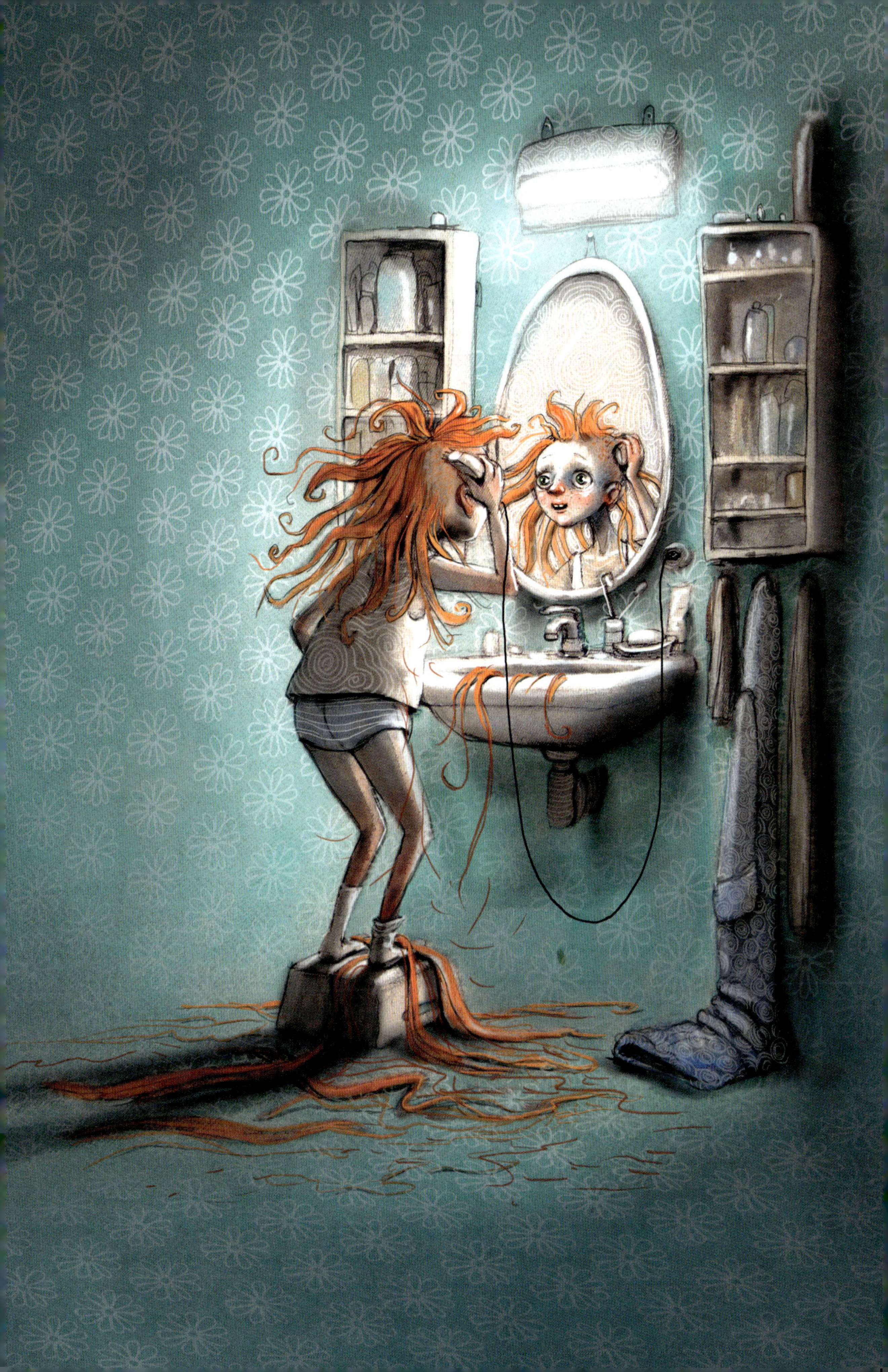

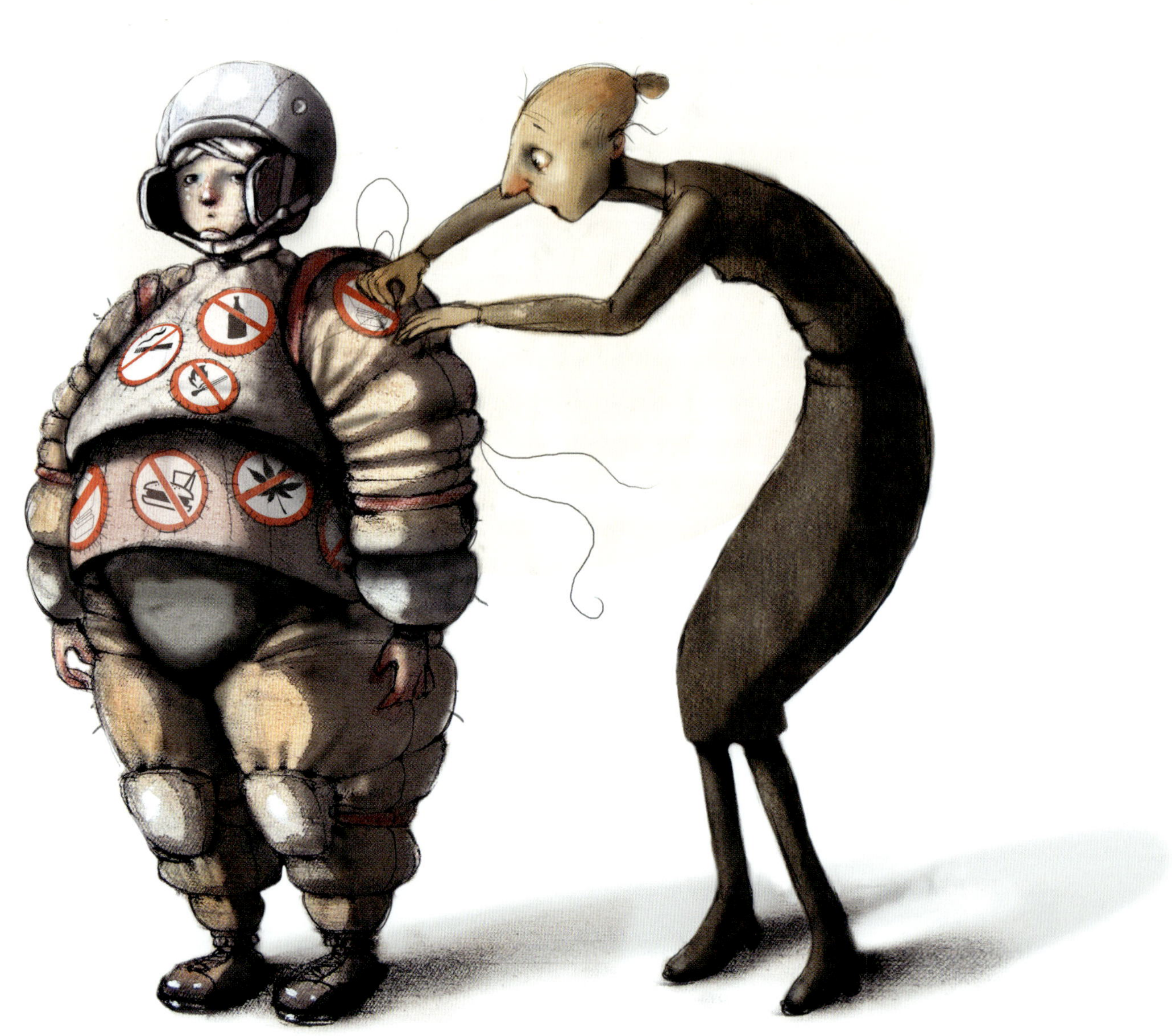

and the grown-ups grew uneasy.

Some days we wanted to rebel.

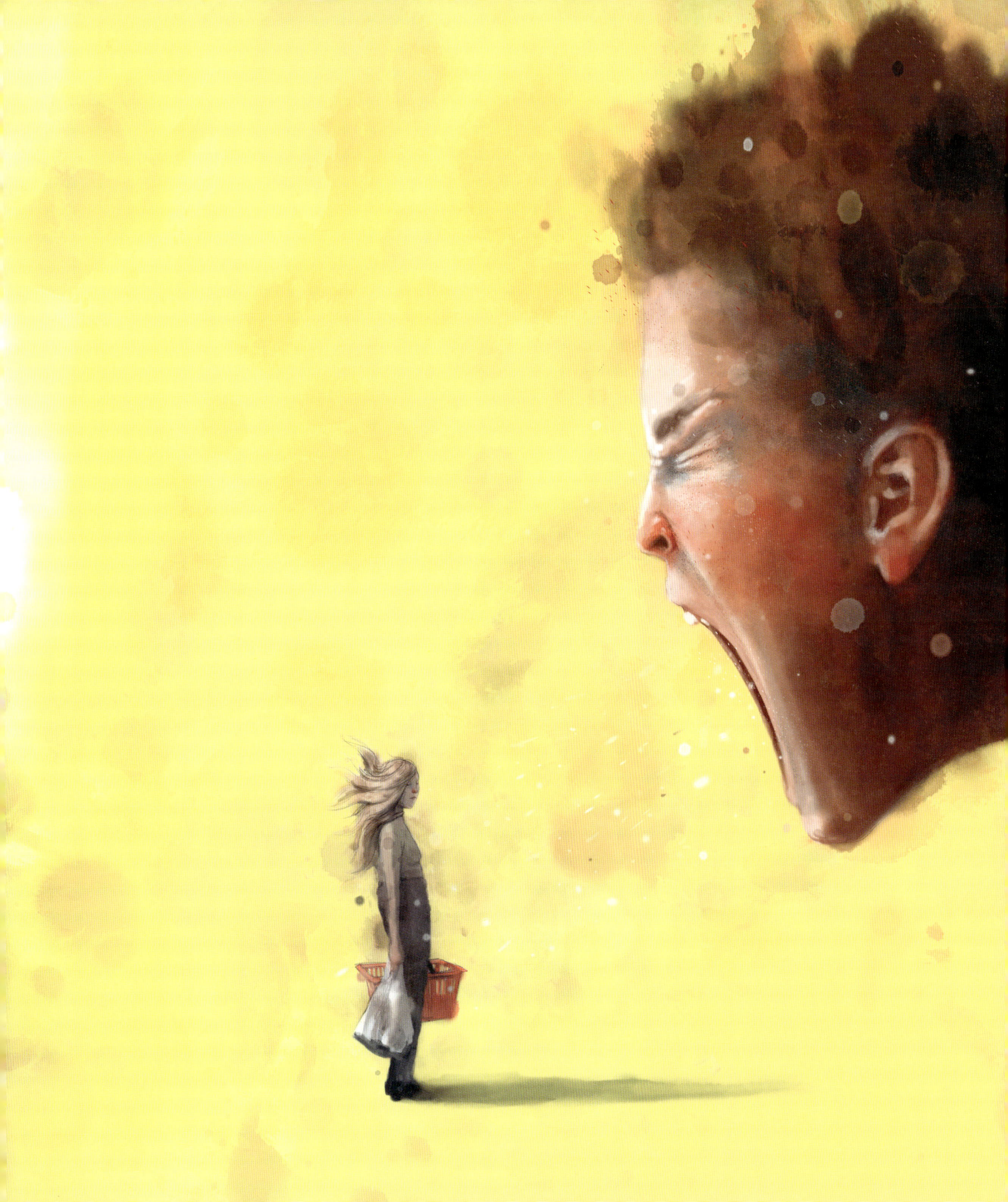

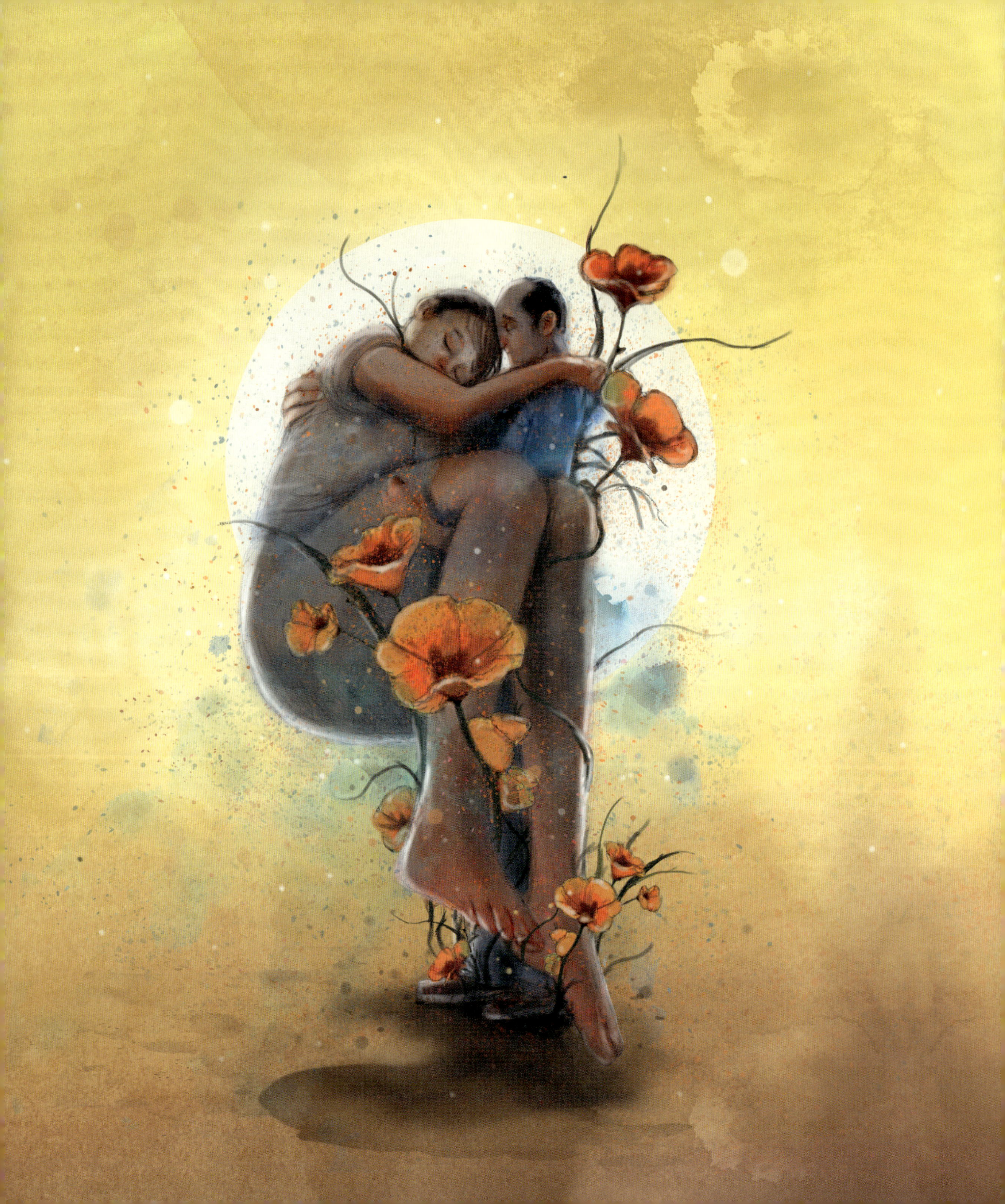

Other days we needed a dad.

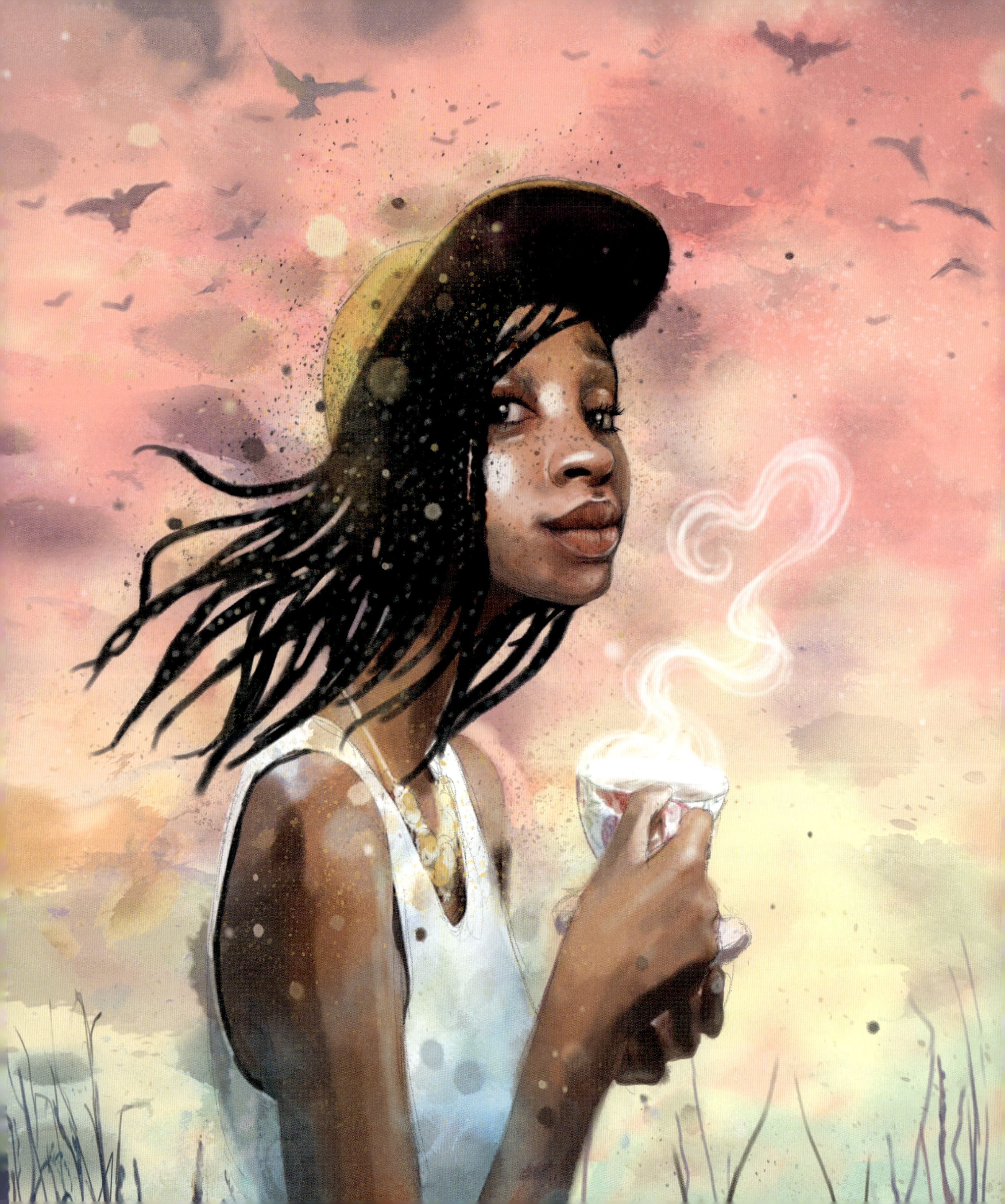

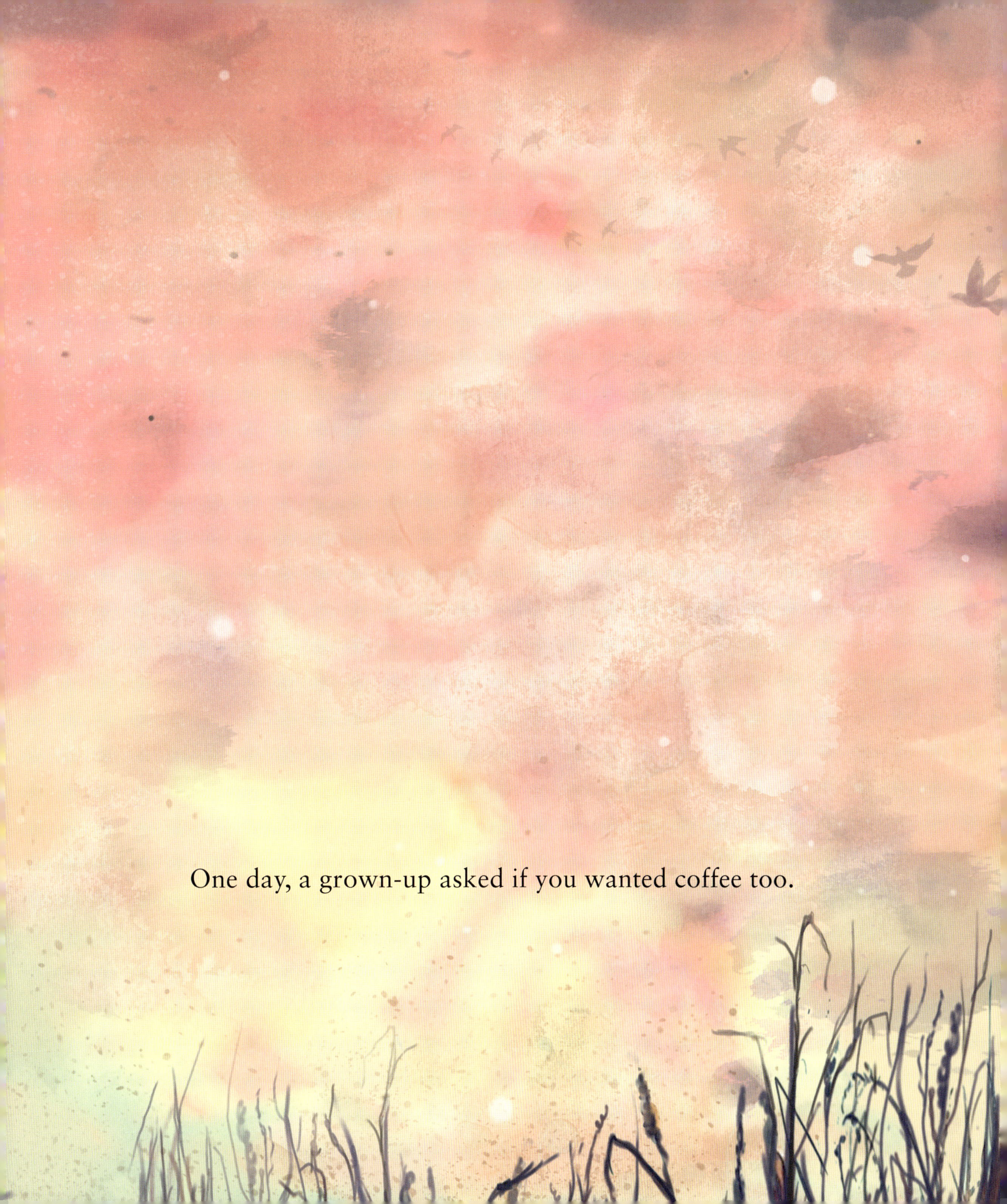
One day, a grown-up asked if you wanted coffee too.

Sometimes the world got messy.

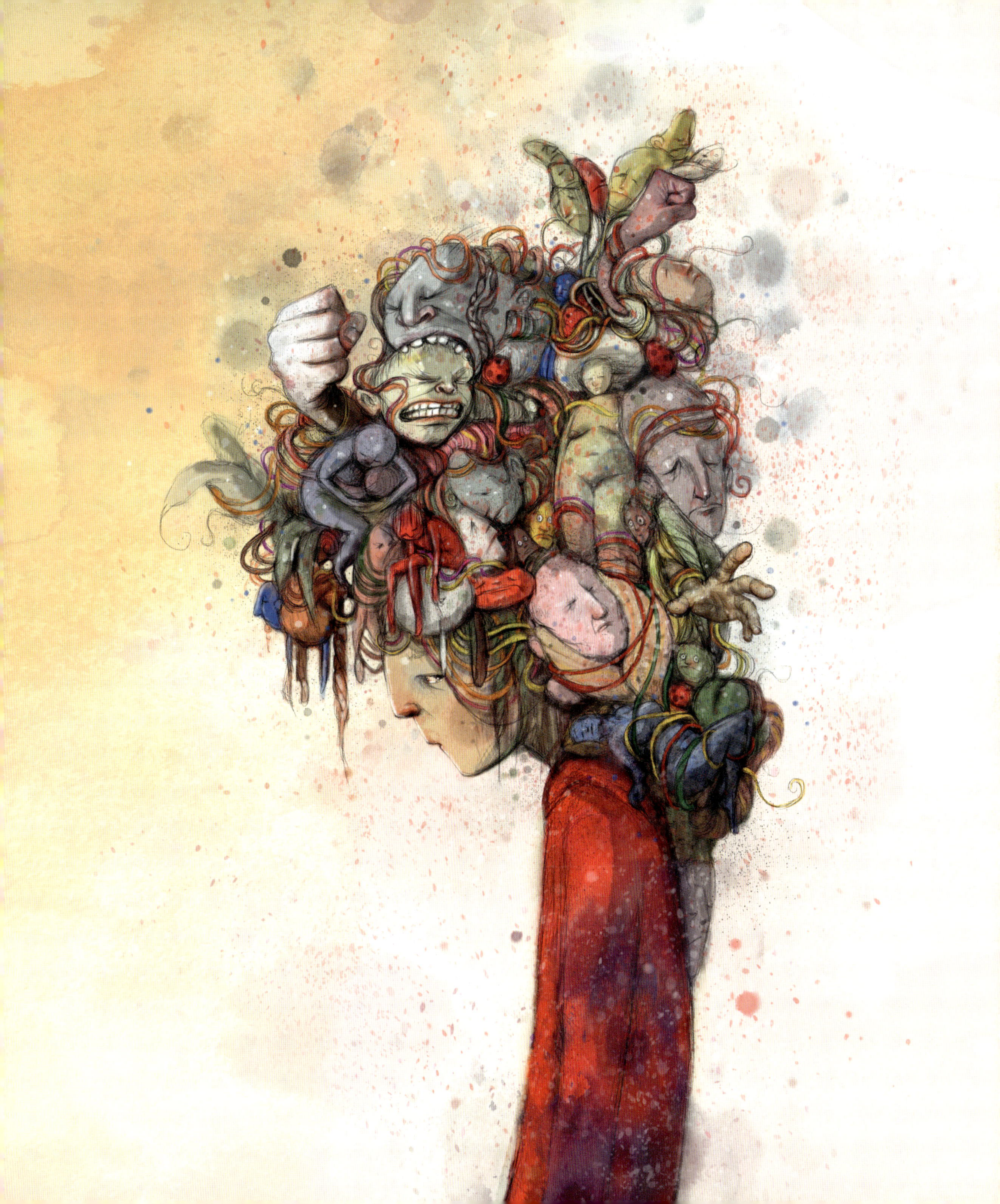

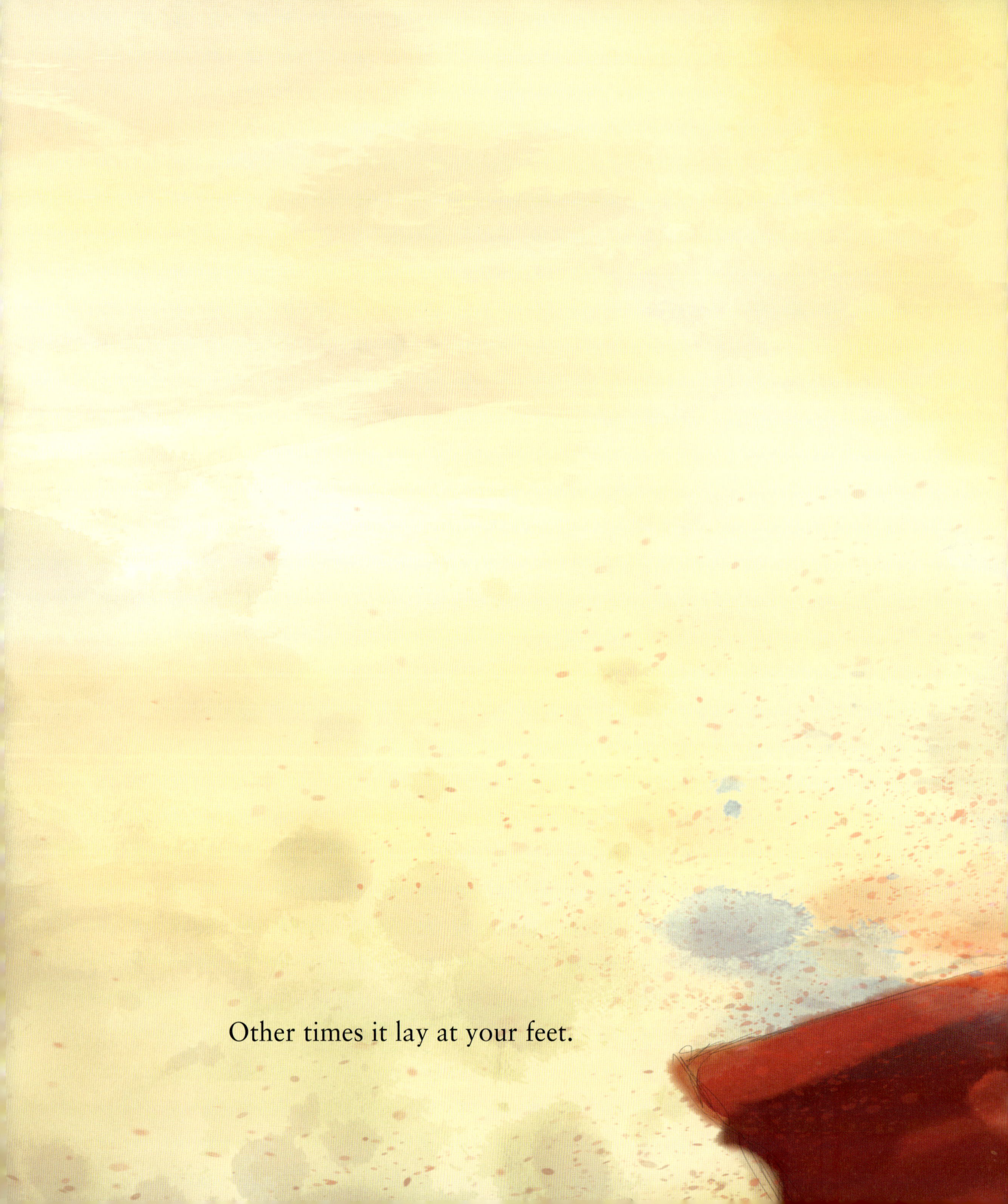

Other times it lay at your feet.

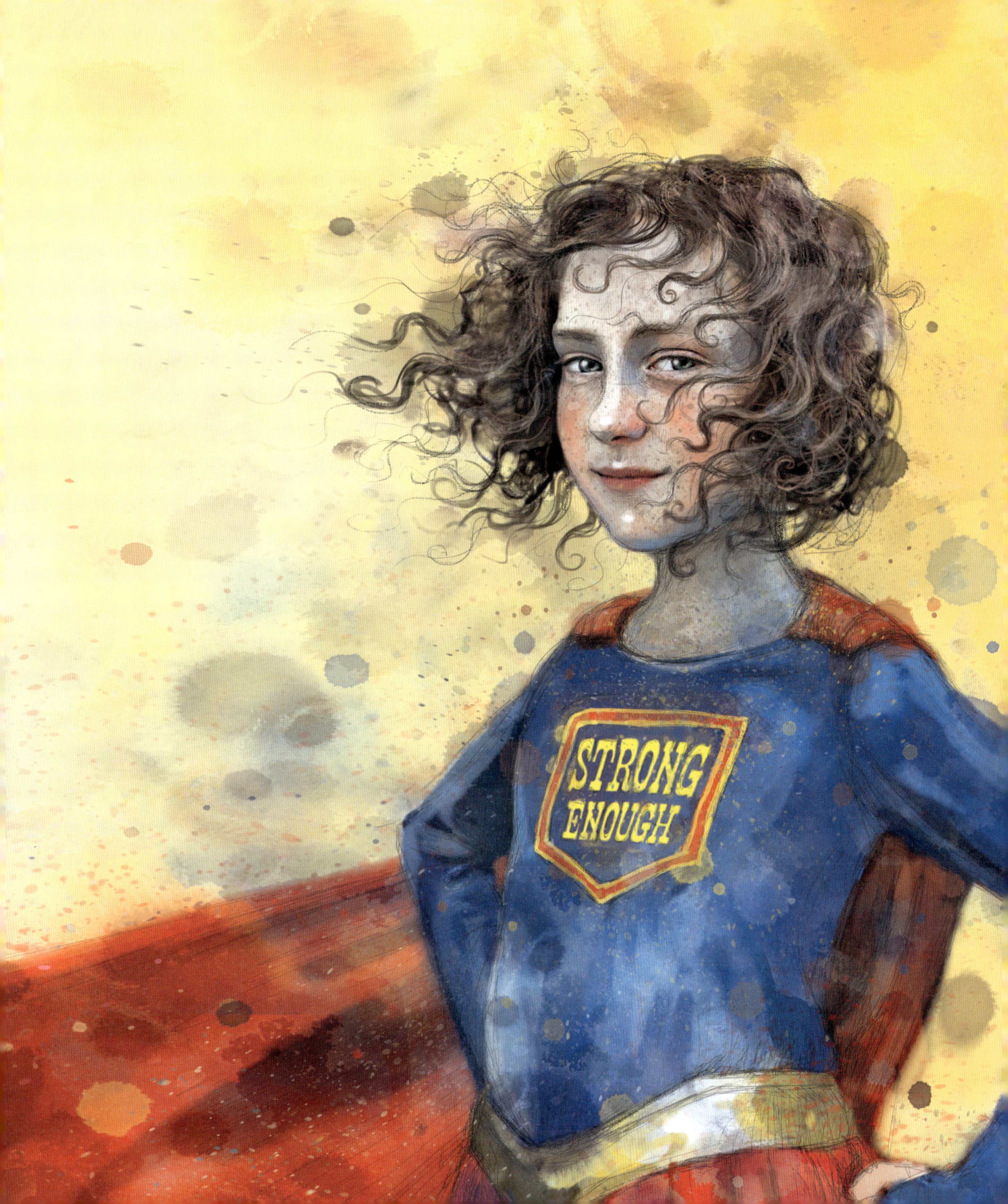

STRONG
ENOUGH

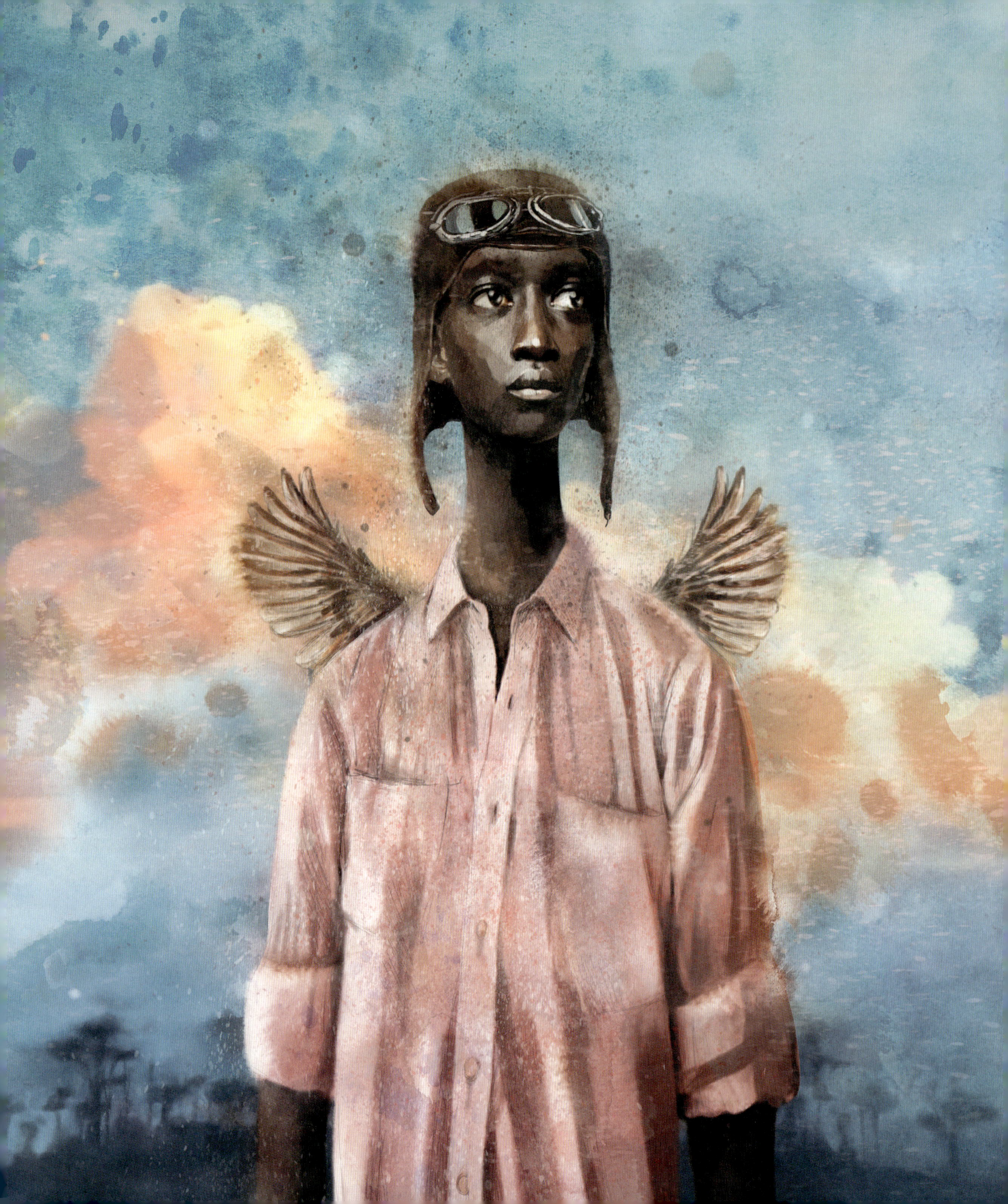

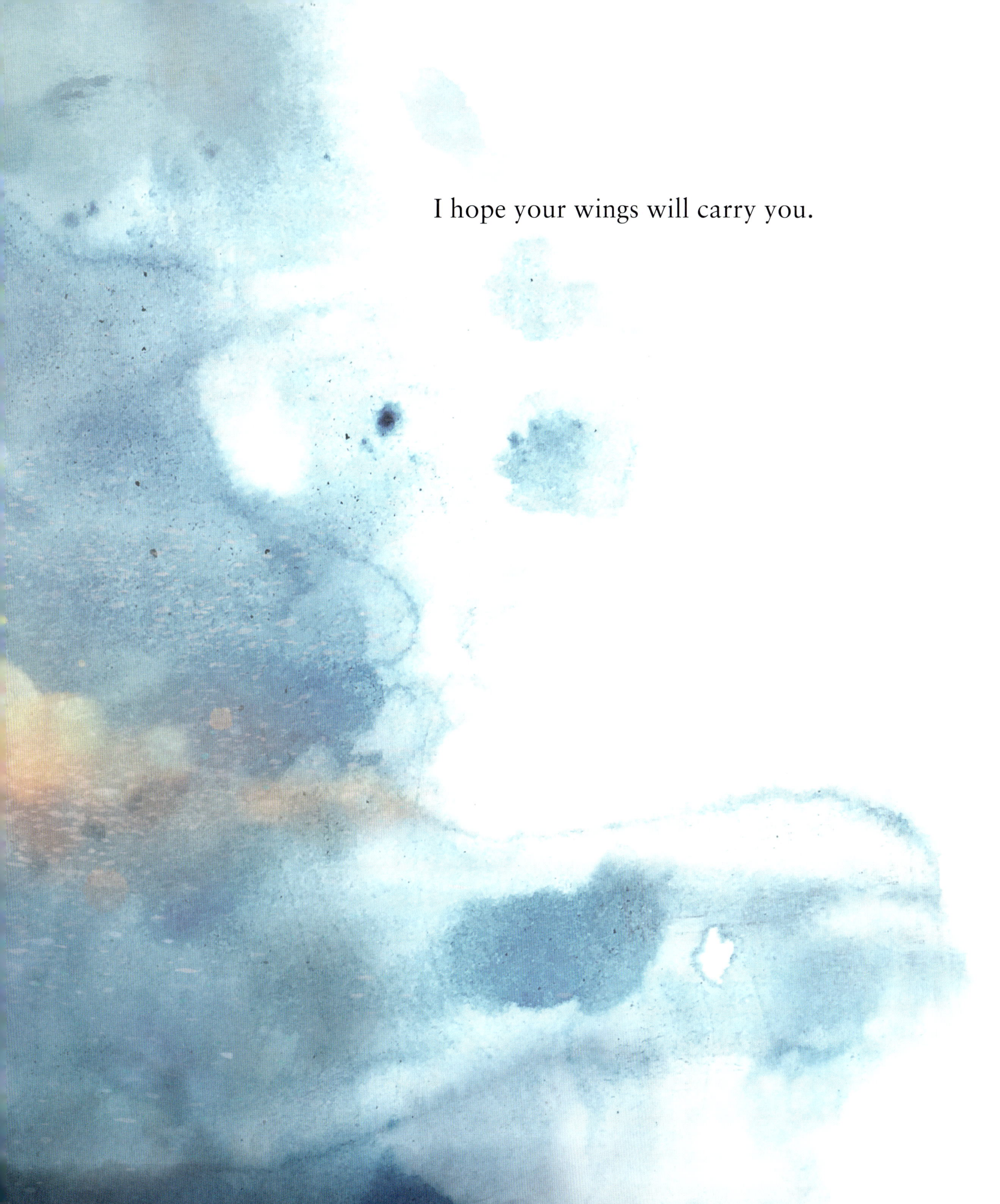
I hope your wings will carry you.

A Life of One's Own

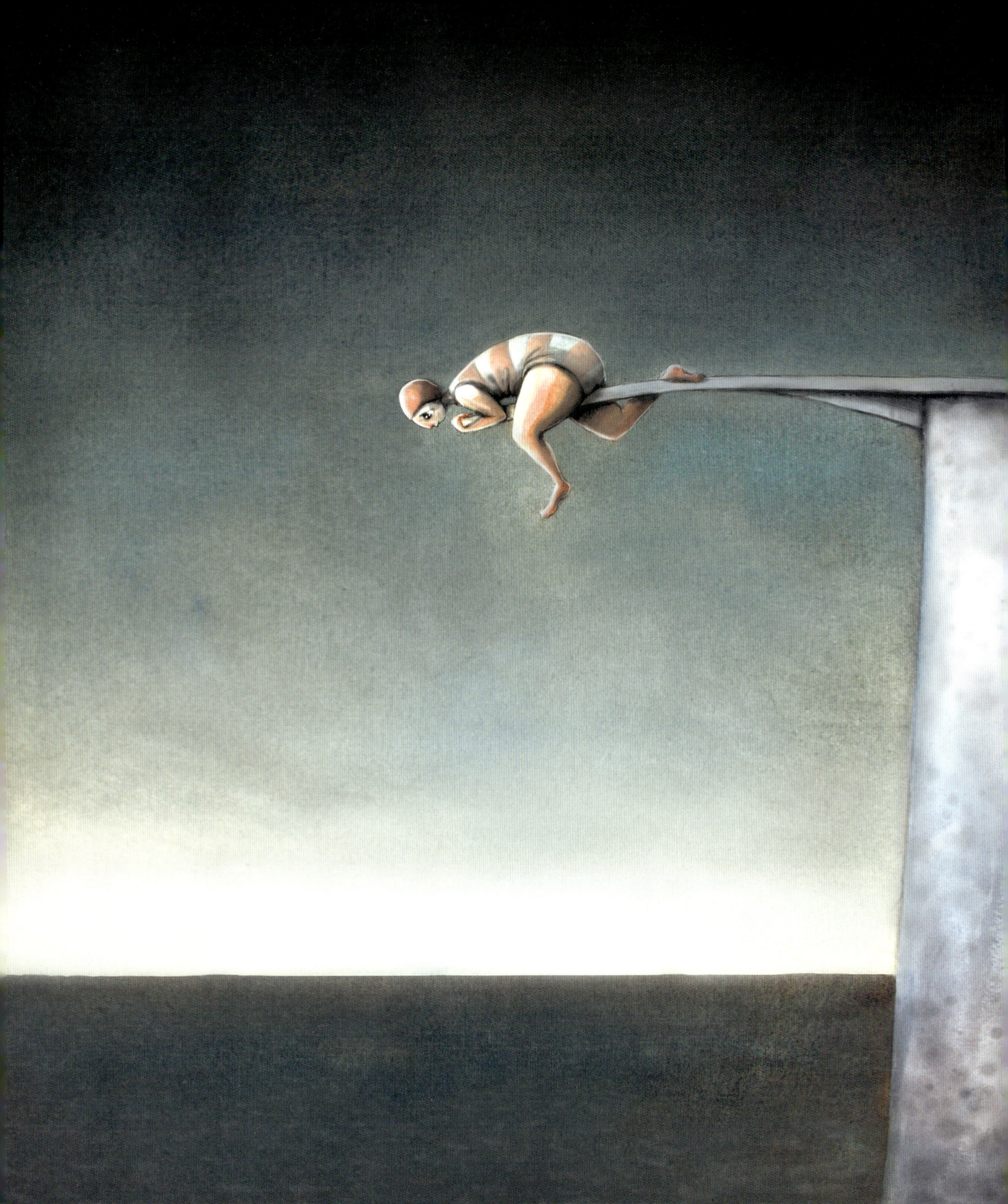

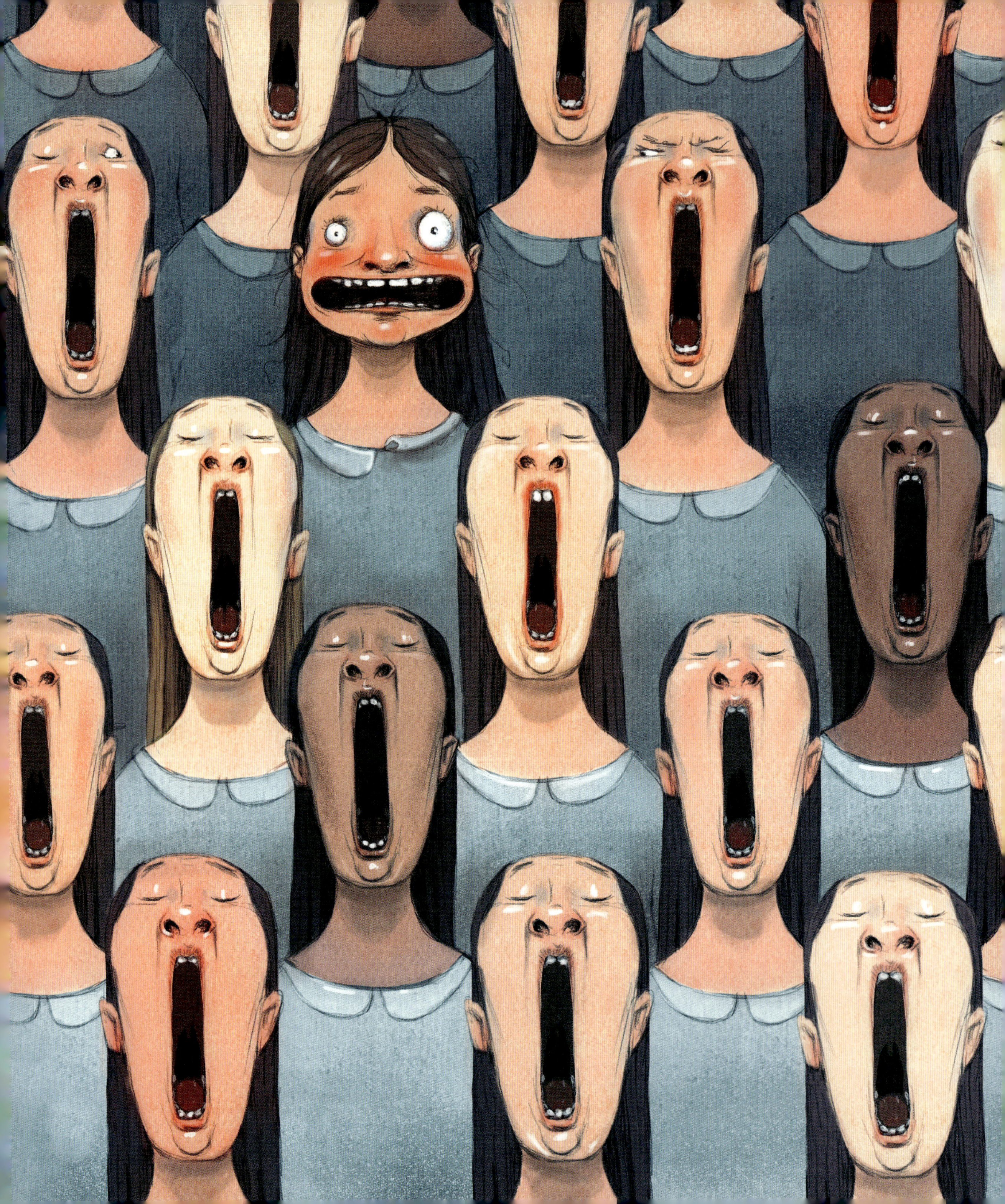

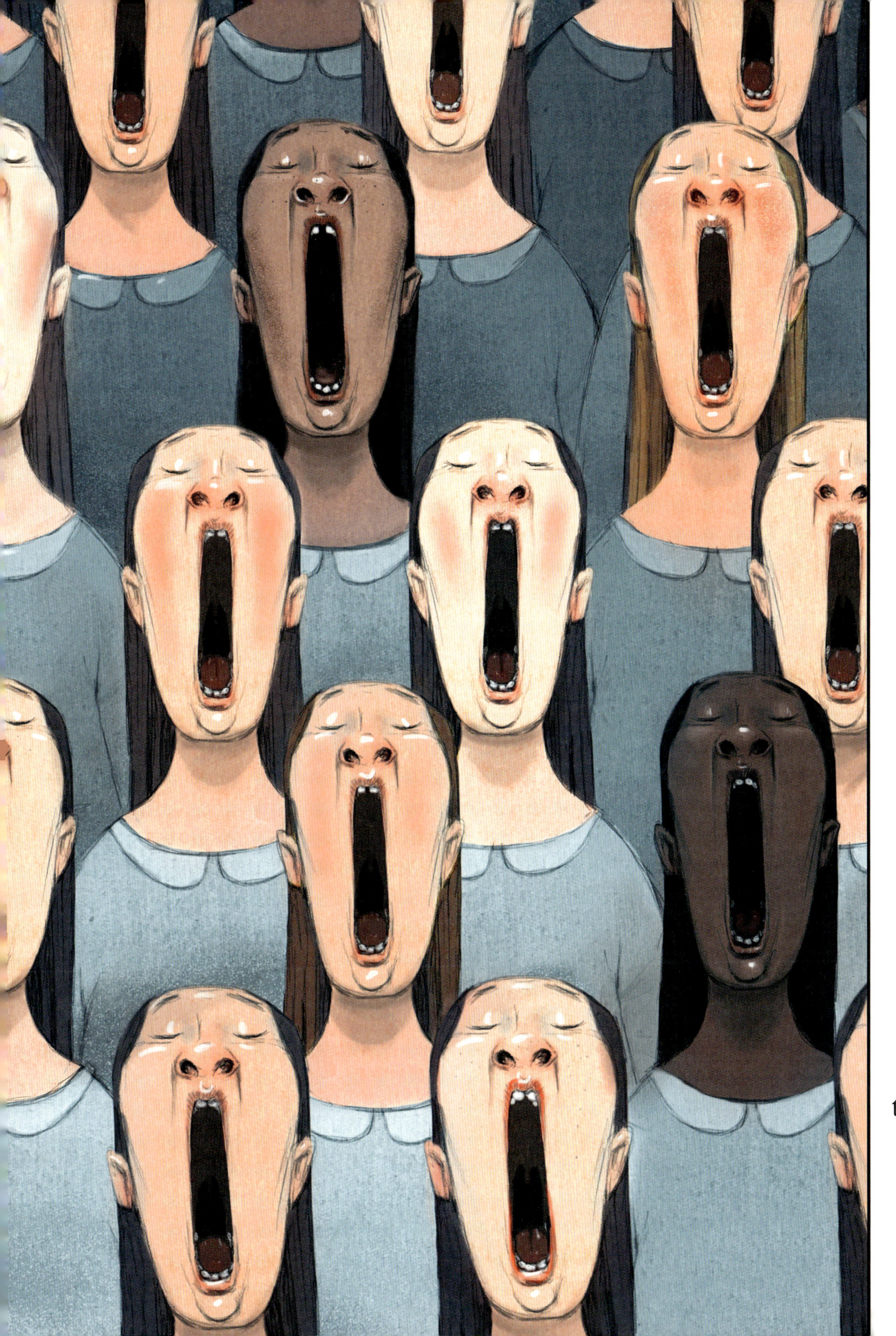

You feel
like you
don't know
the words
to the song
the grown-ups
are singing.

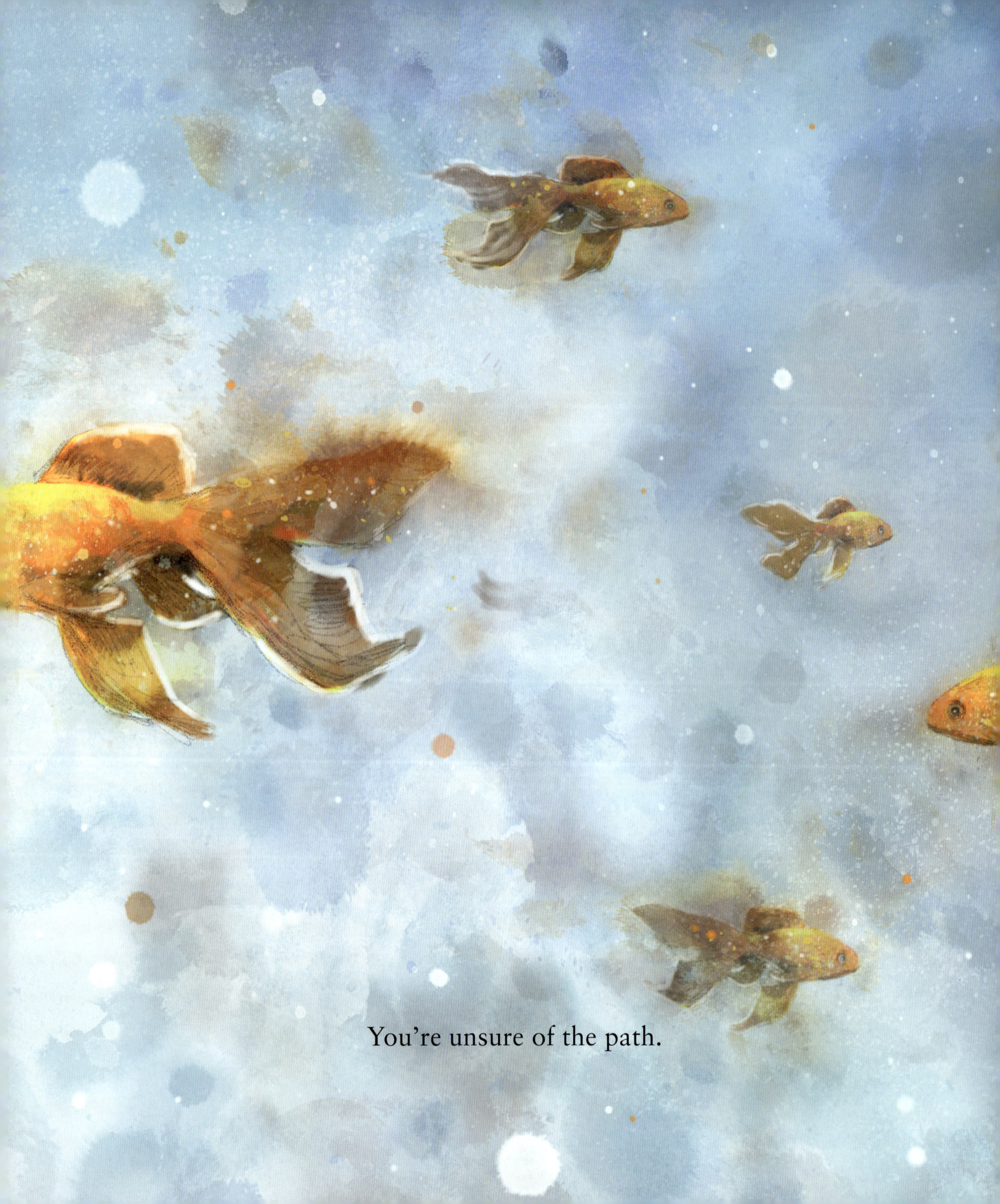

You're unsure of the path.

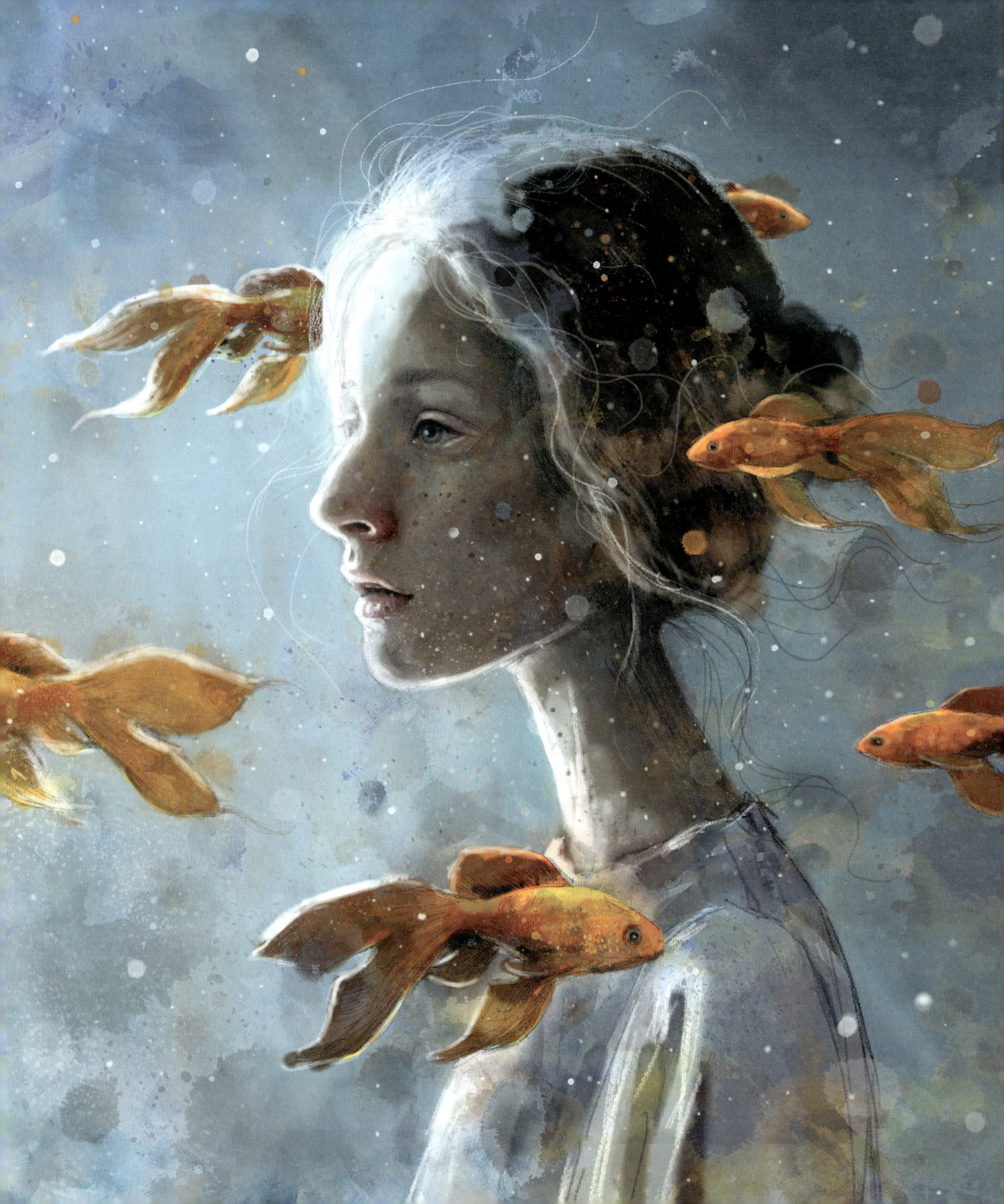

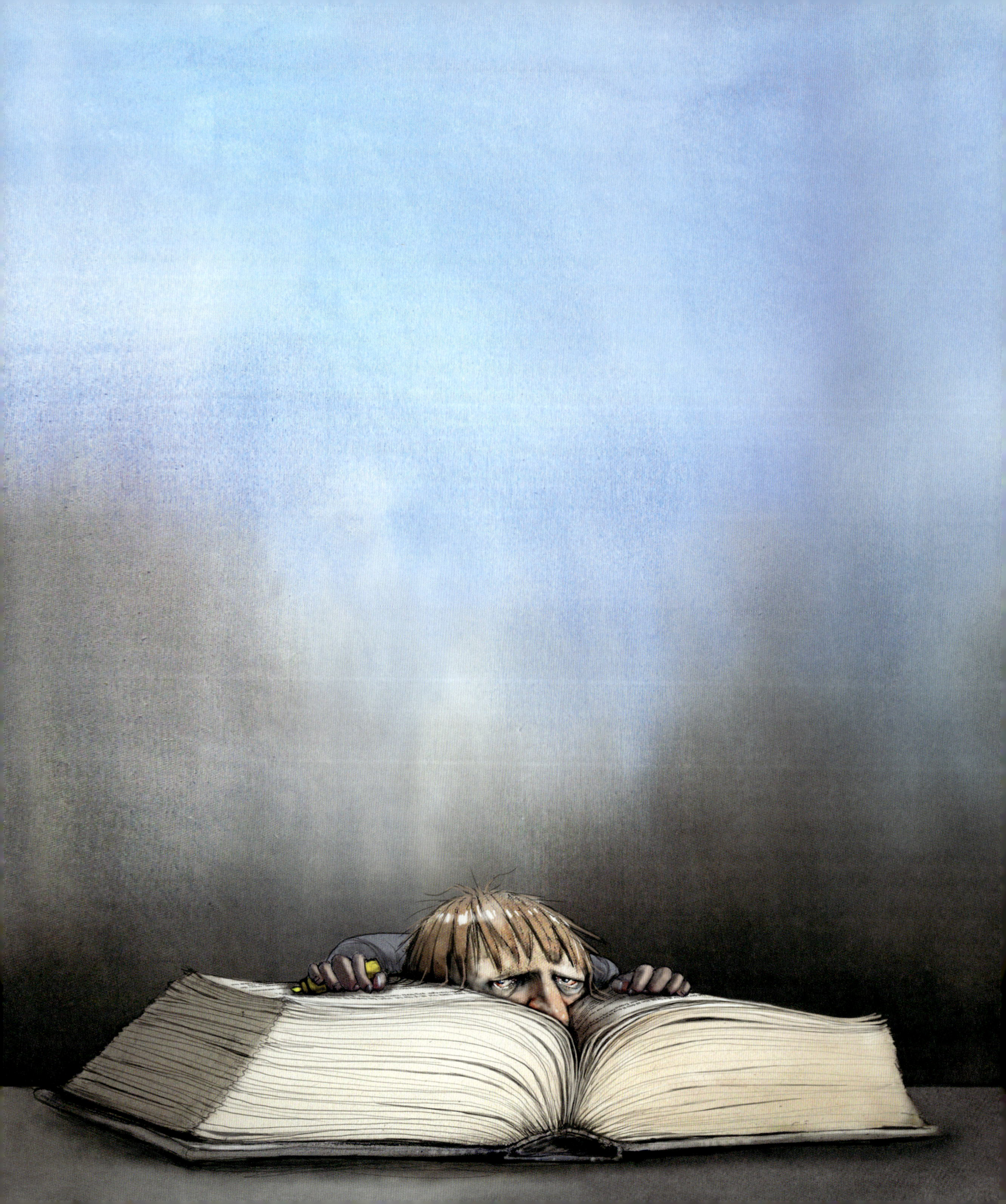

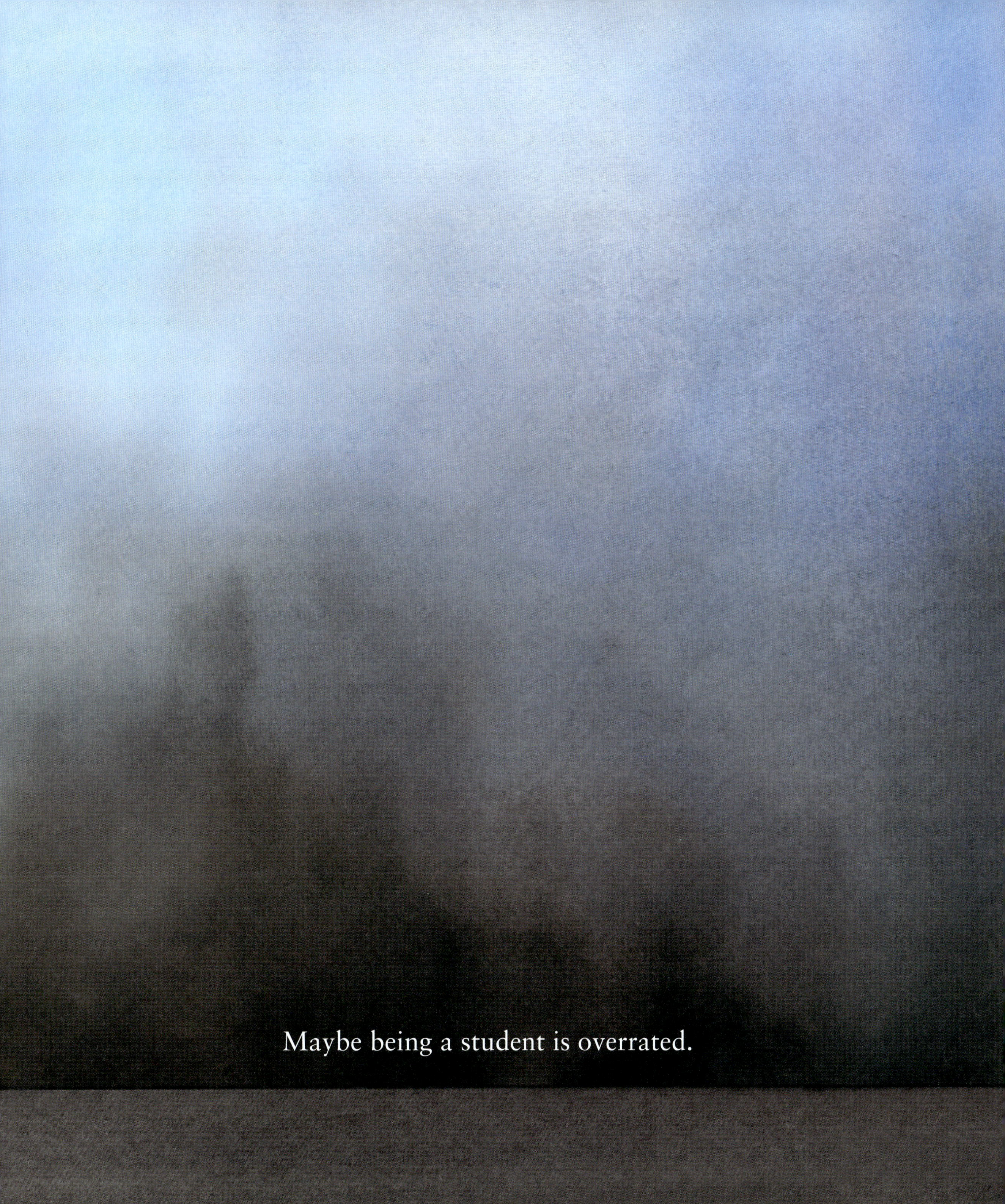

Maybe being a student is overrated.

Maybe it's the best time of your life.

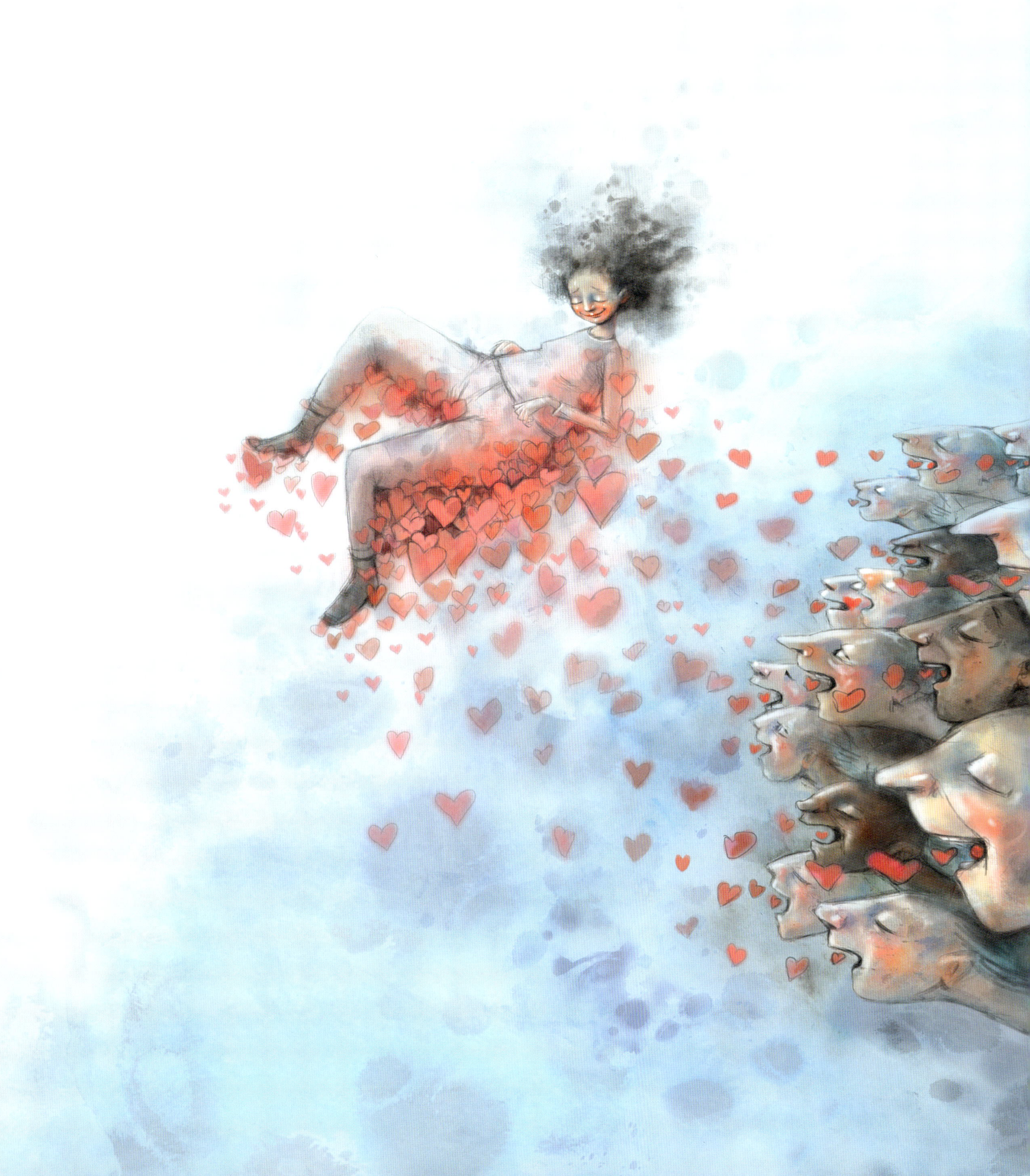

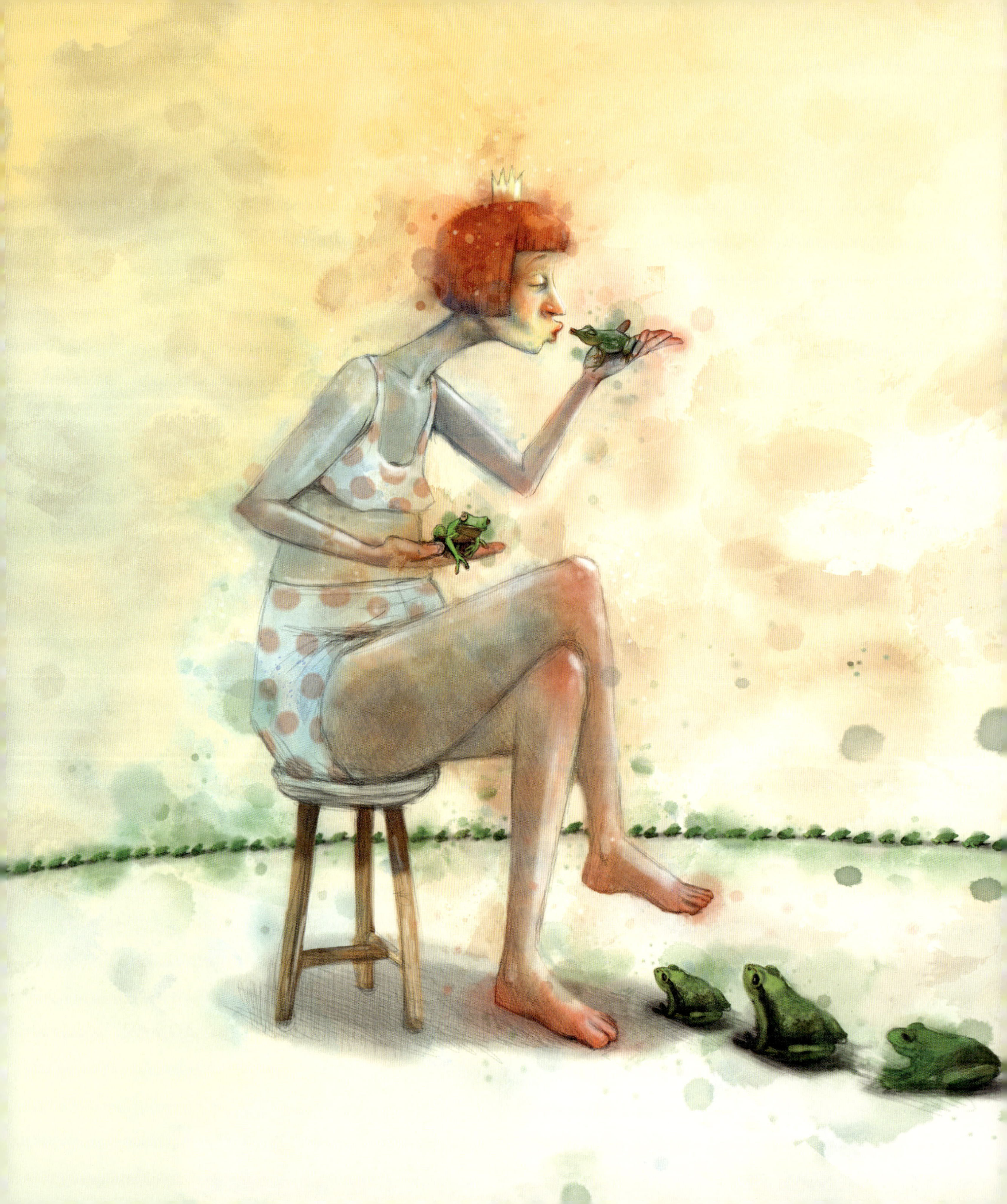

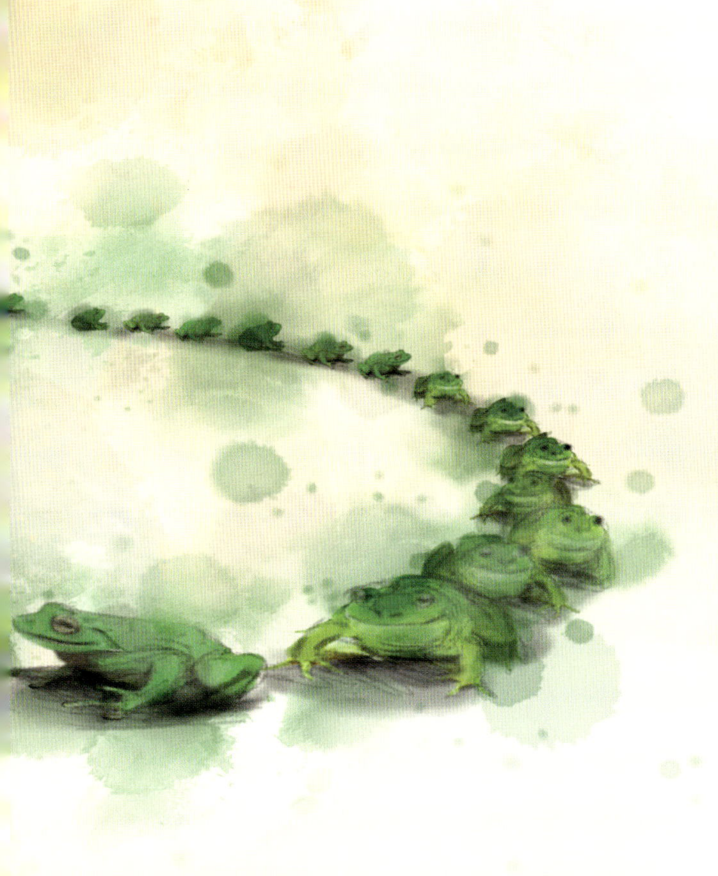

We seek,

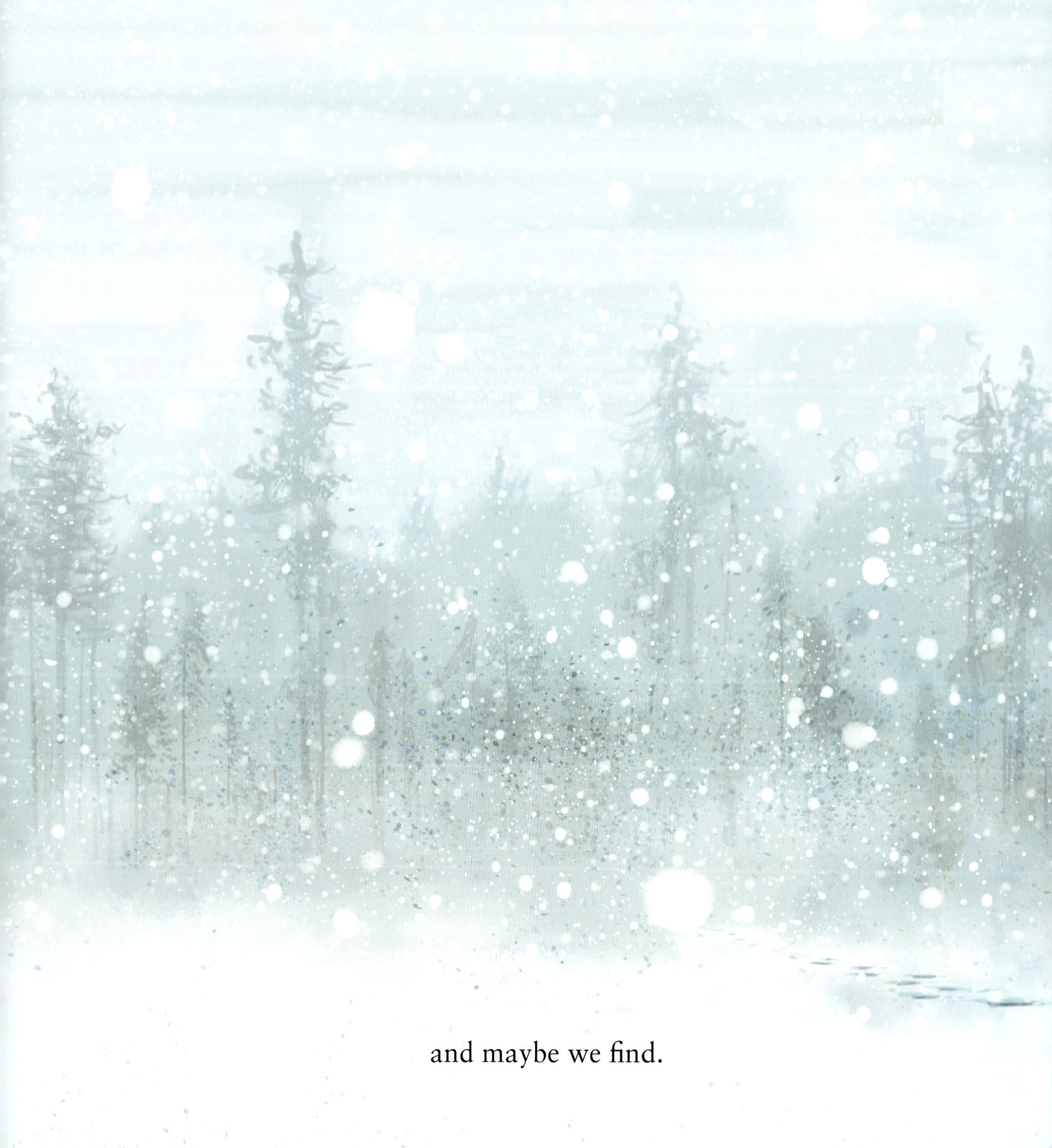

and maybe we find.

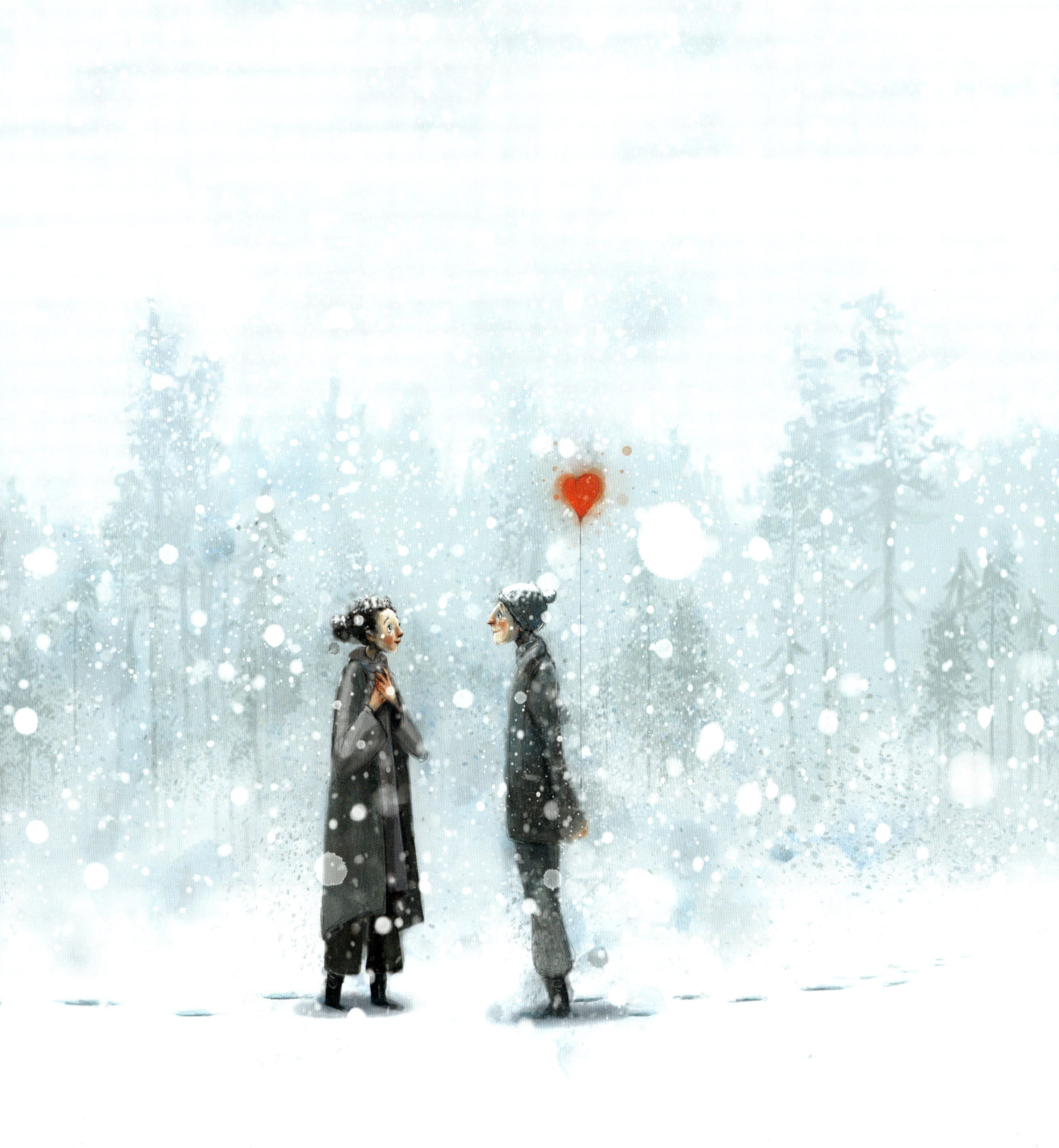

Such bliss!

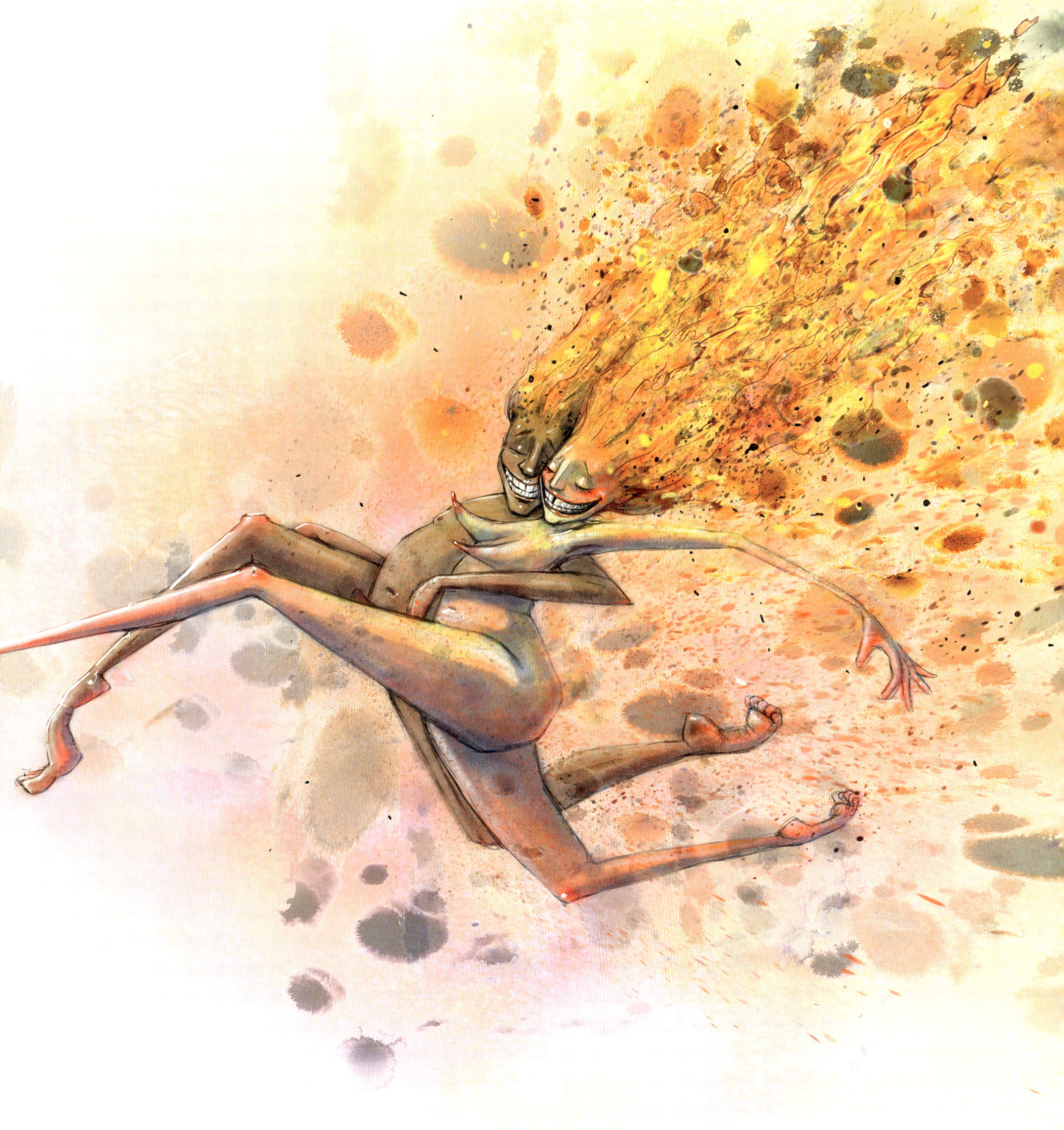

To find …

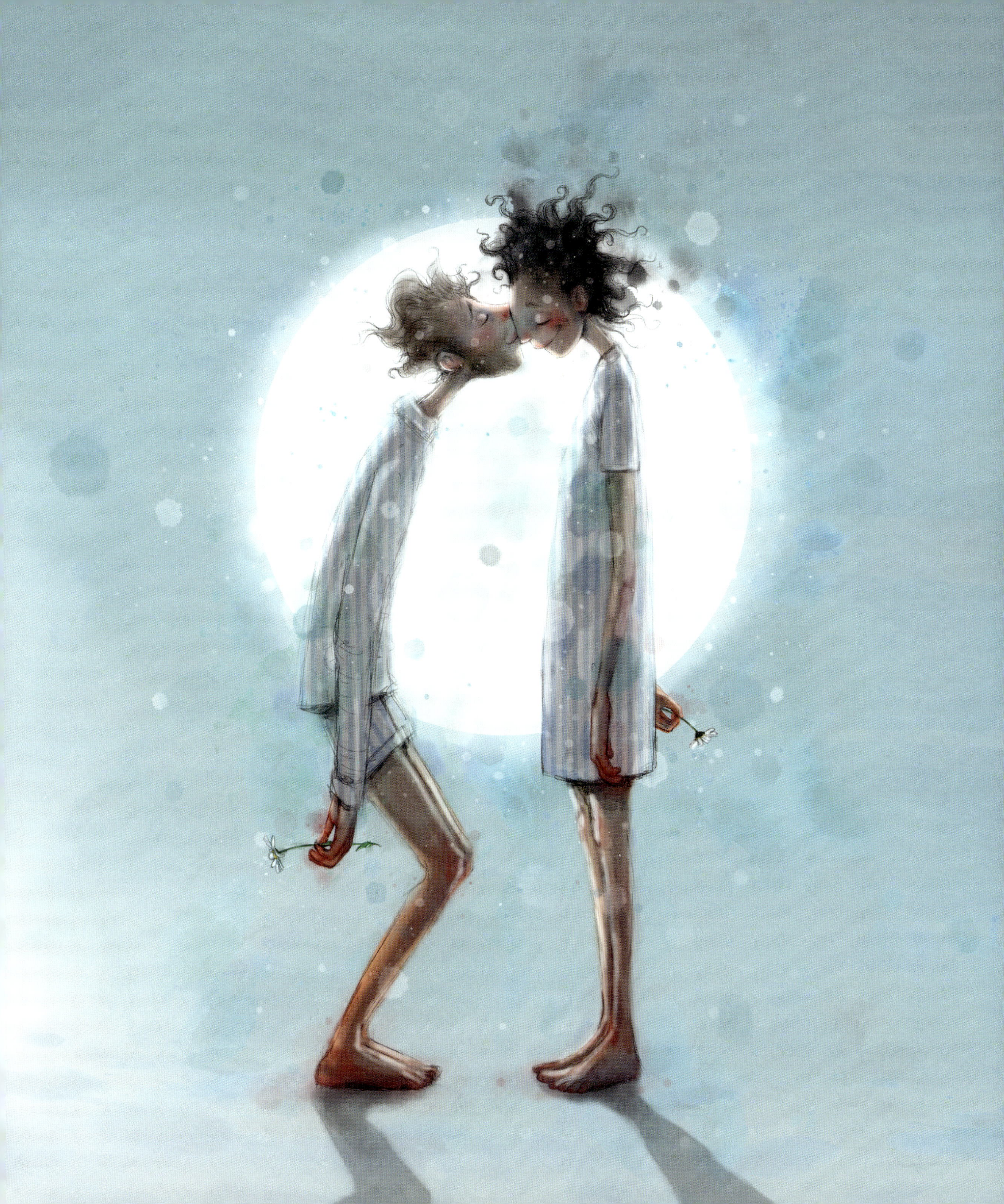

the one ...

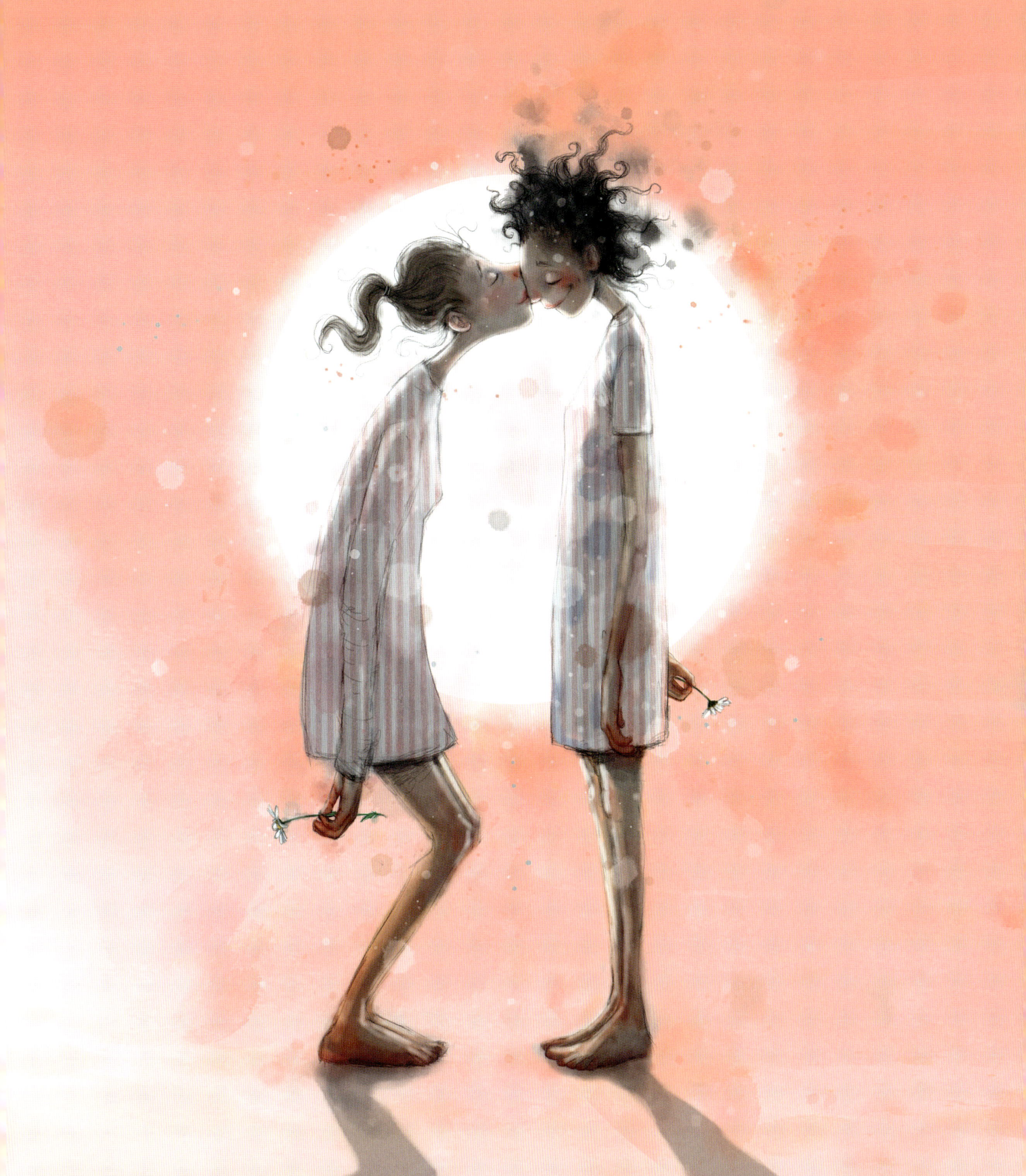

to love.

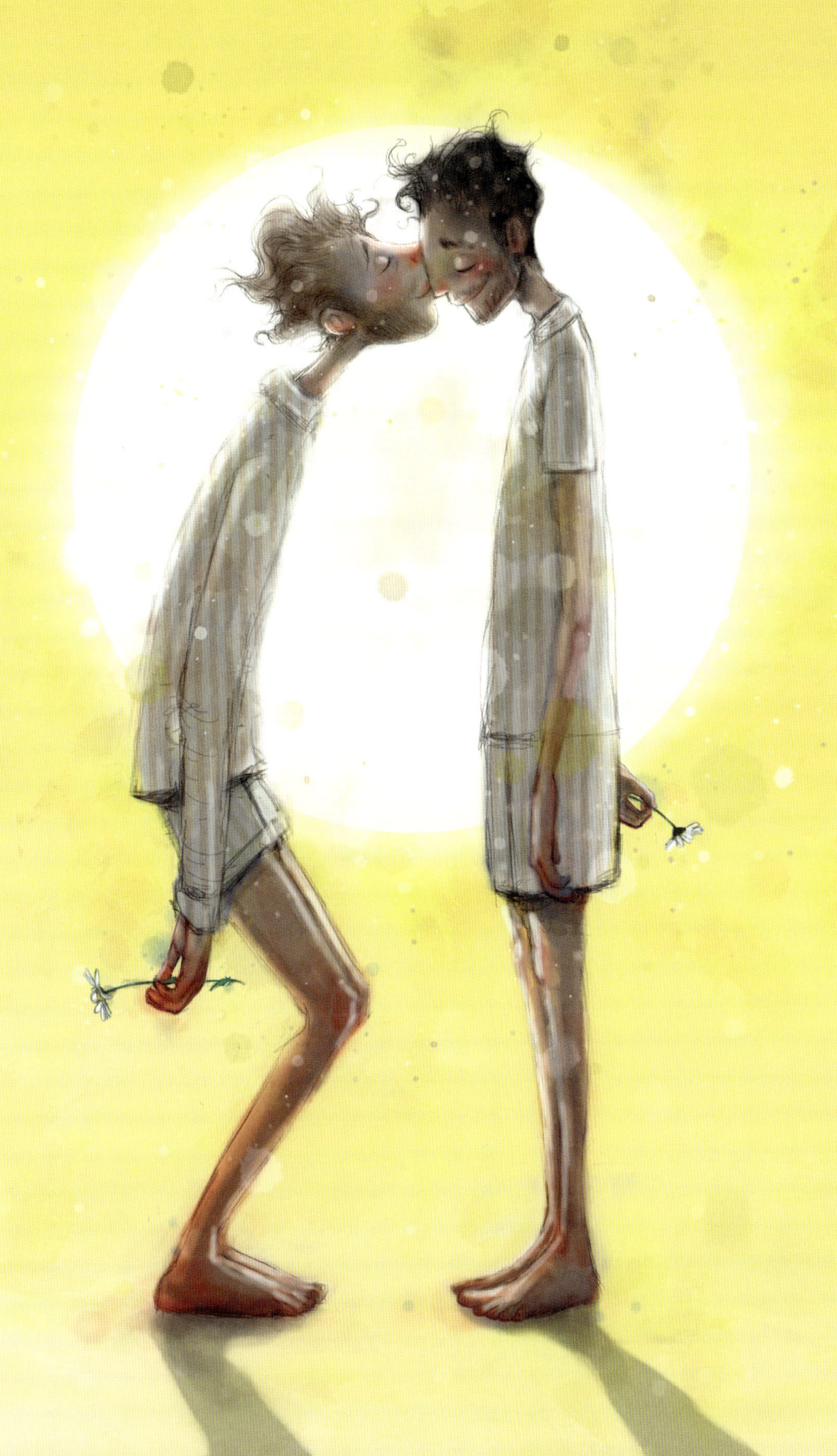

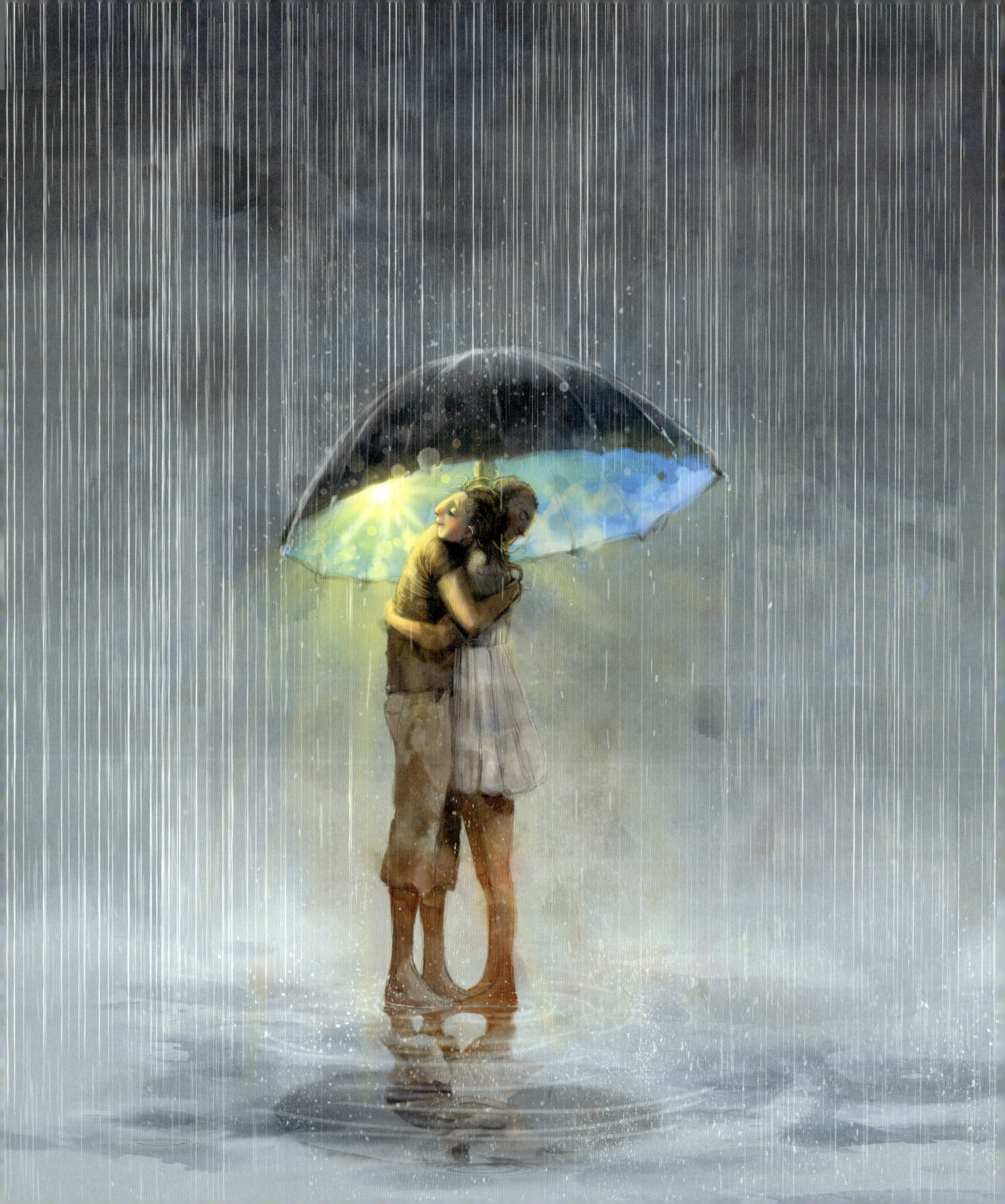

But then everyday life comes along,

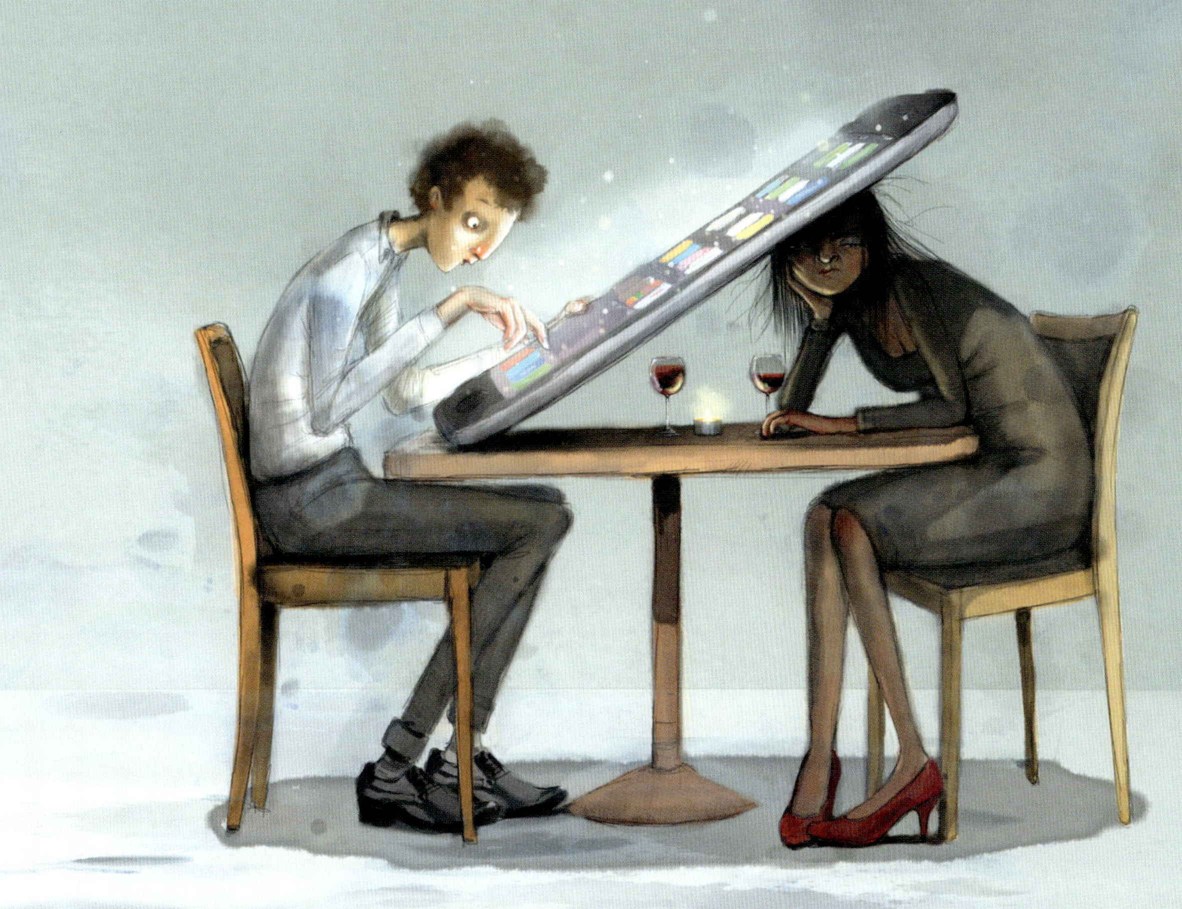

and you need to keep pace.

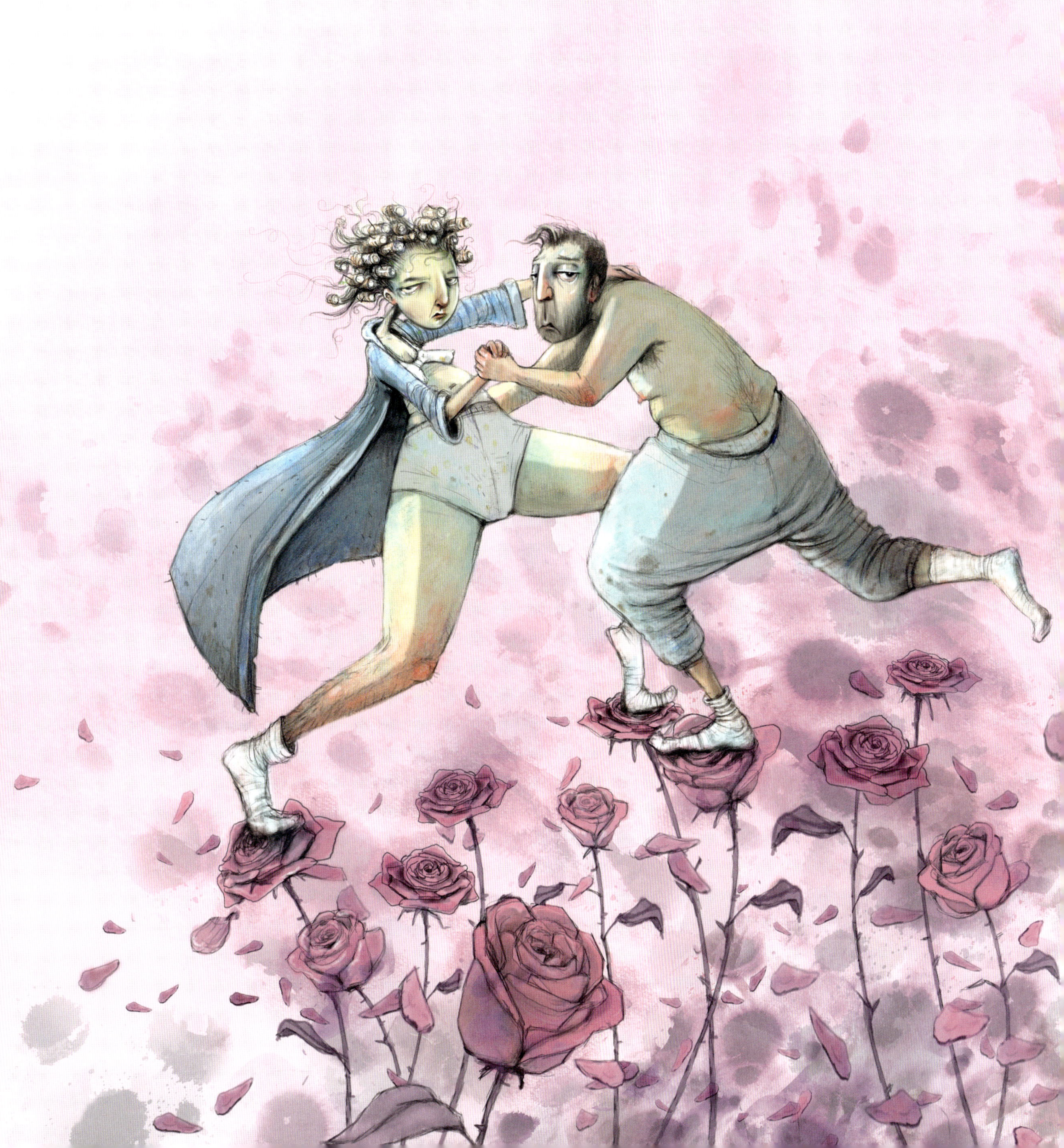

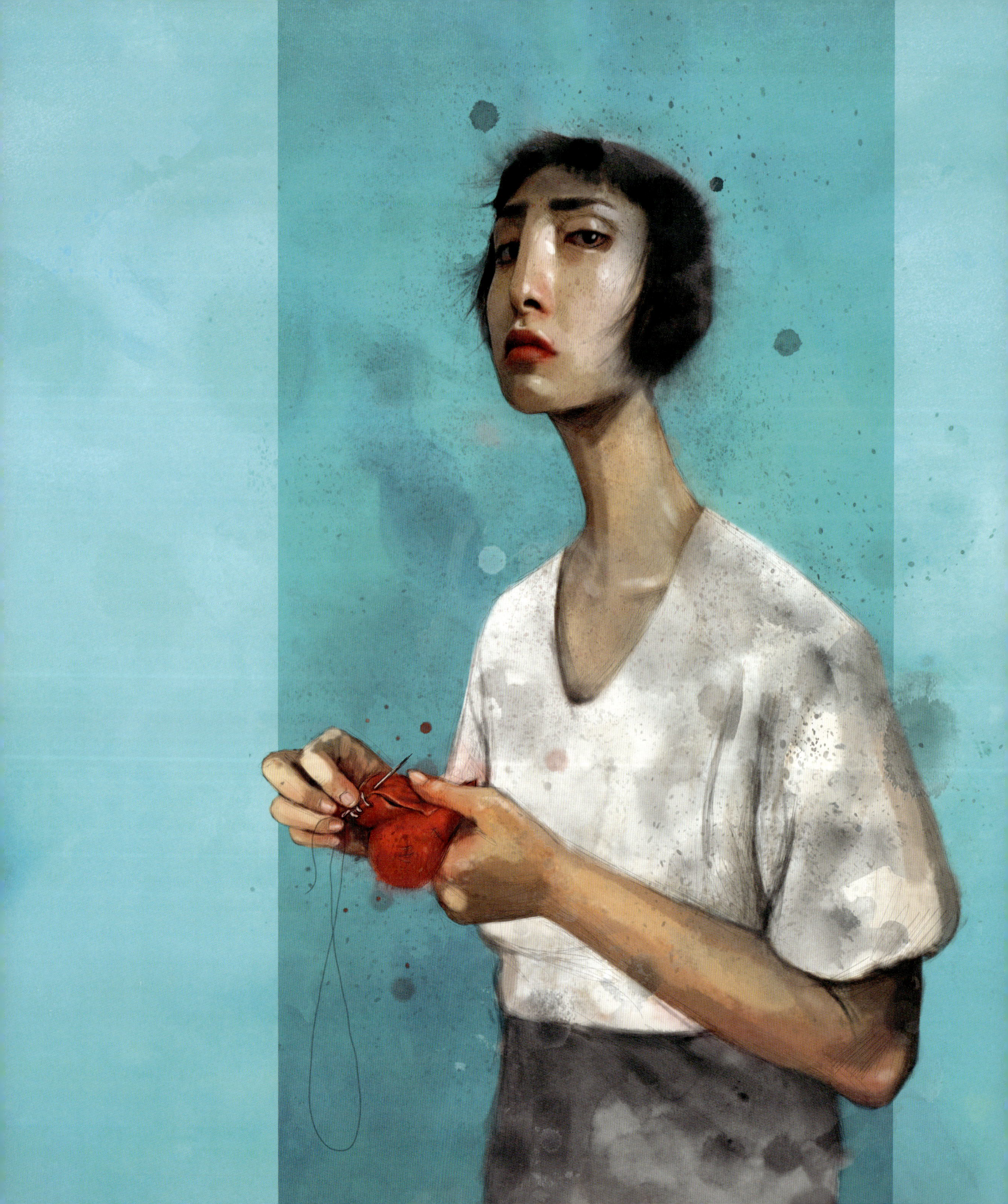

Maybe it all falls apart.

Or maybe it's the two of you.

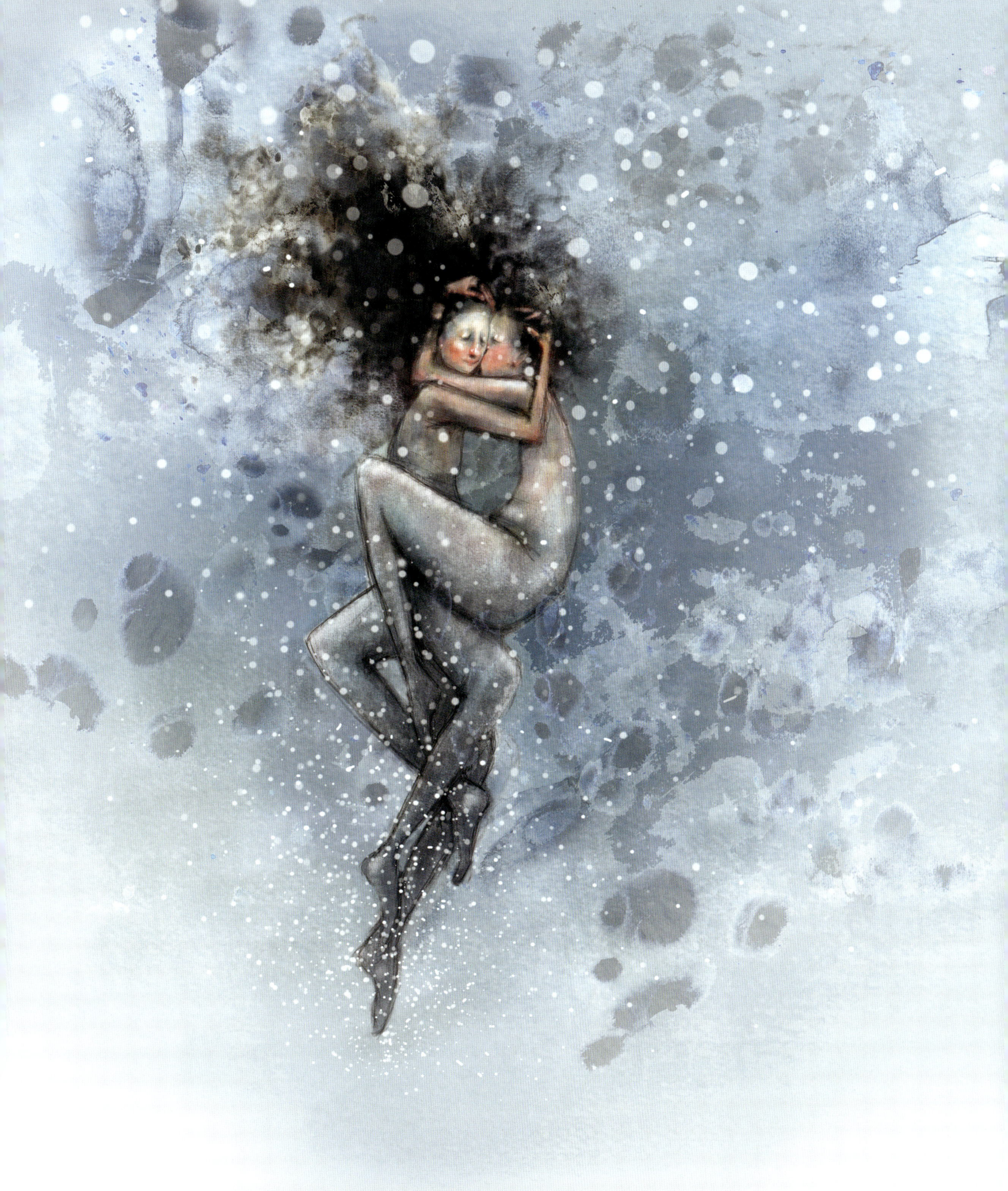

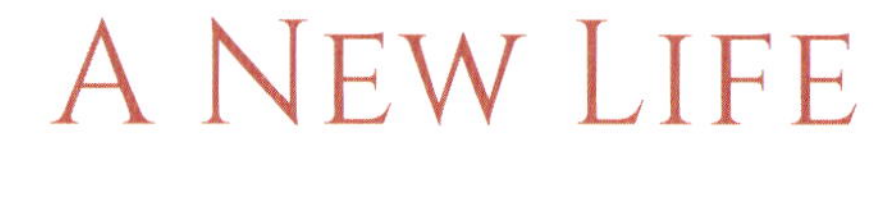

A NEW LIFE

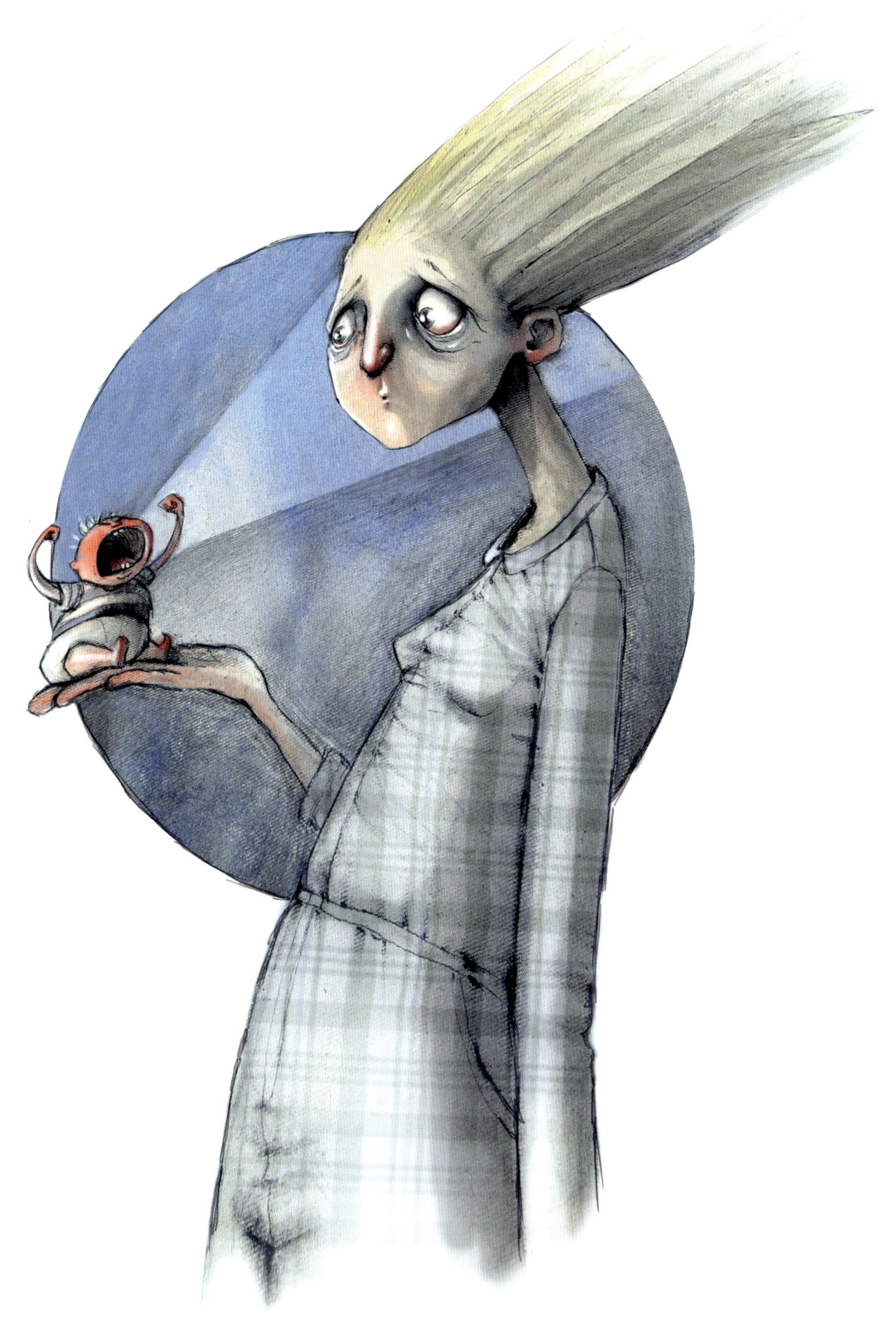

You wish there were a user manual

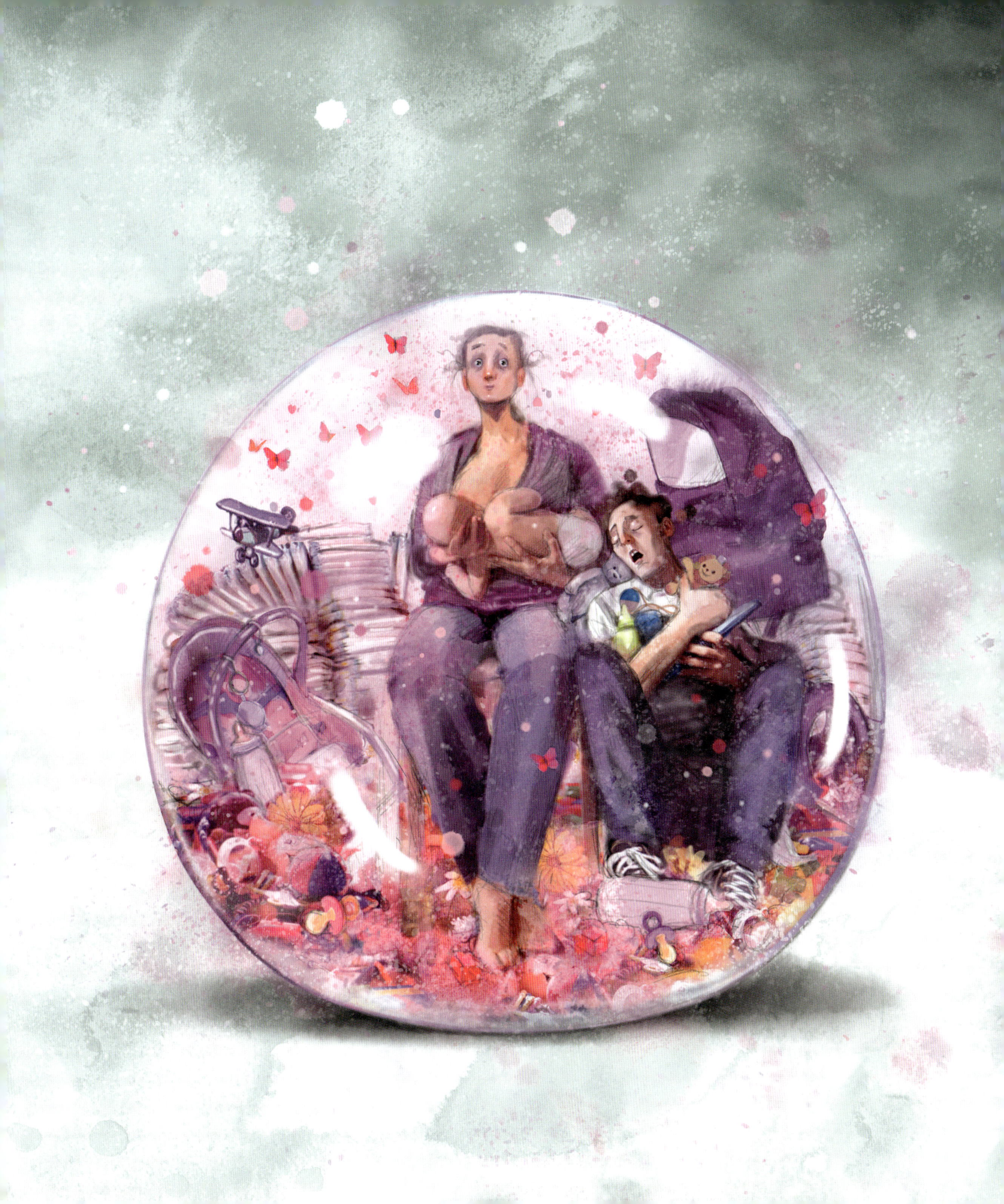

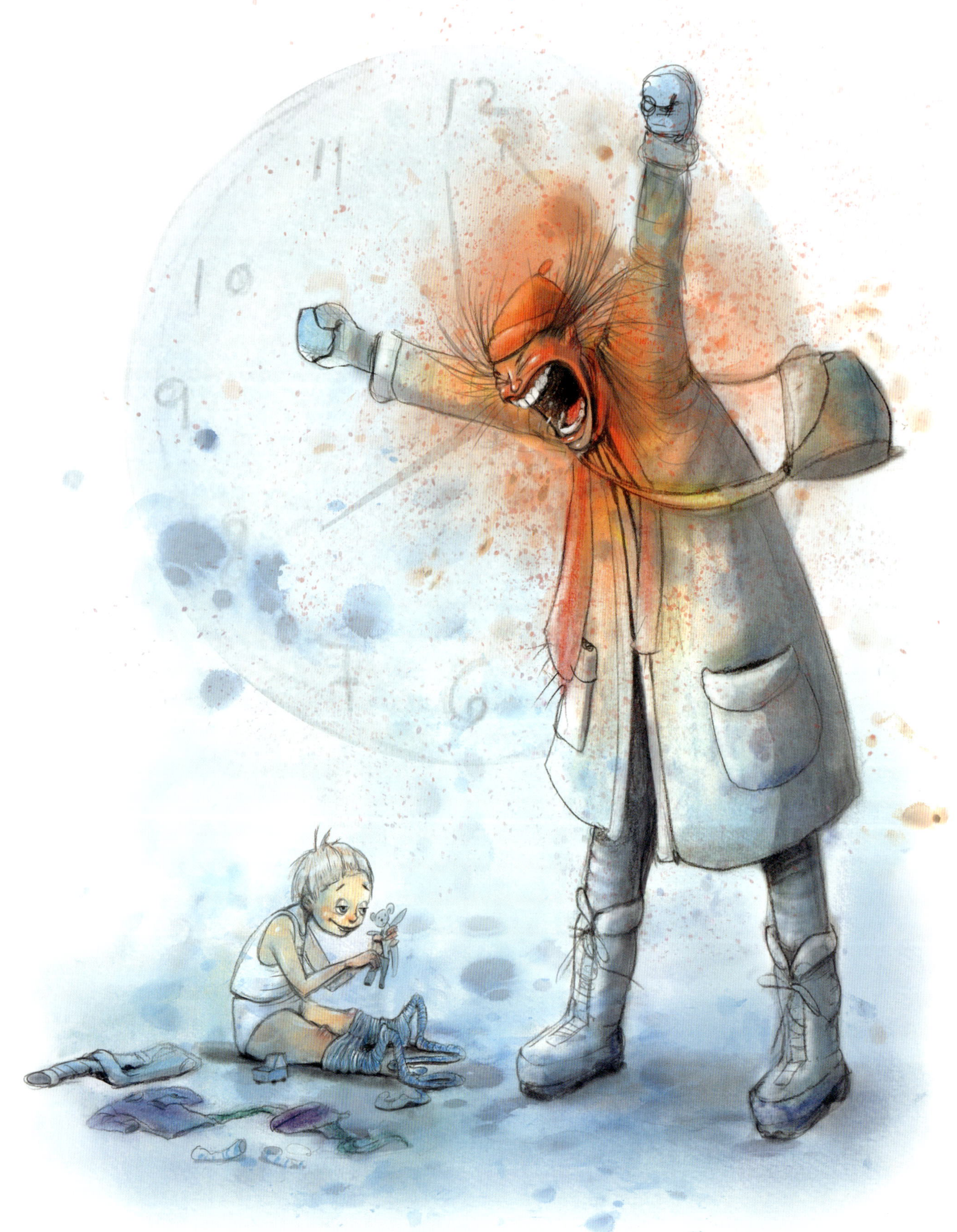

for difficult mornings,

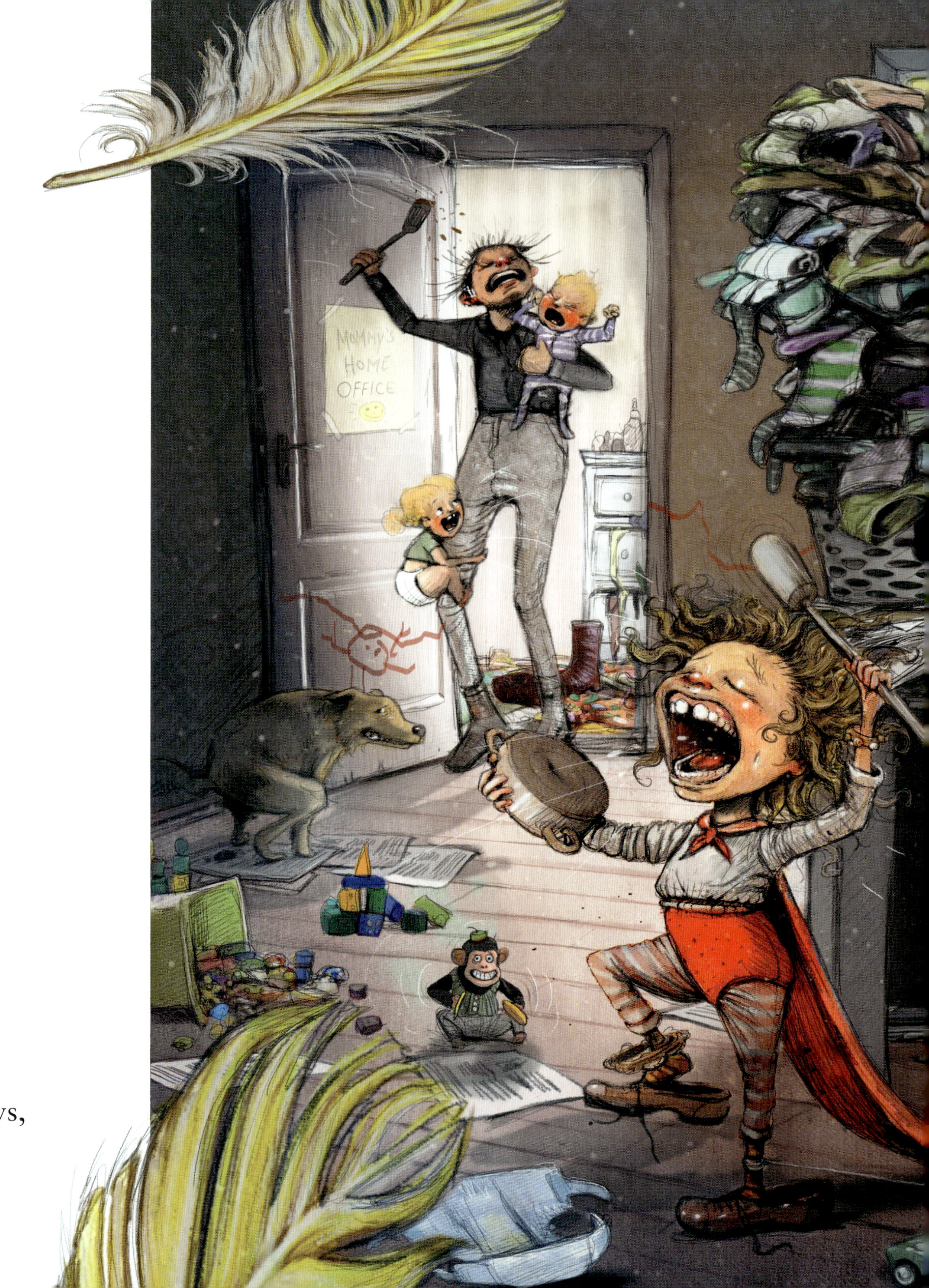

days,

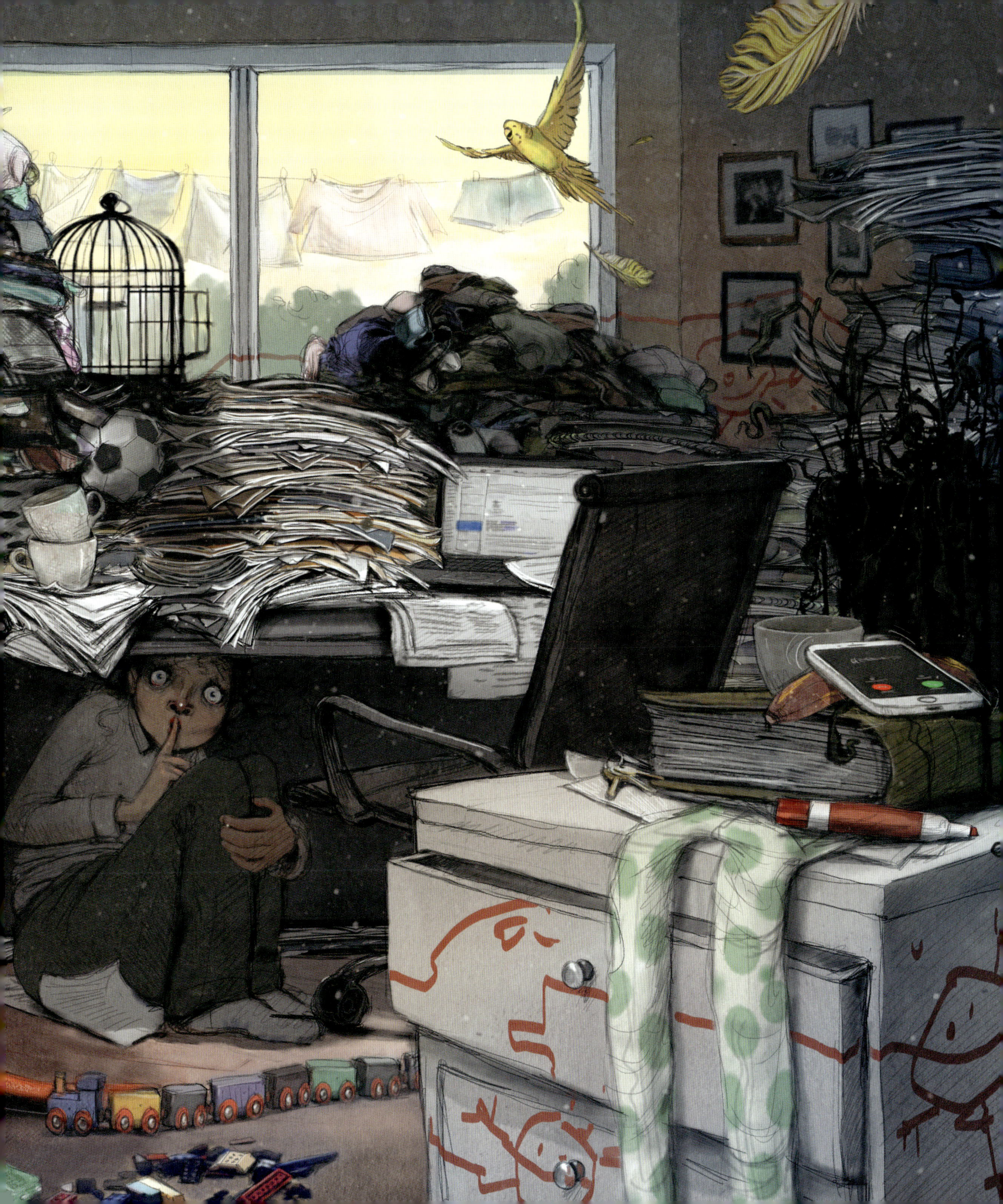

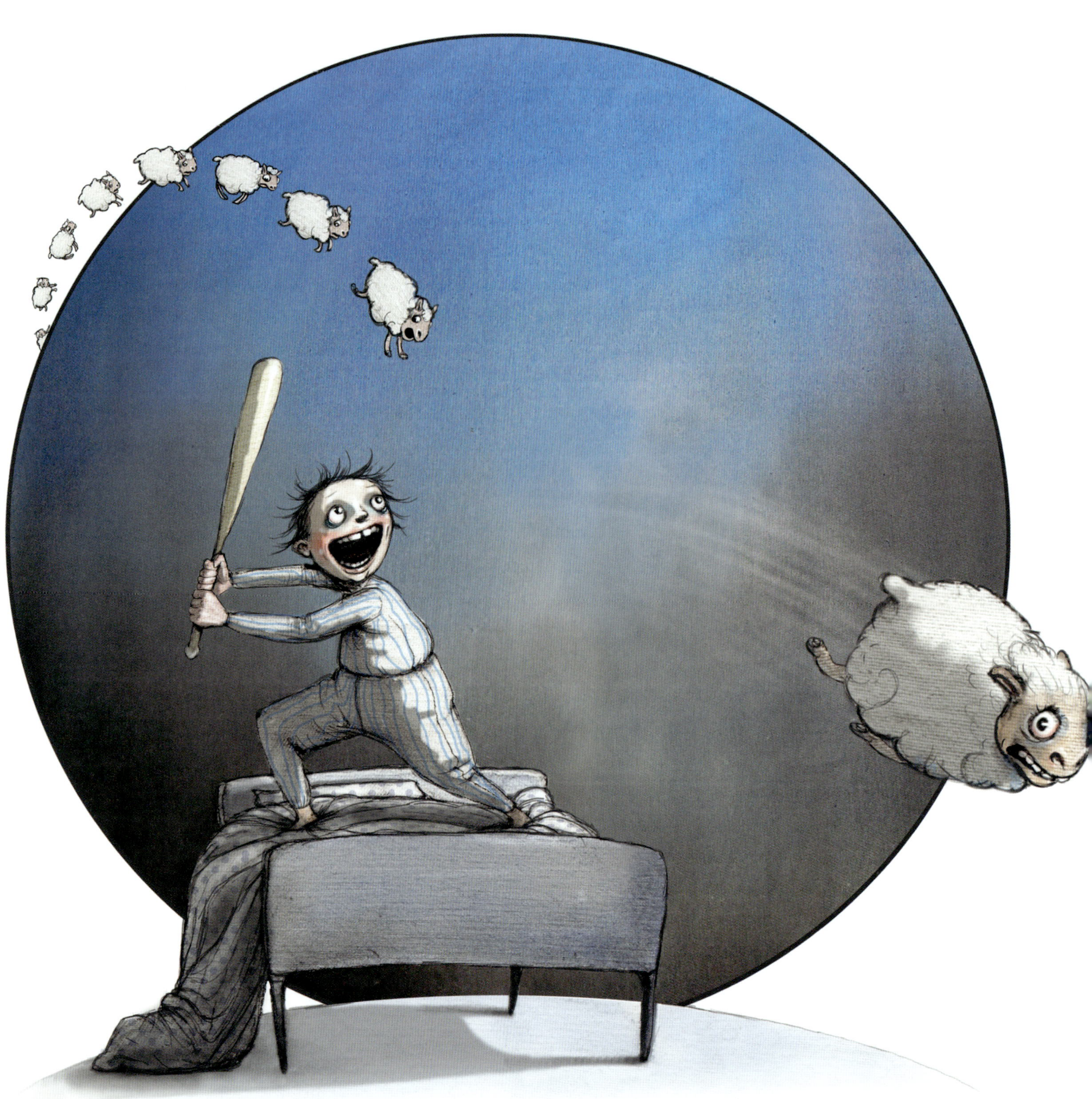

and nights.

It takes a toll.

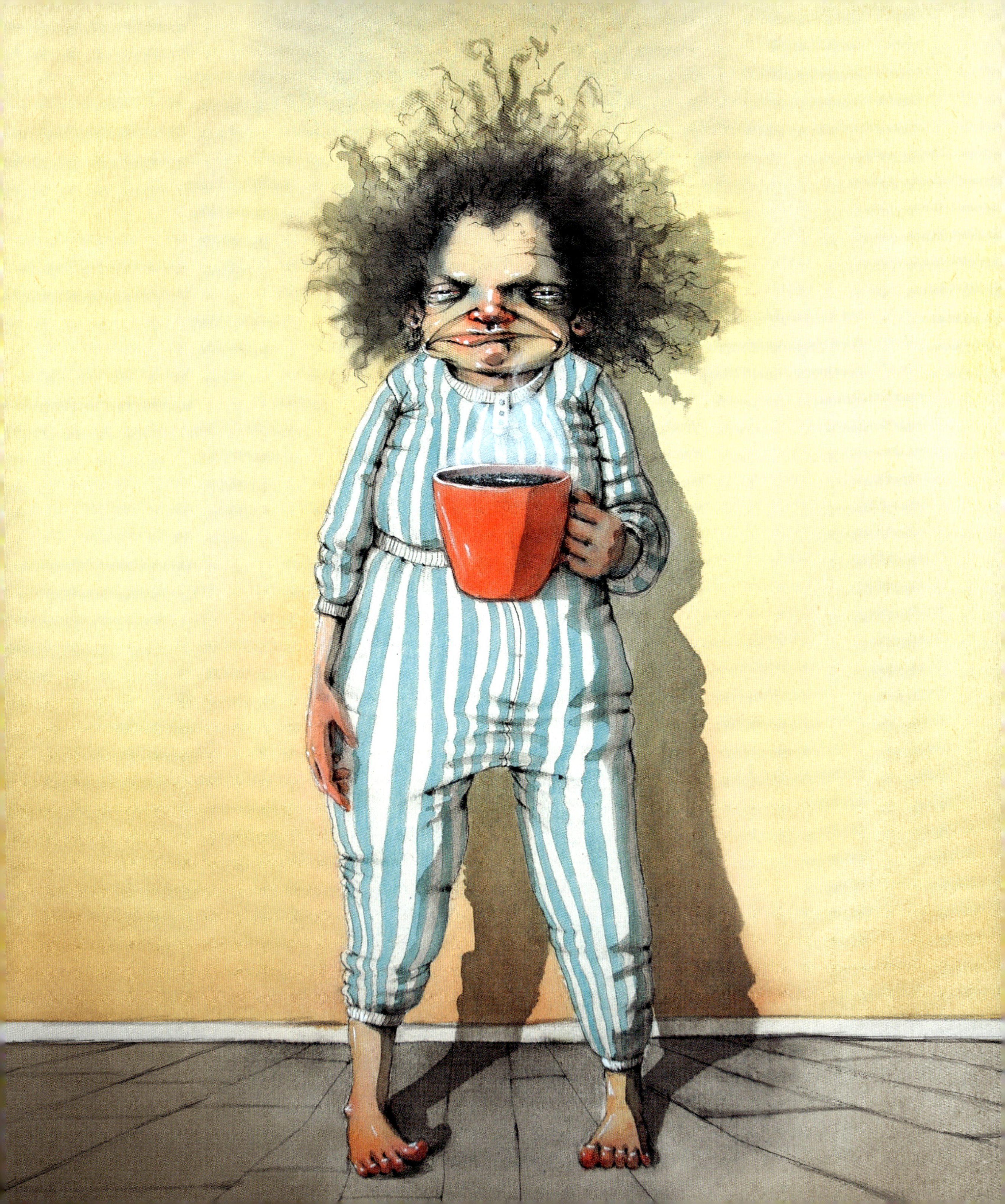

You discover new sides of yourself,

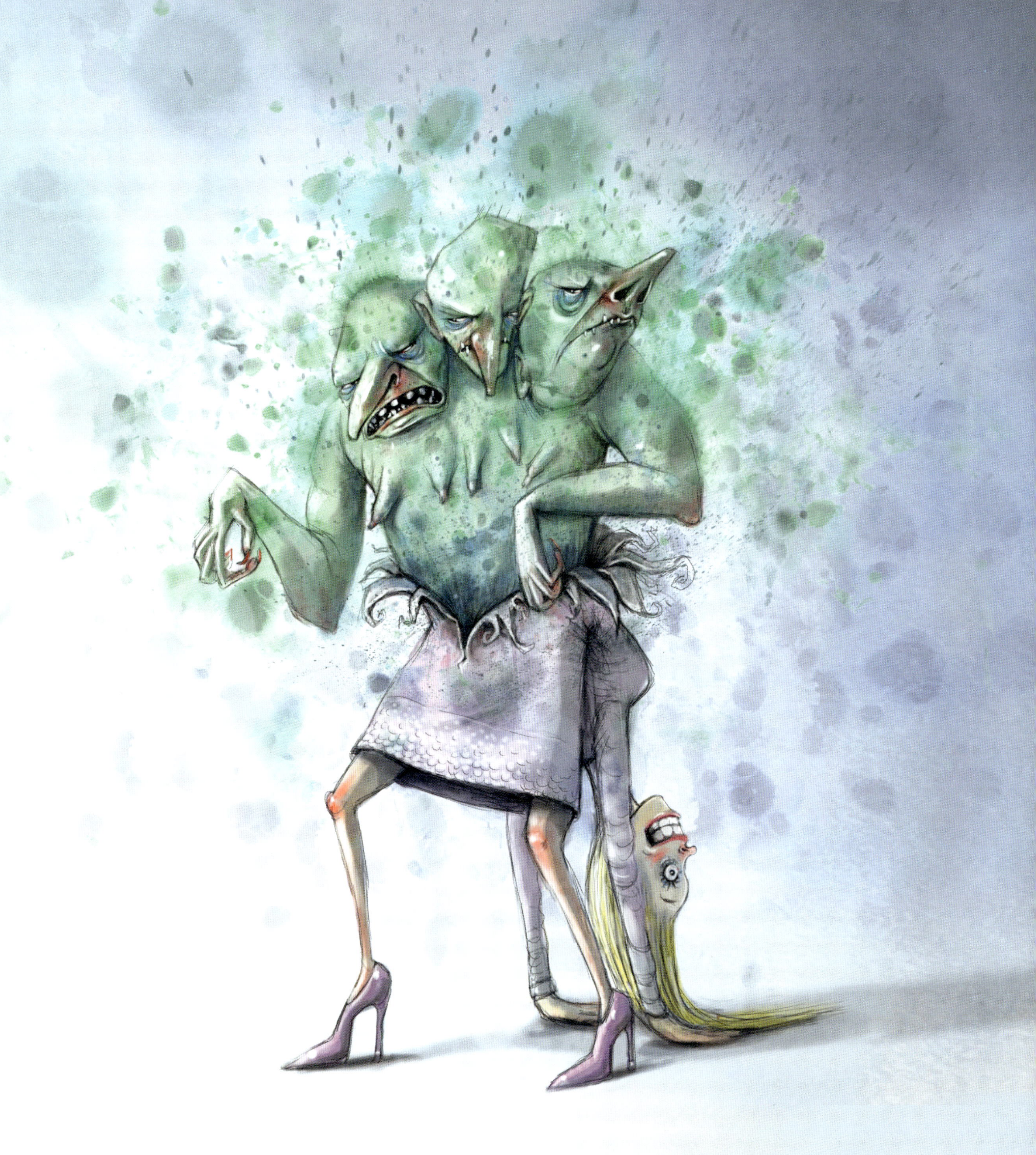

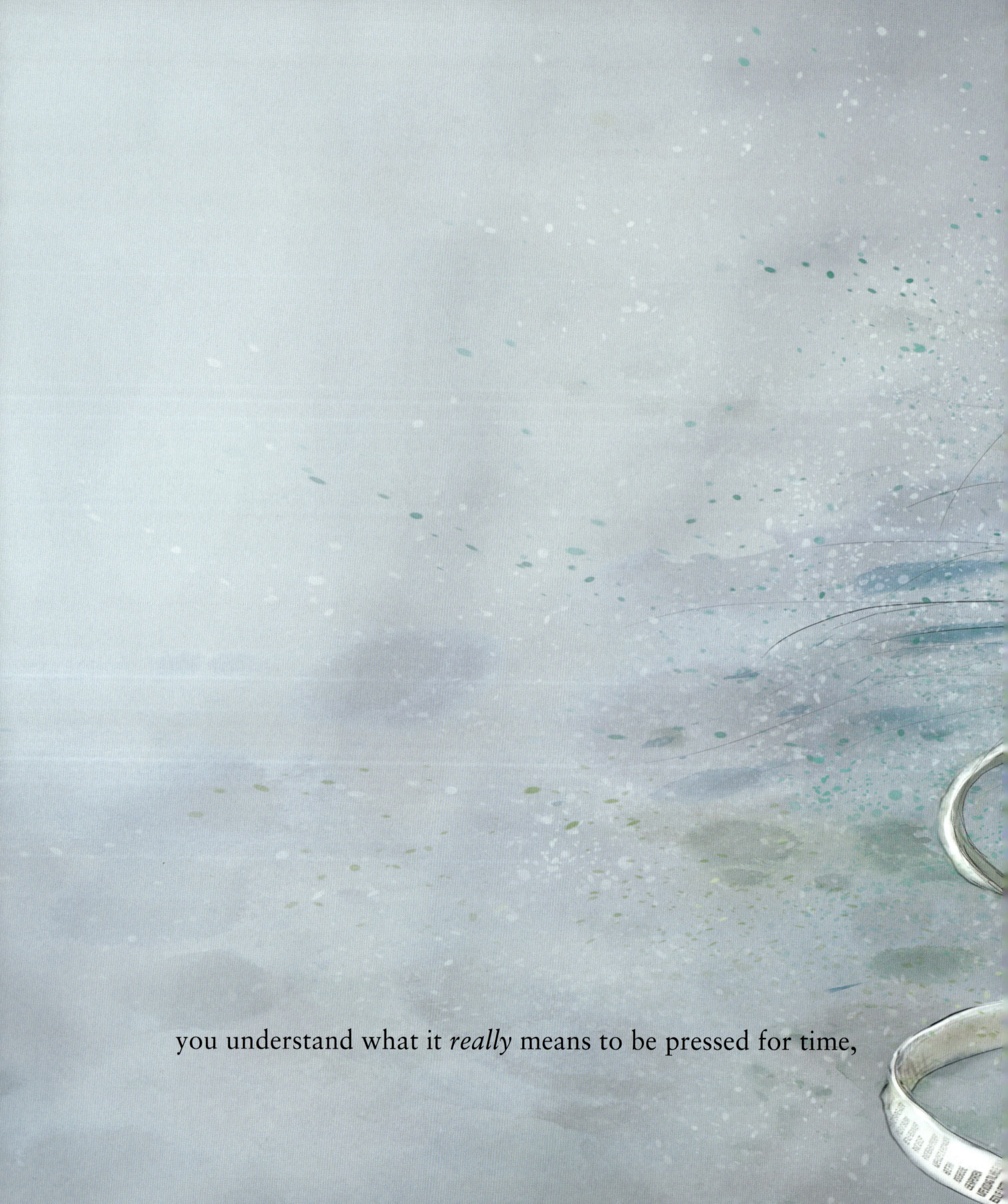

you understand what it *really* means to be pressed for time,

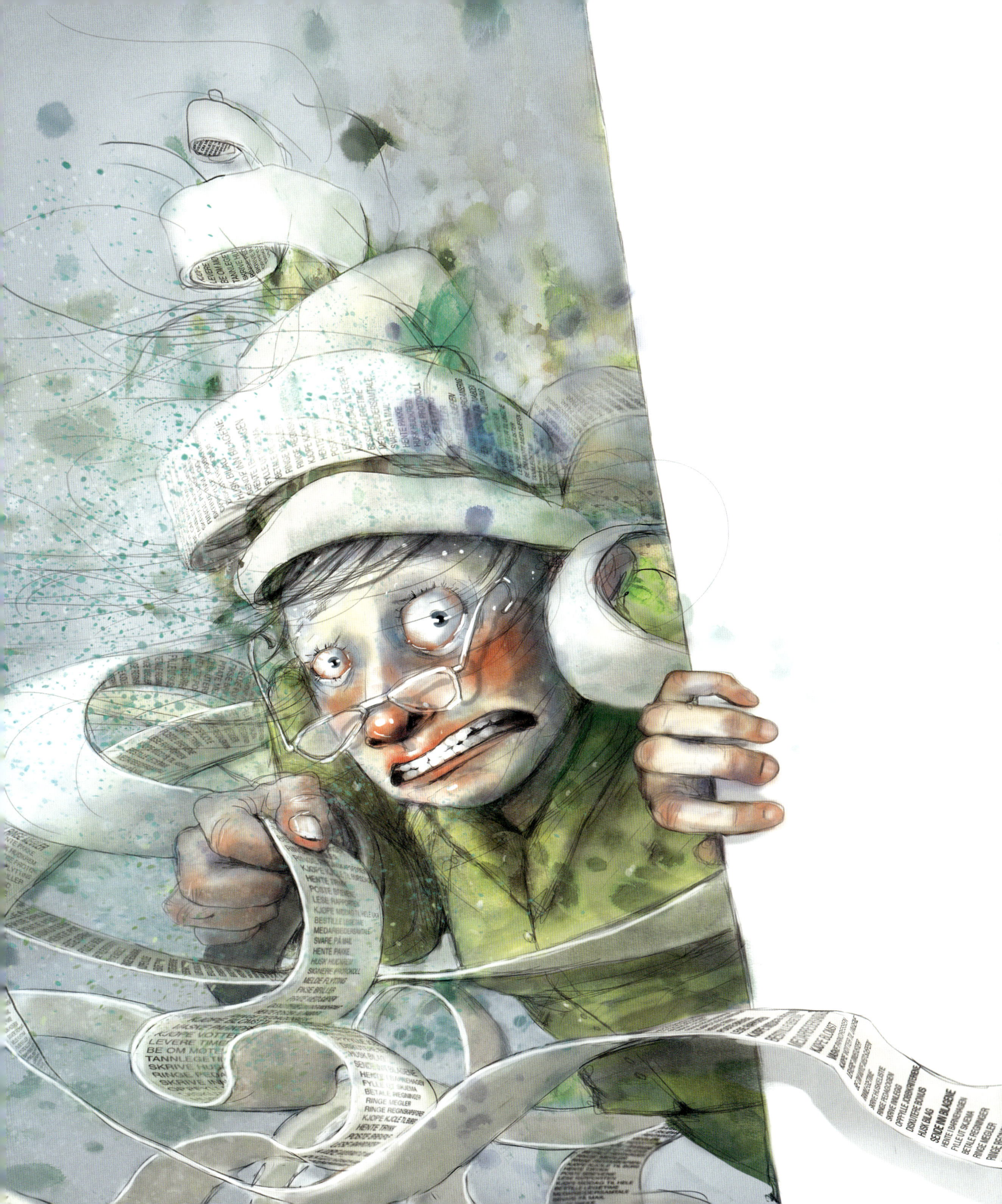

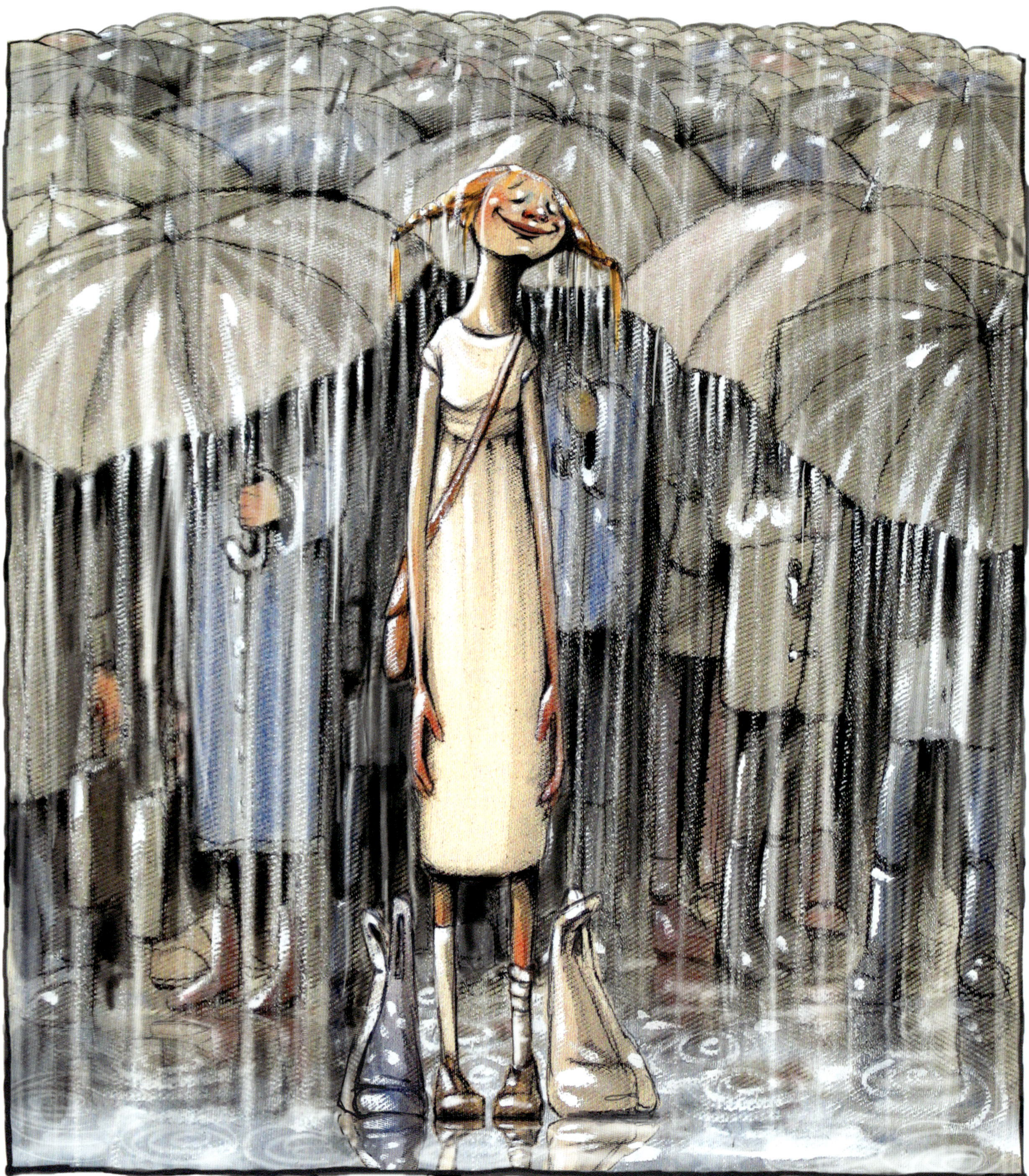

and a moment alone is simply golden.

But now and then time stands still.

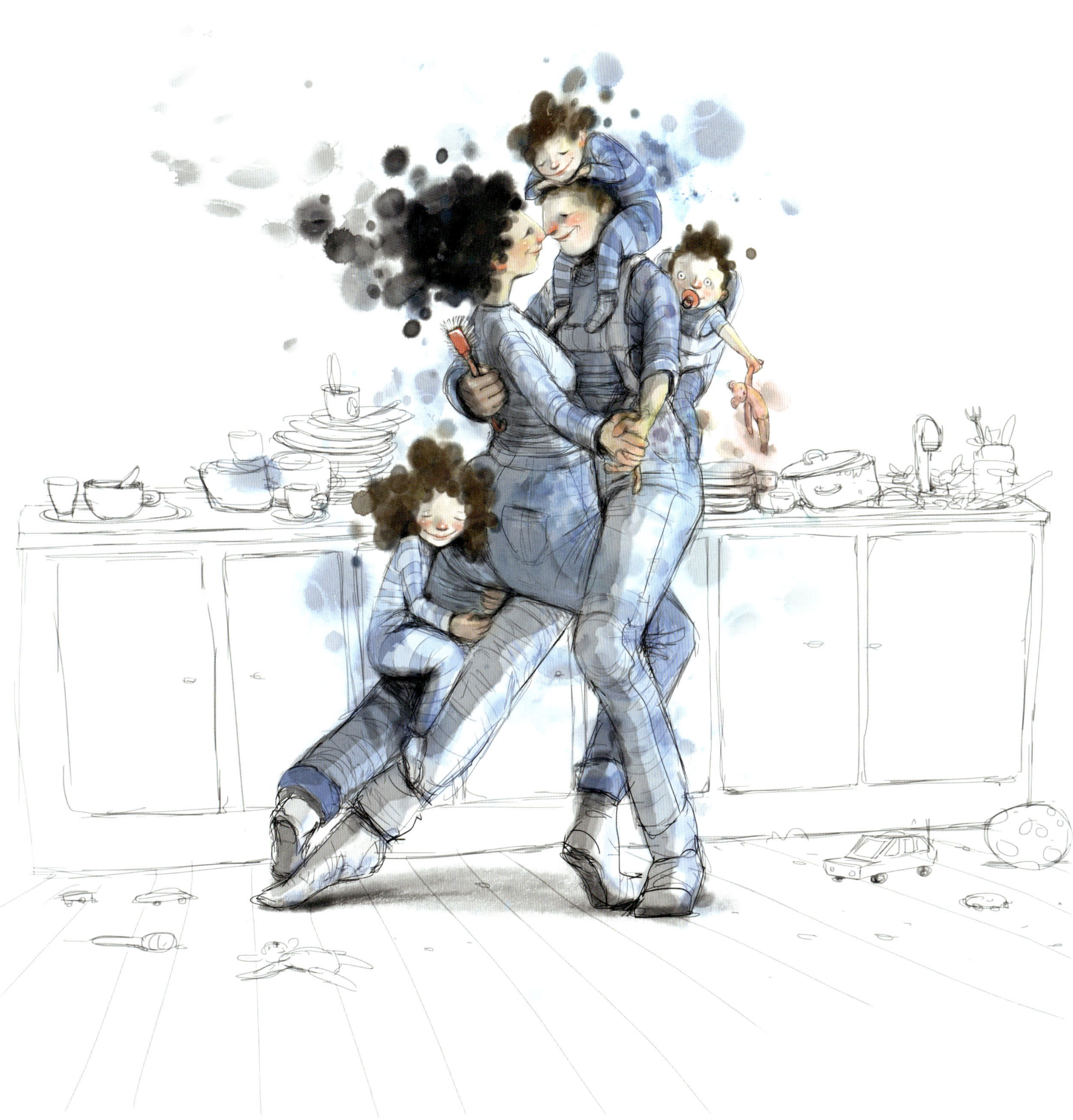

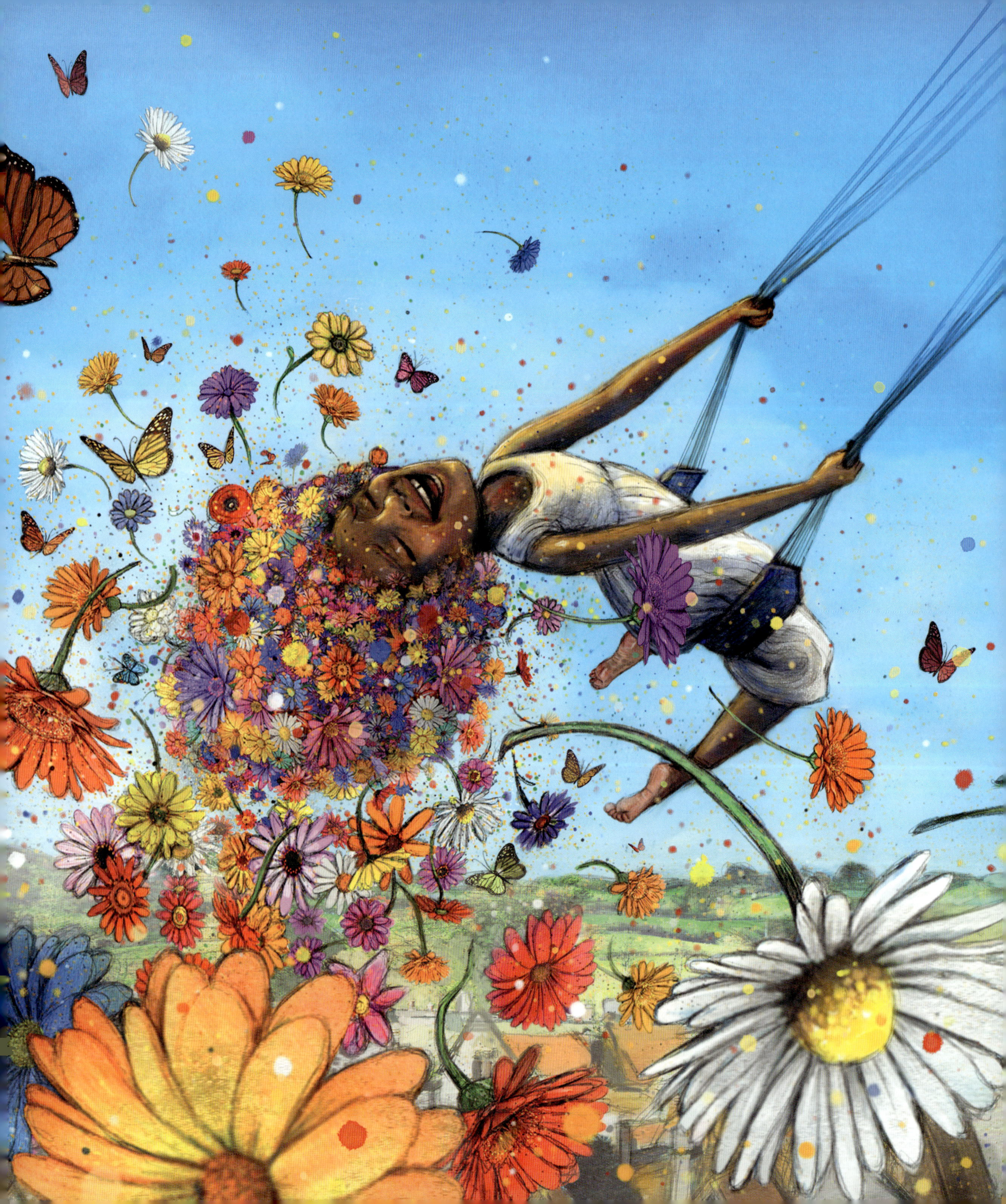

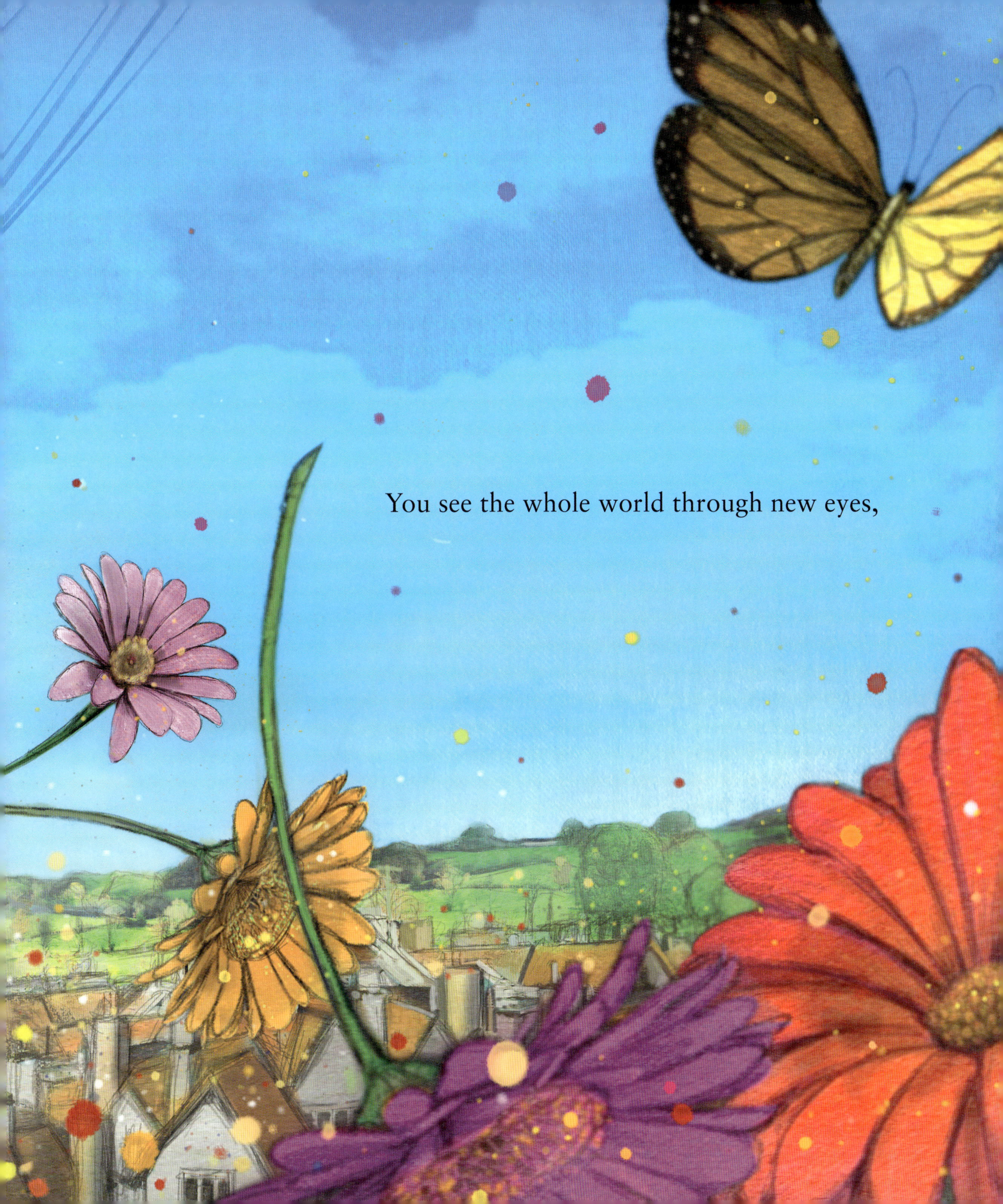
You see the whole world through new eyes,

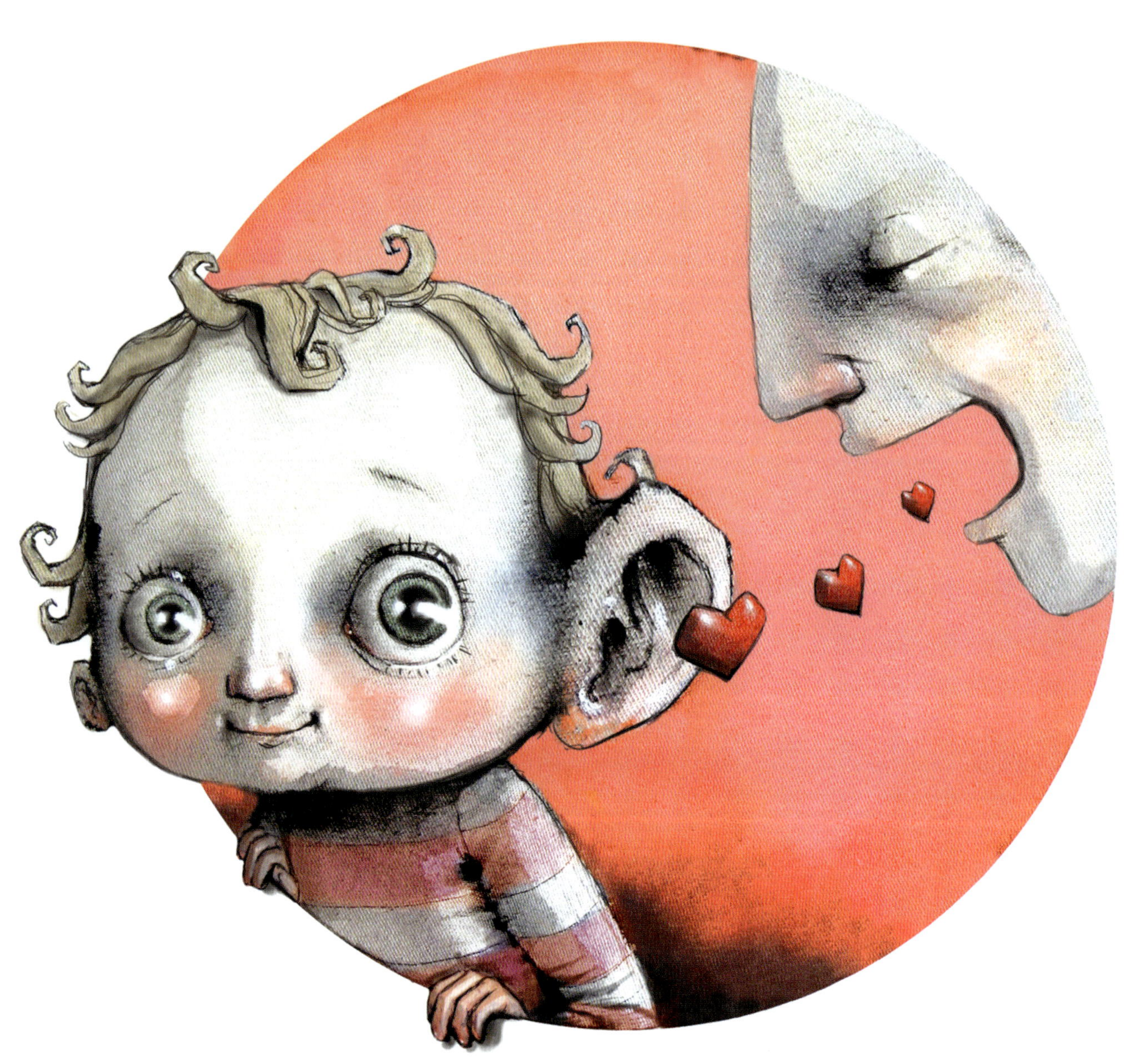

and you've never been filled with so much love.

A Grown-Up's Life

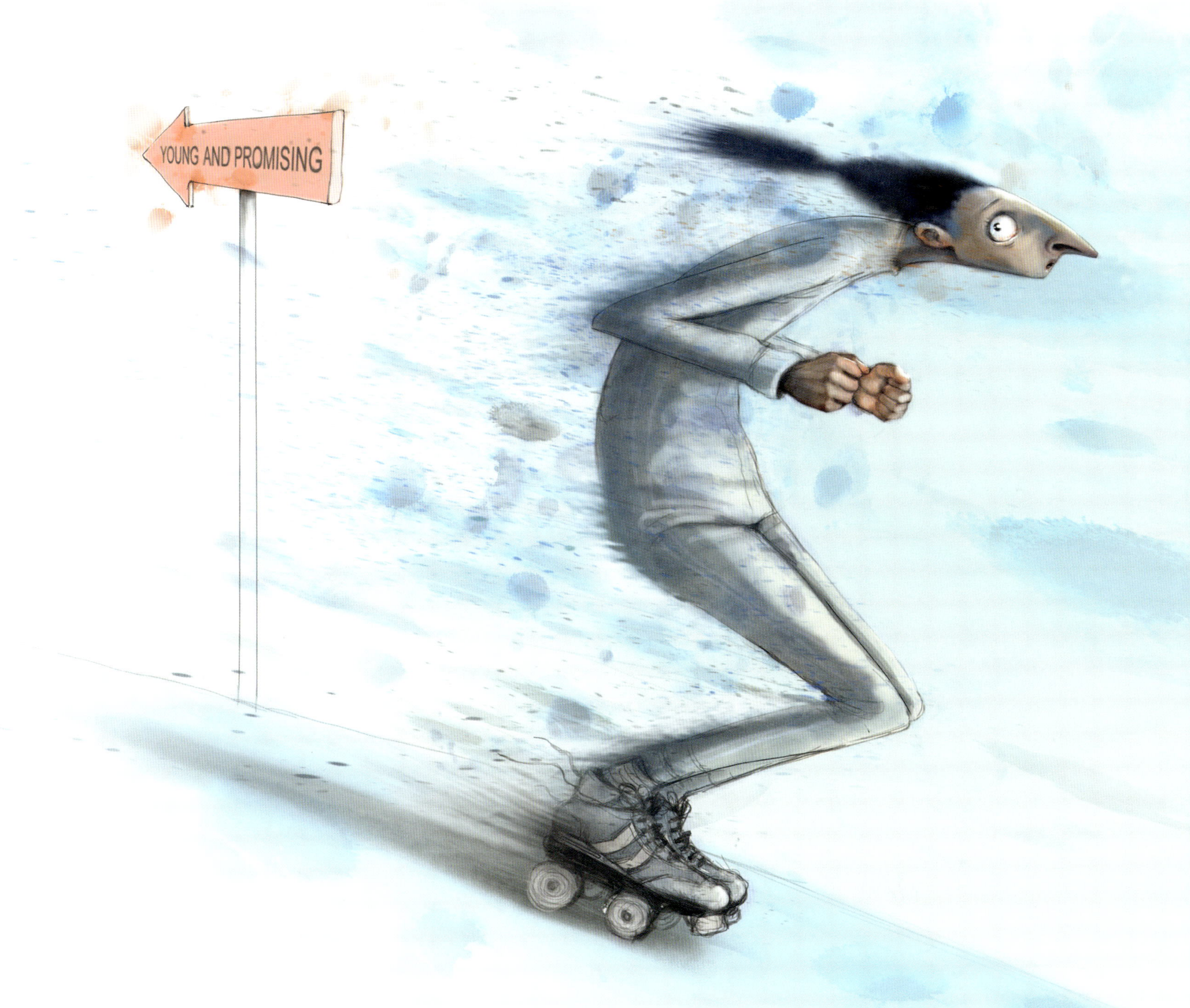

YOUNG AND PROMISING

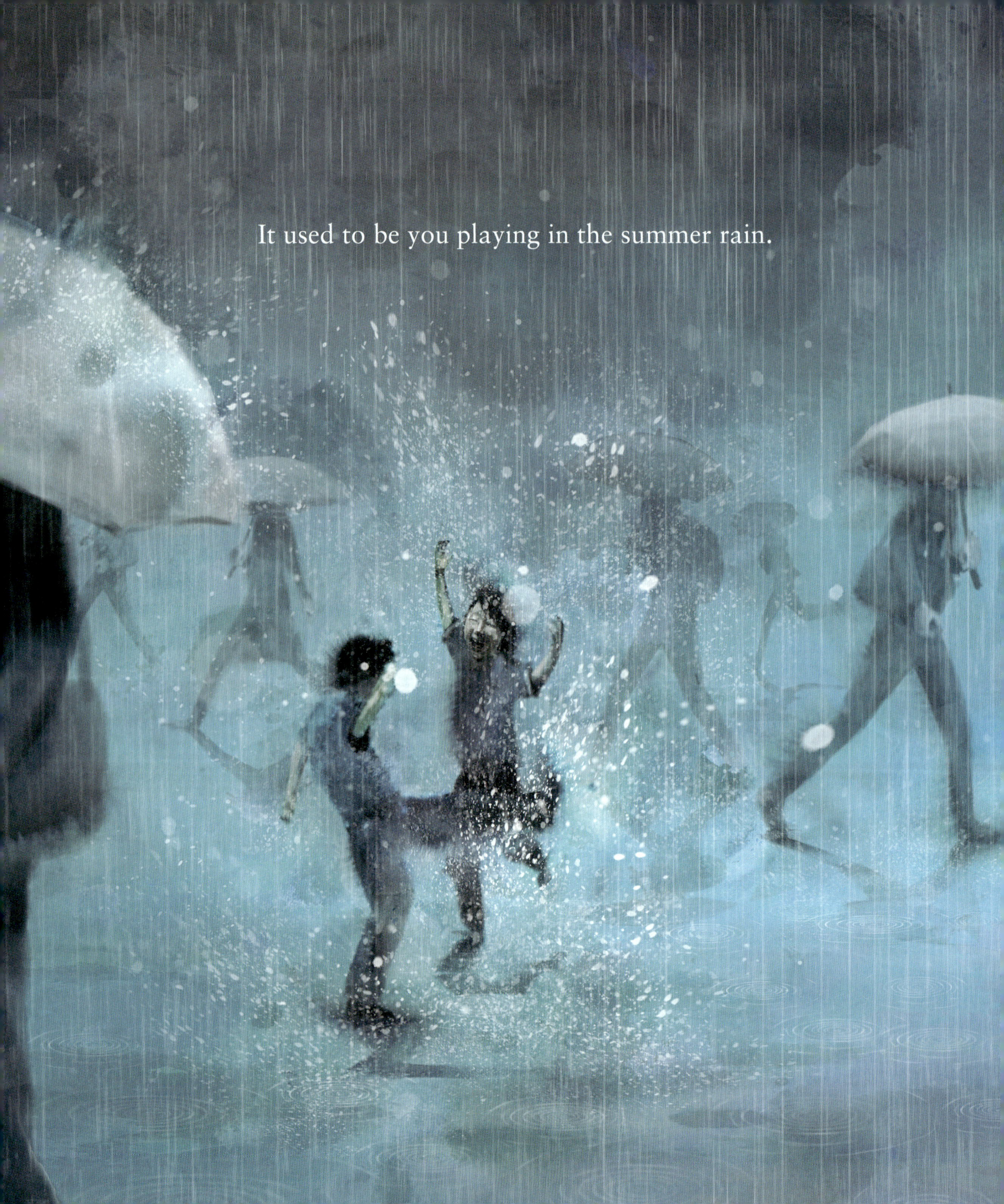
It used to be you playing in the summer rain.

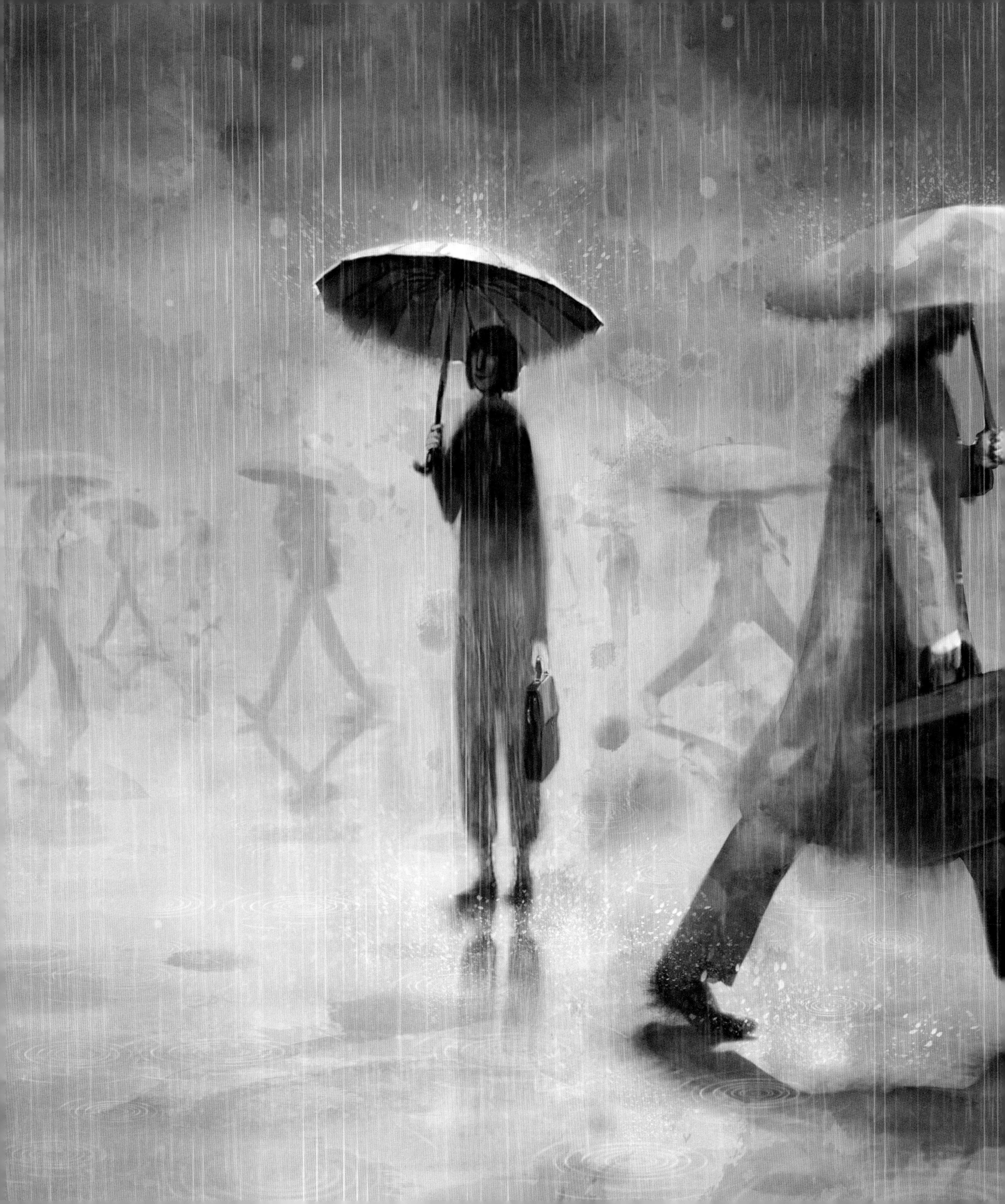

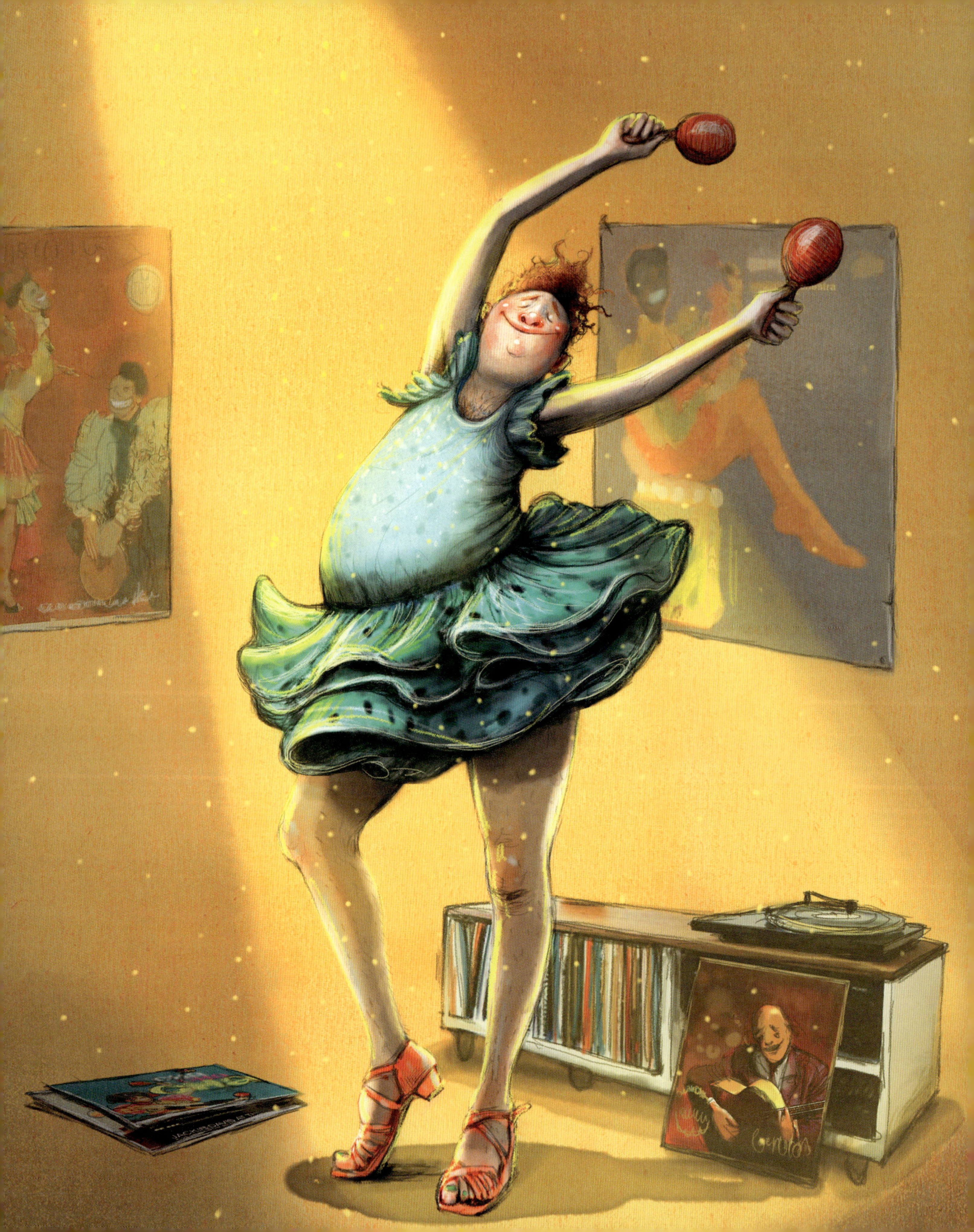

Maybe you've finally figured out who you are.

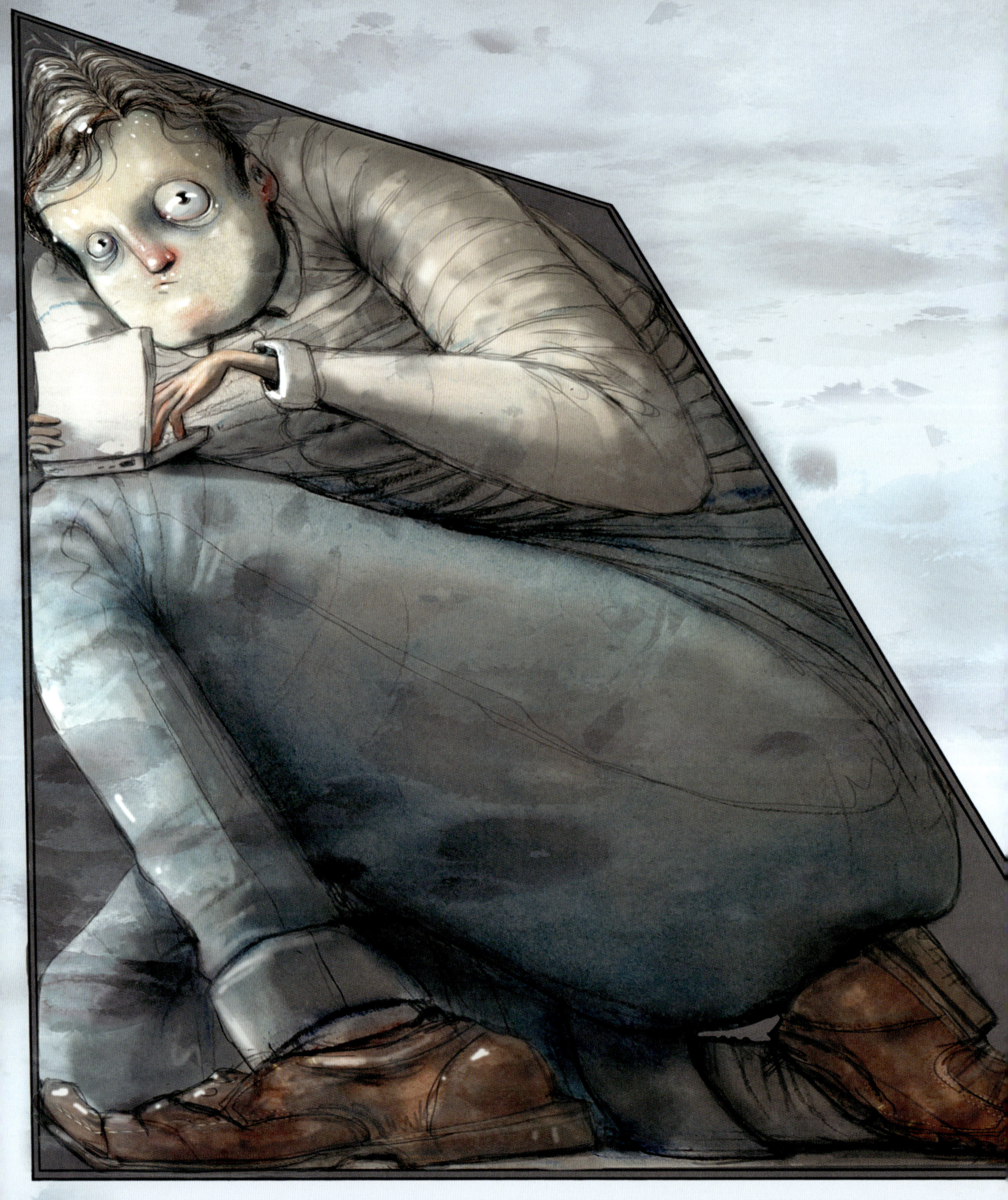

Or maybe you're still searching.

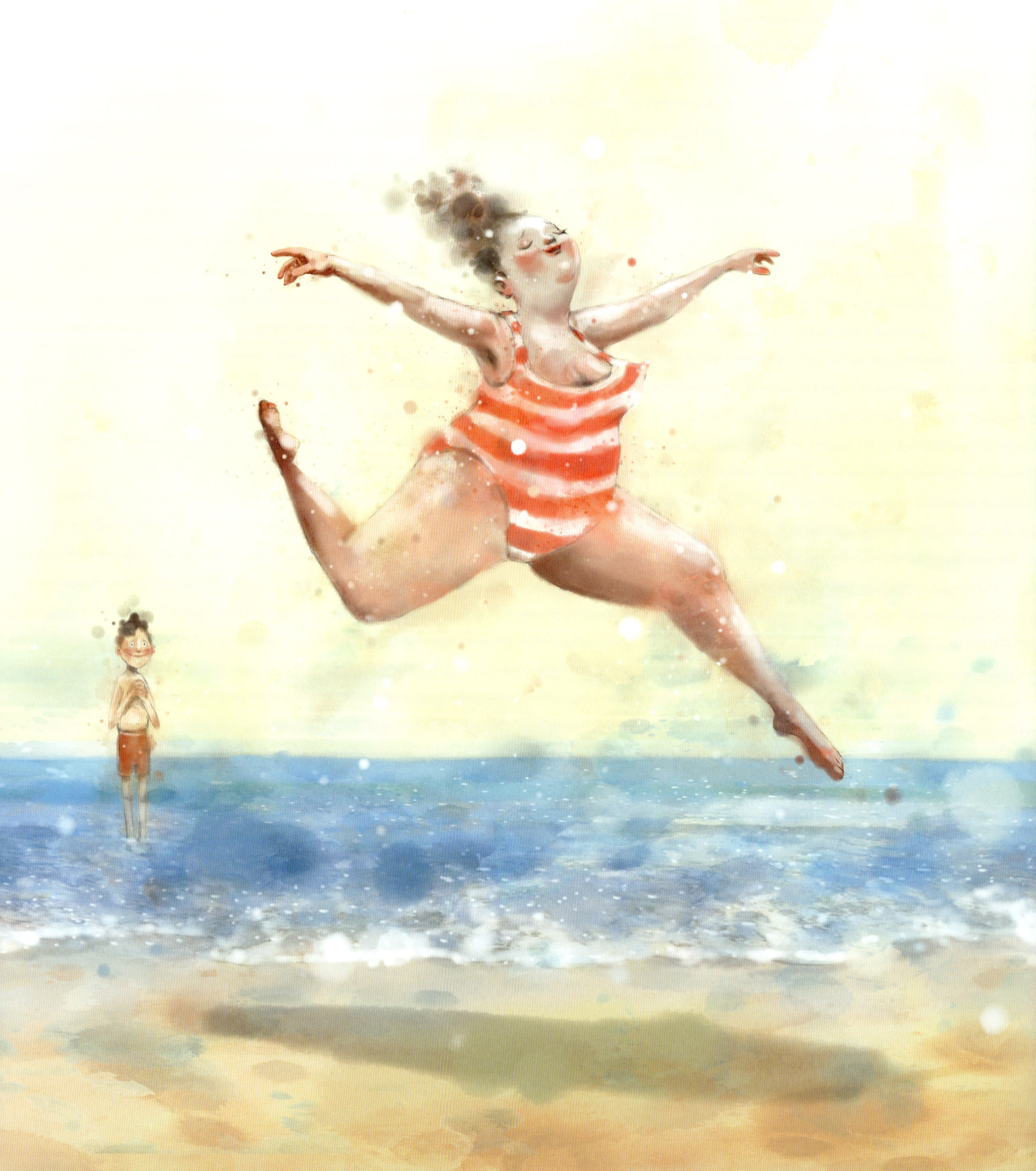

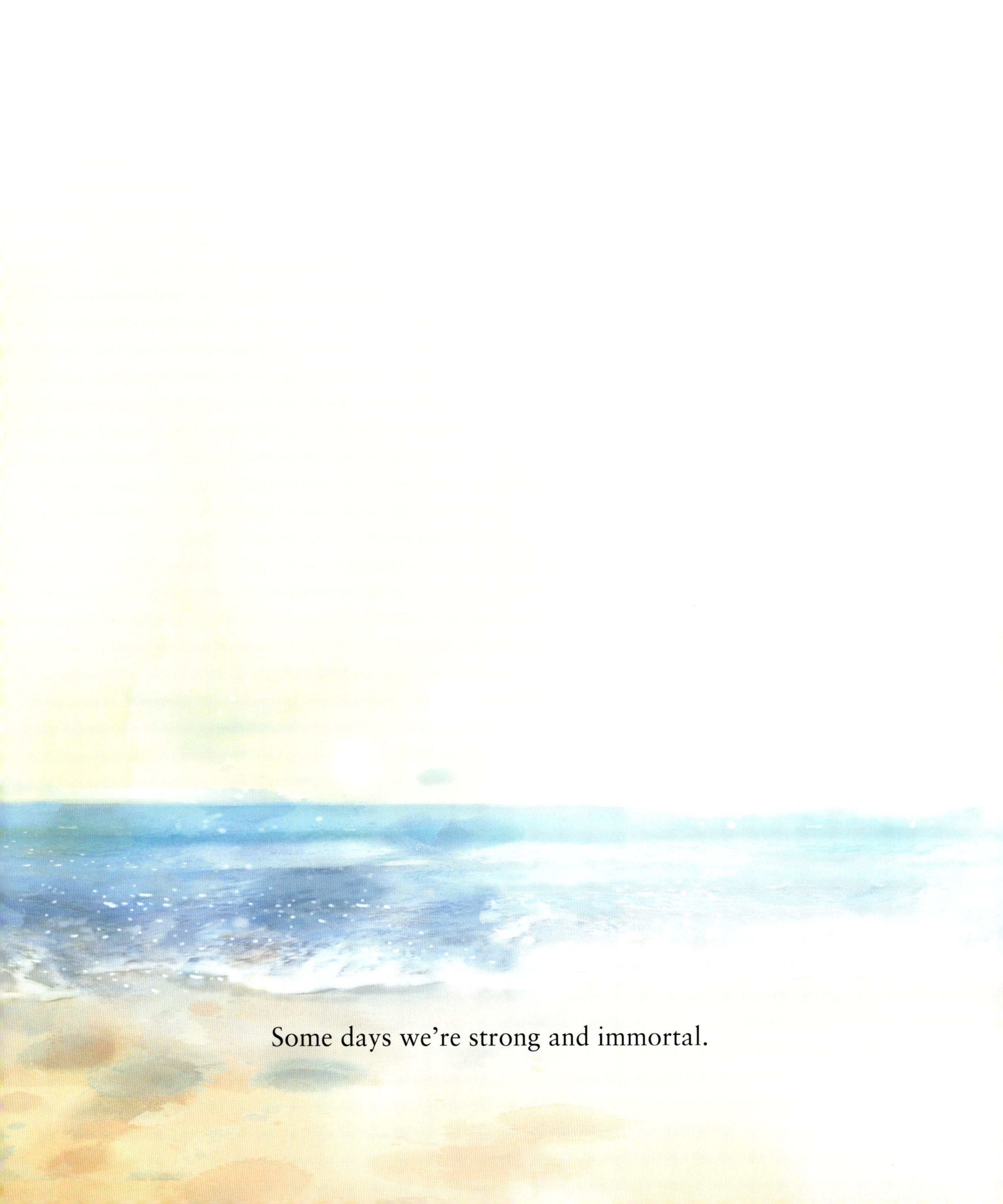

Some days we're strong and immortal.

Other days we're just plain run-down.

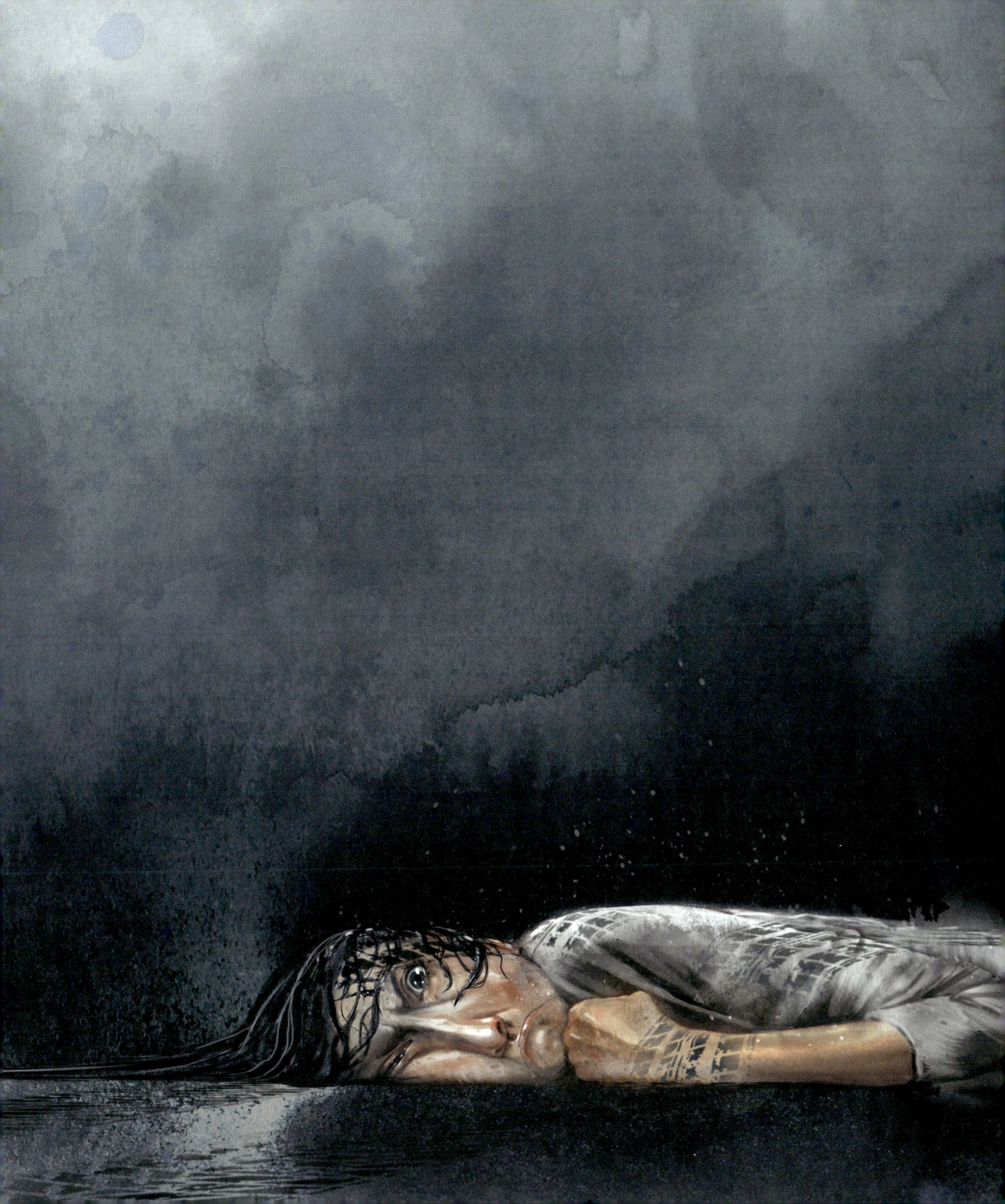

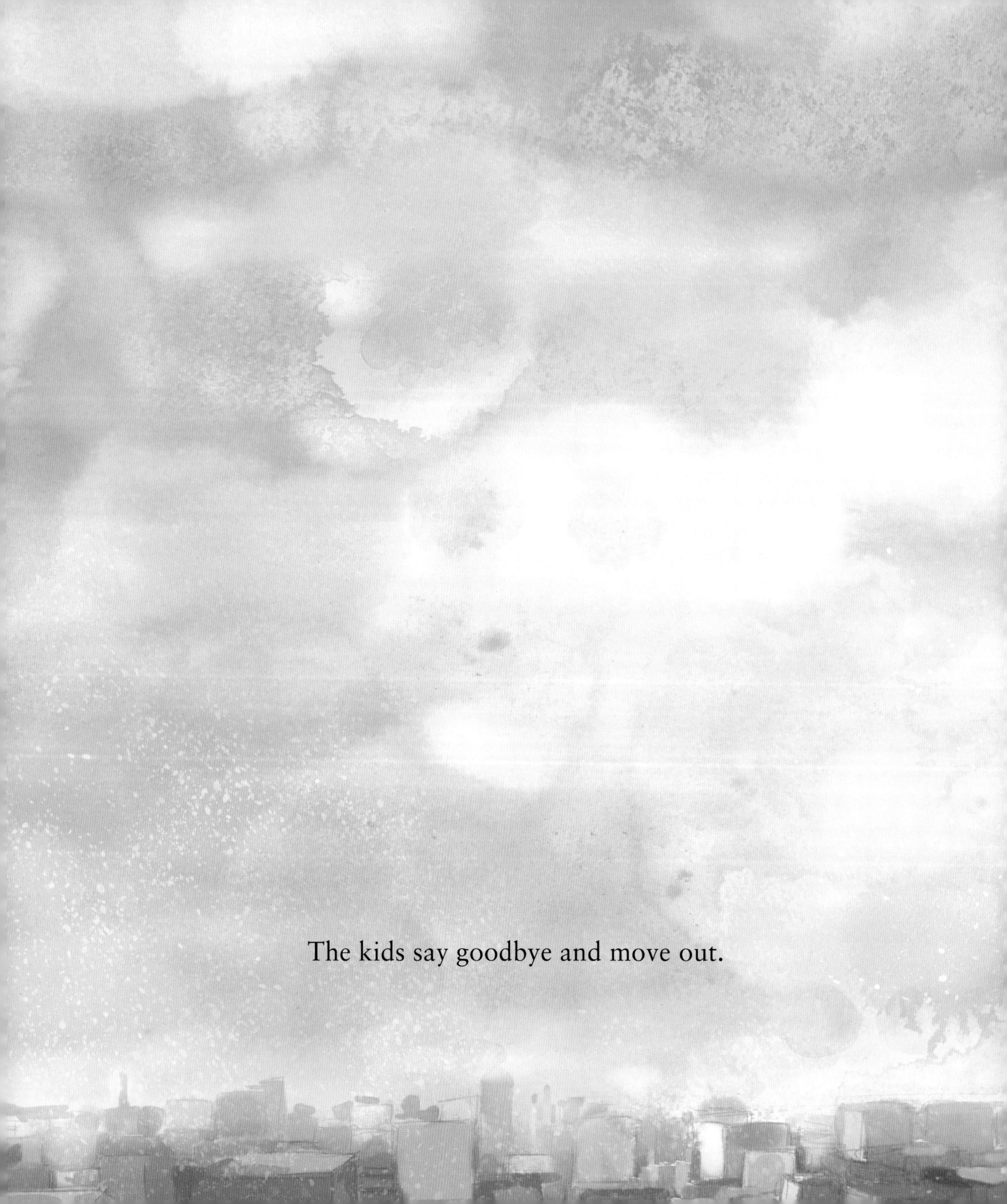

The kids say goodbye and move out.

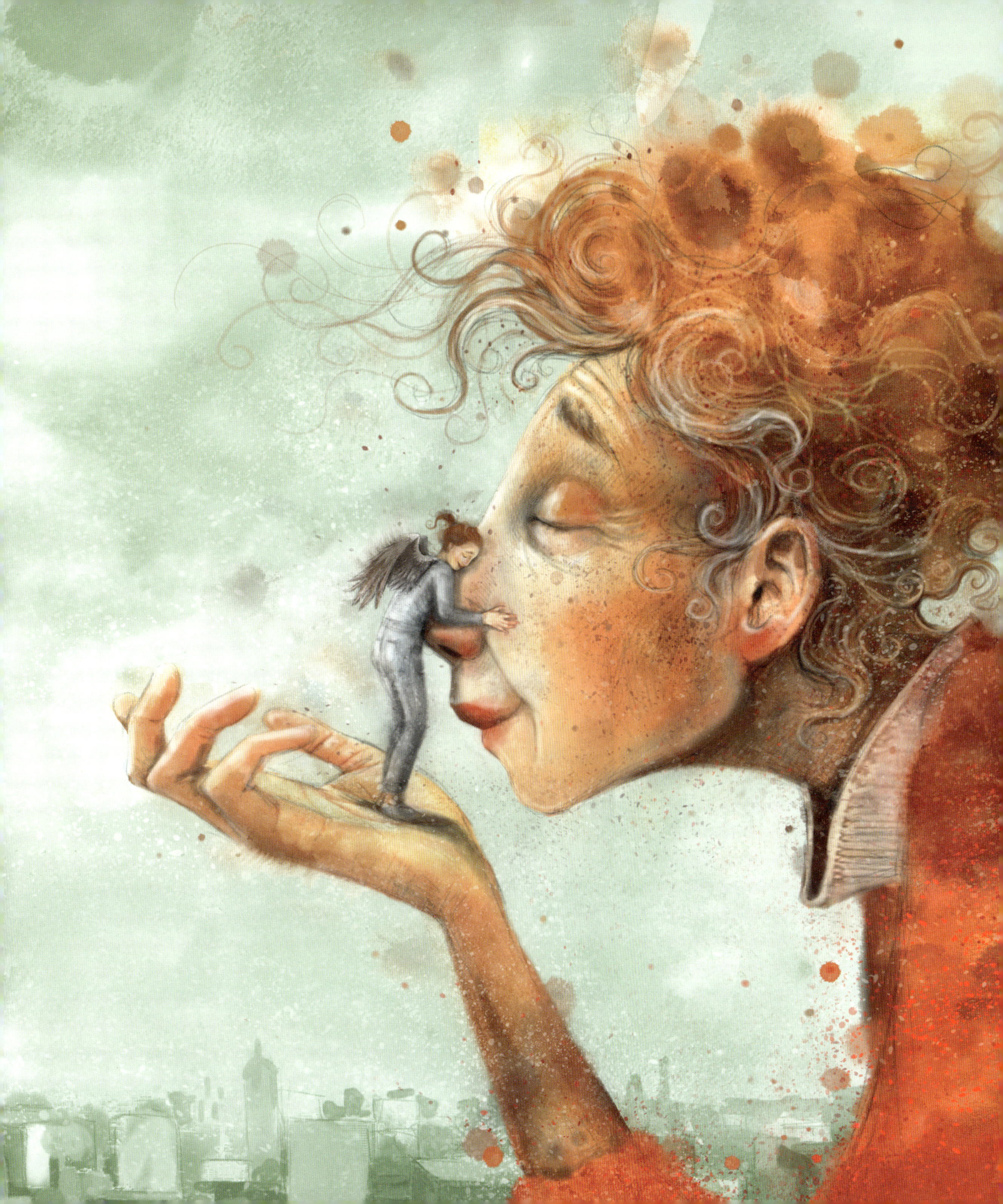

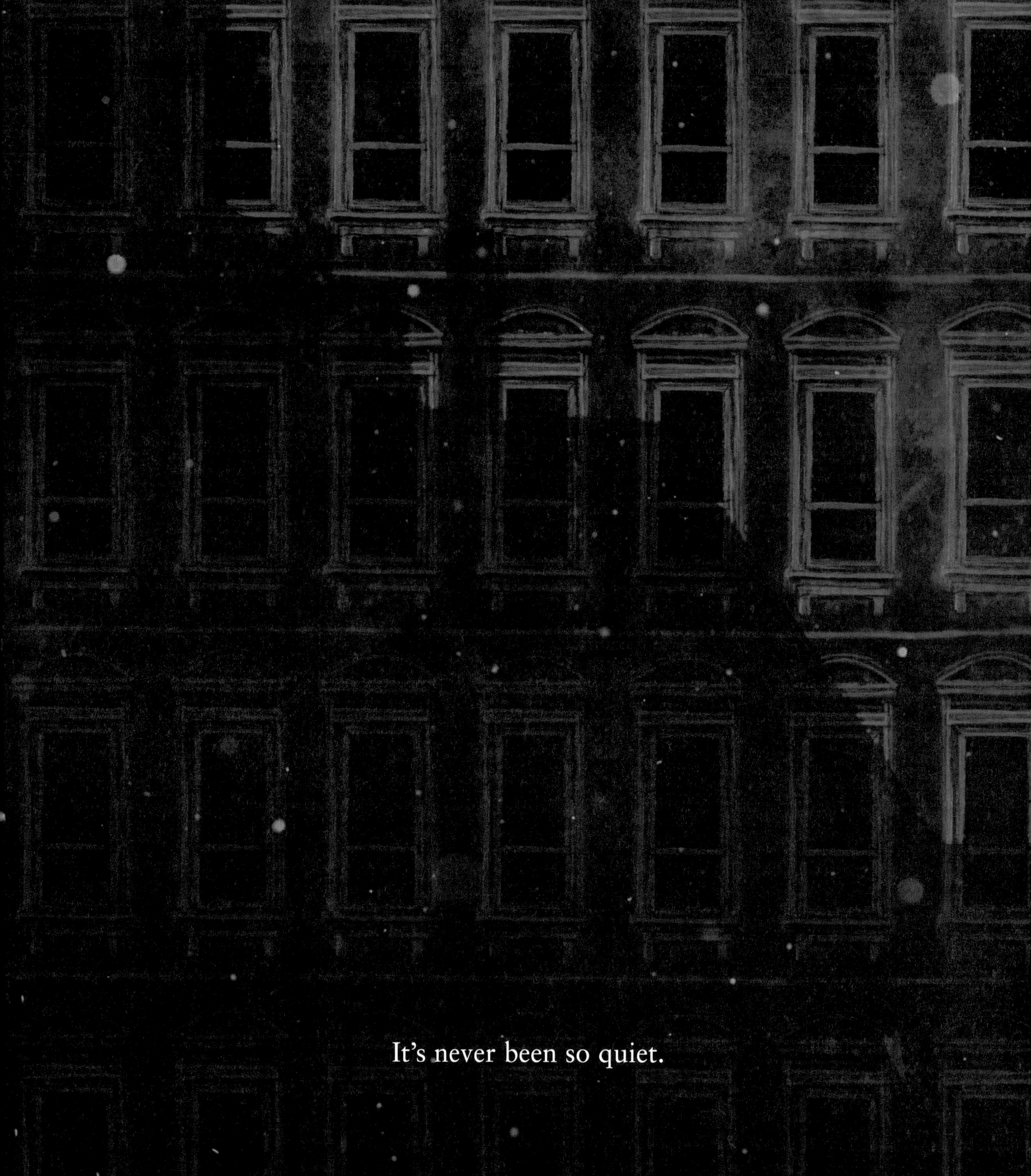
It's never been so quiet.

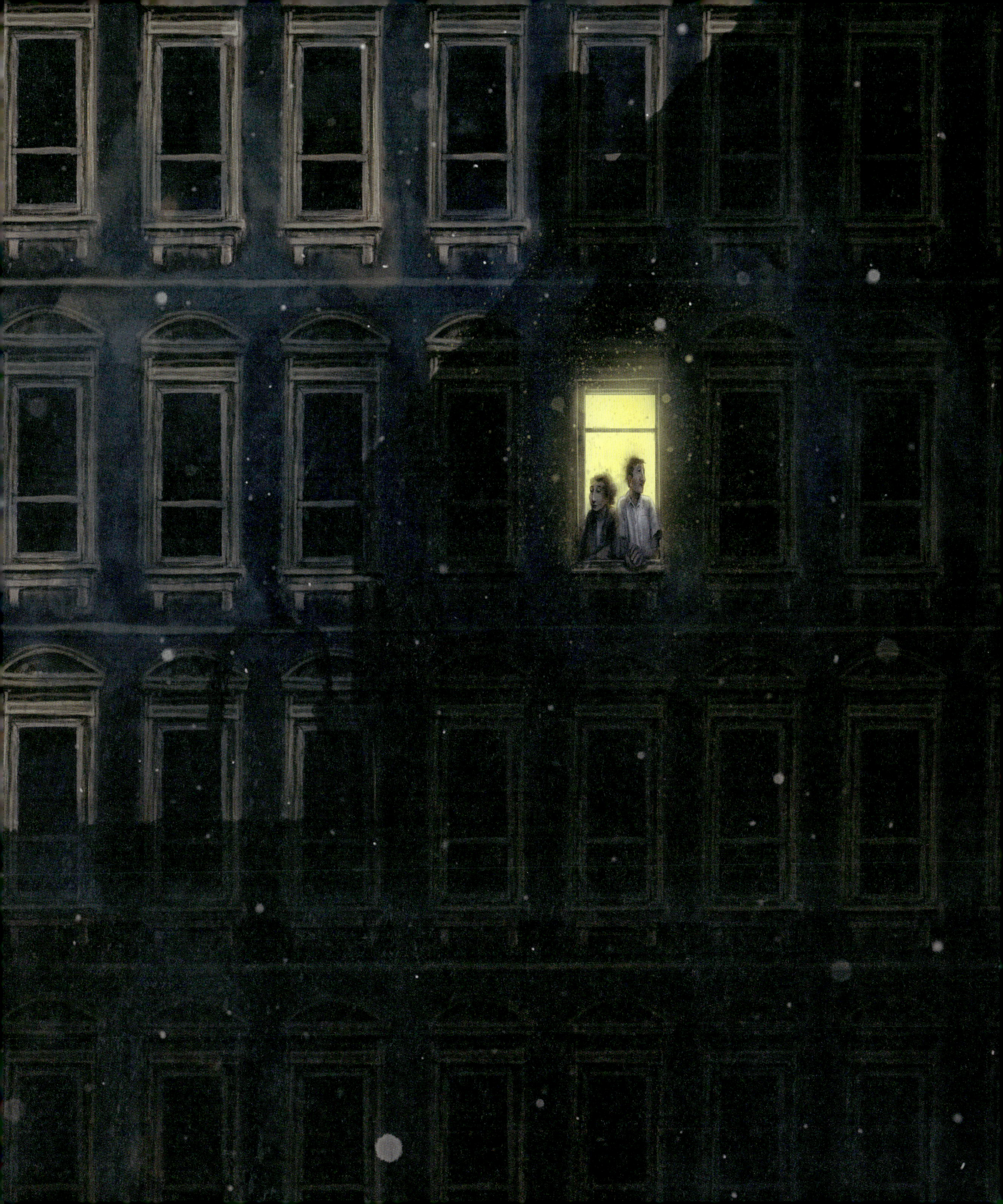

Maybe you grow closer,

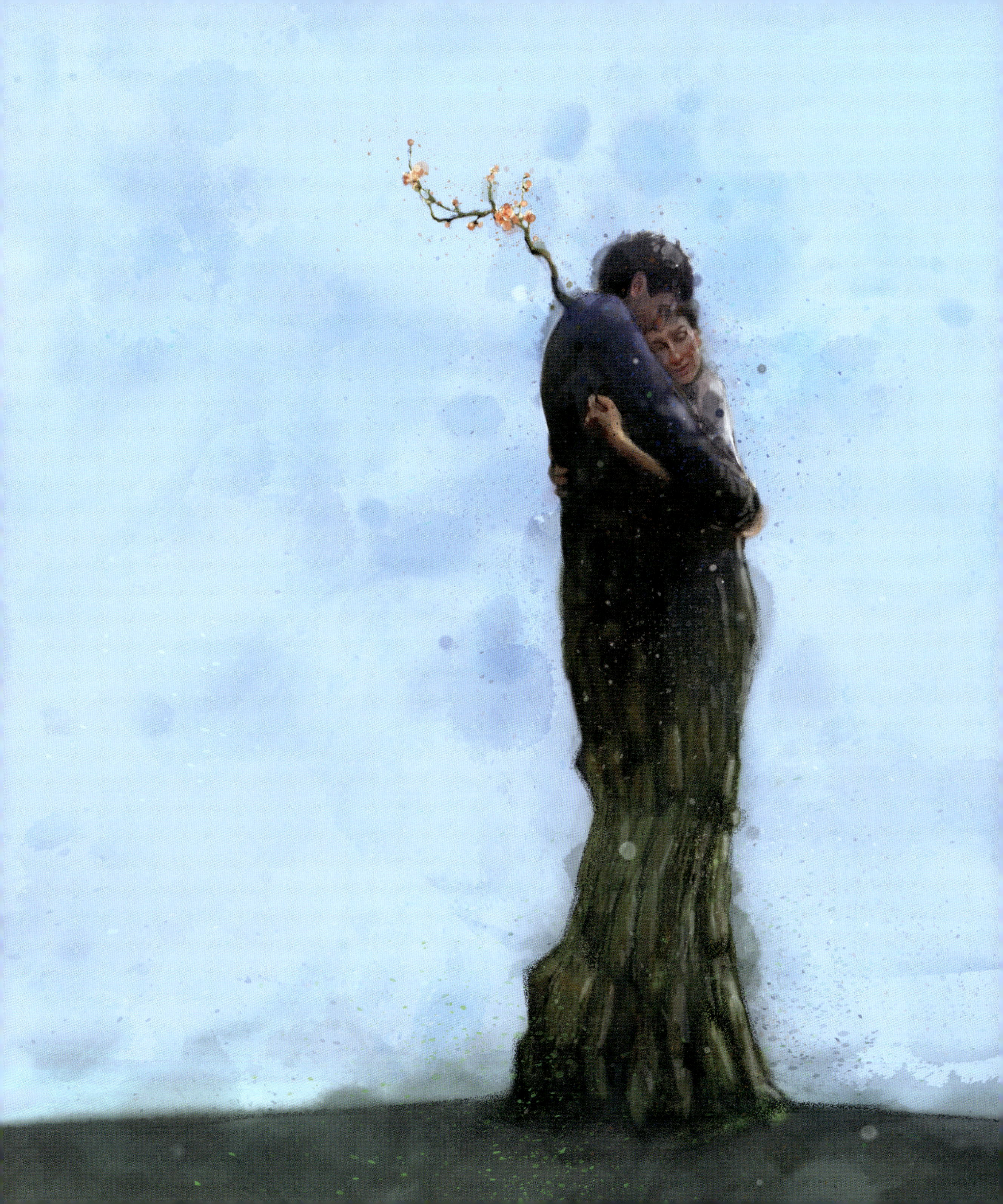

or maybe it all falls apart.

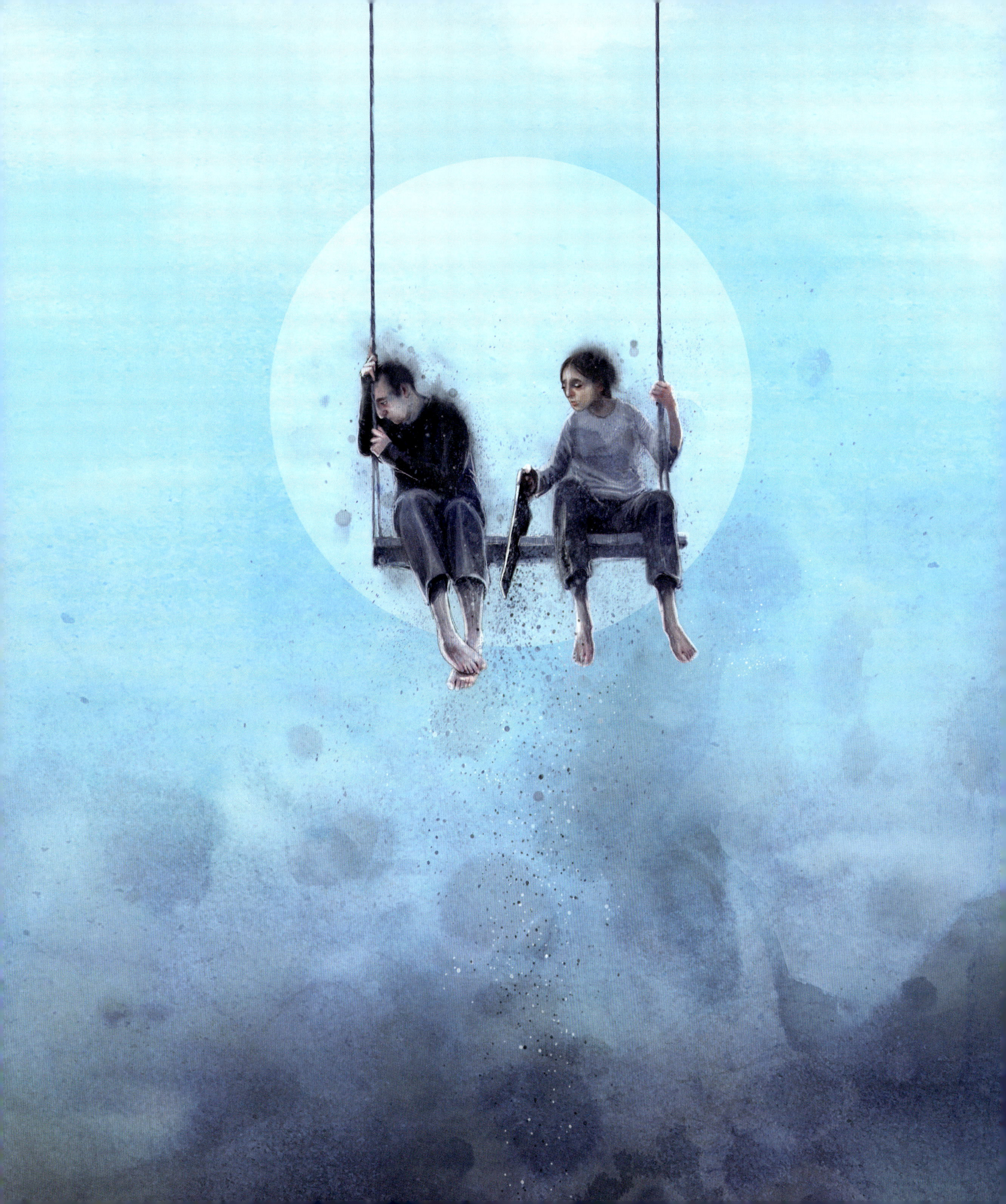

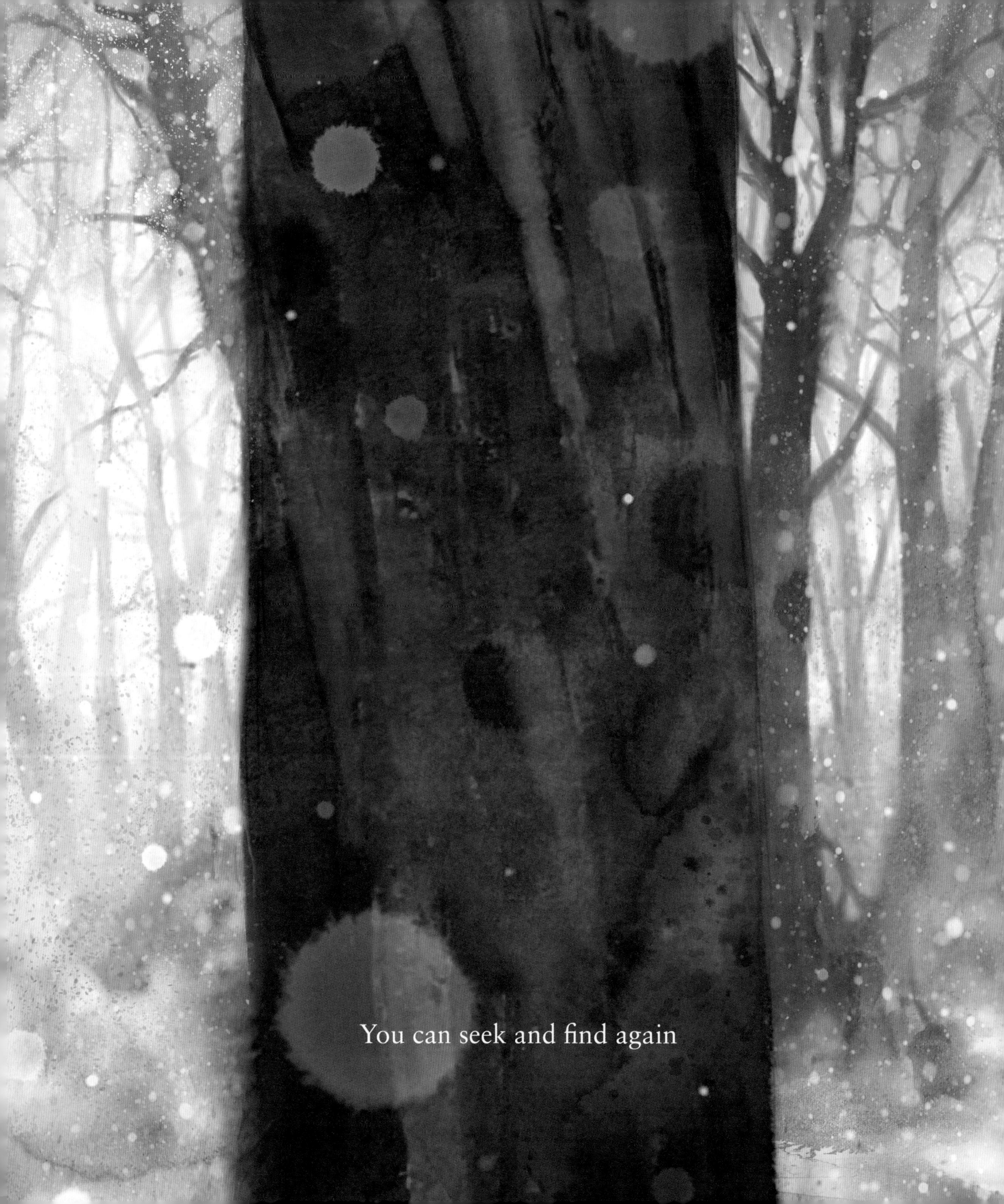
You can seek and find again

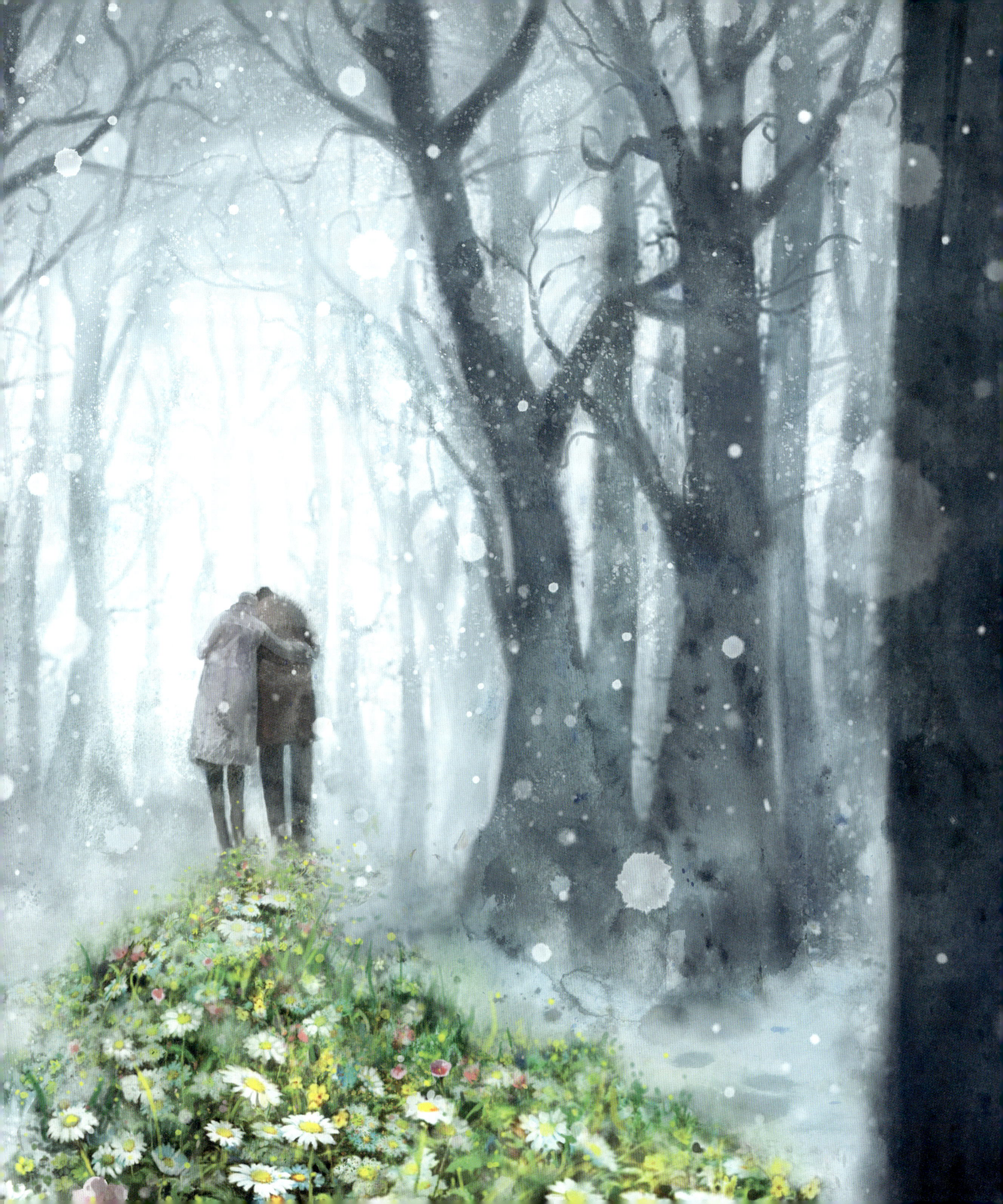

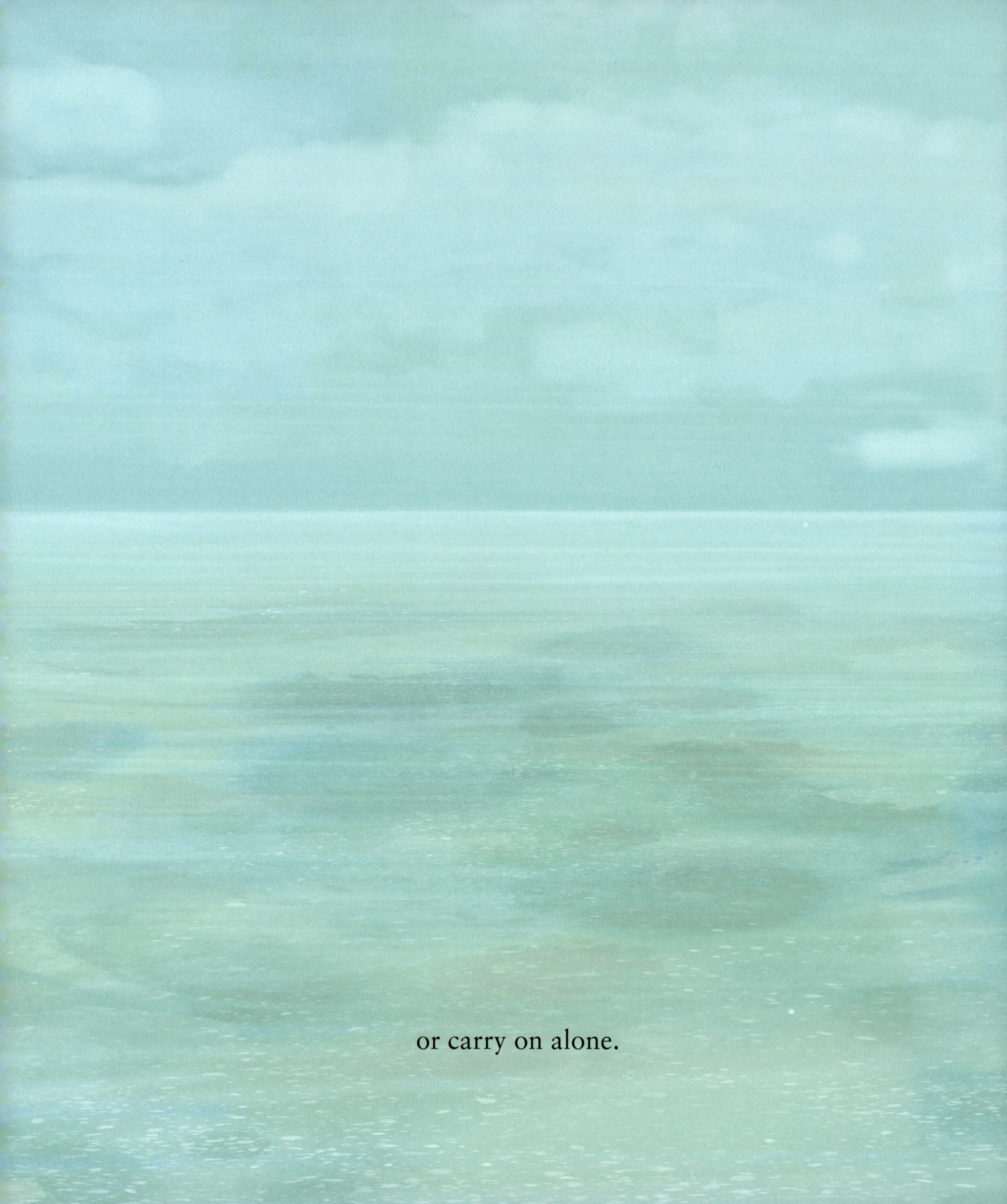

or carry on alone.

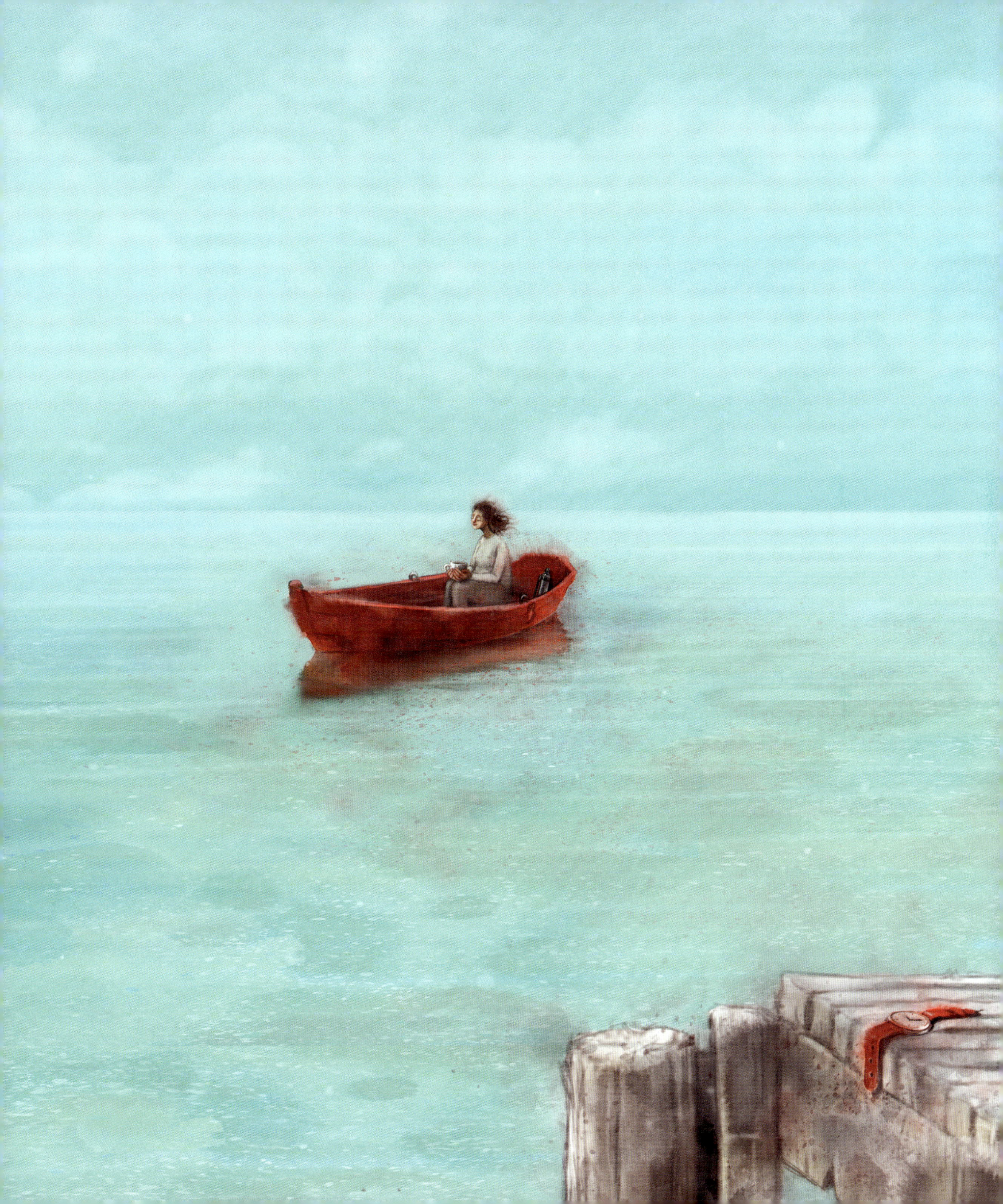

Now we are the ones who have to take care of Mom and Dad.

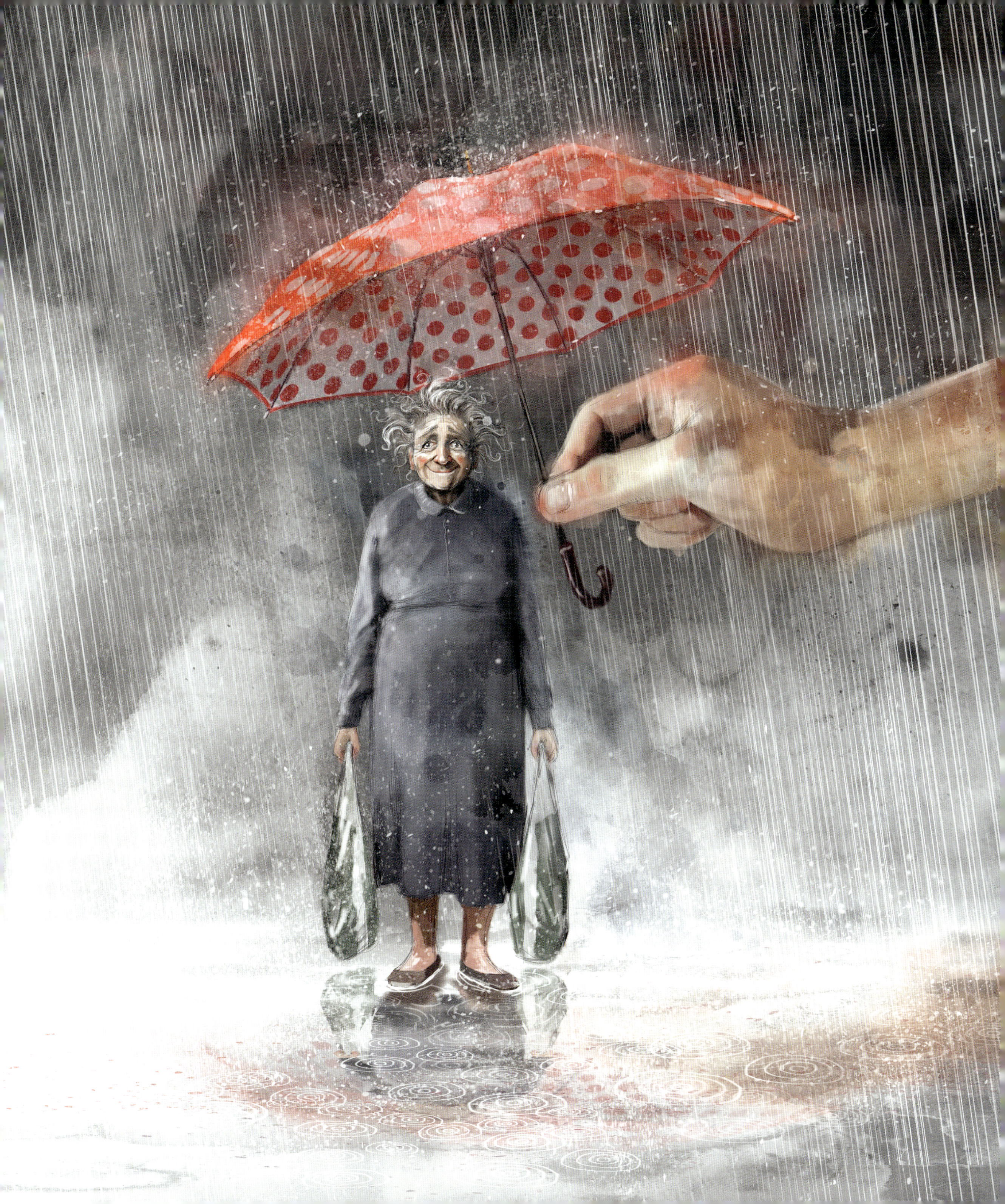

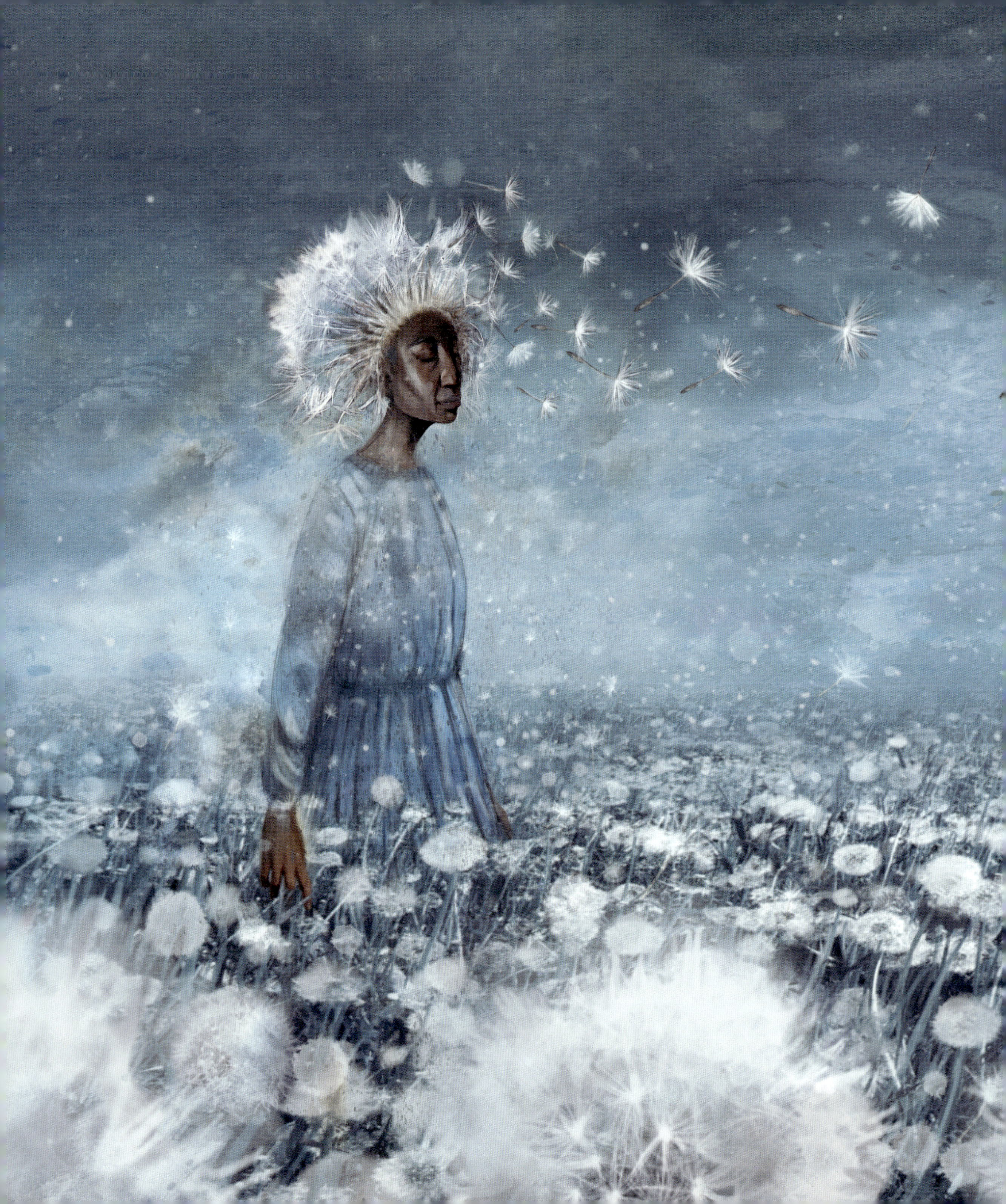

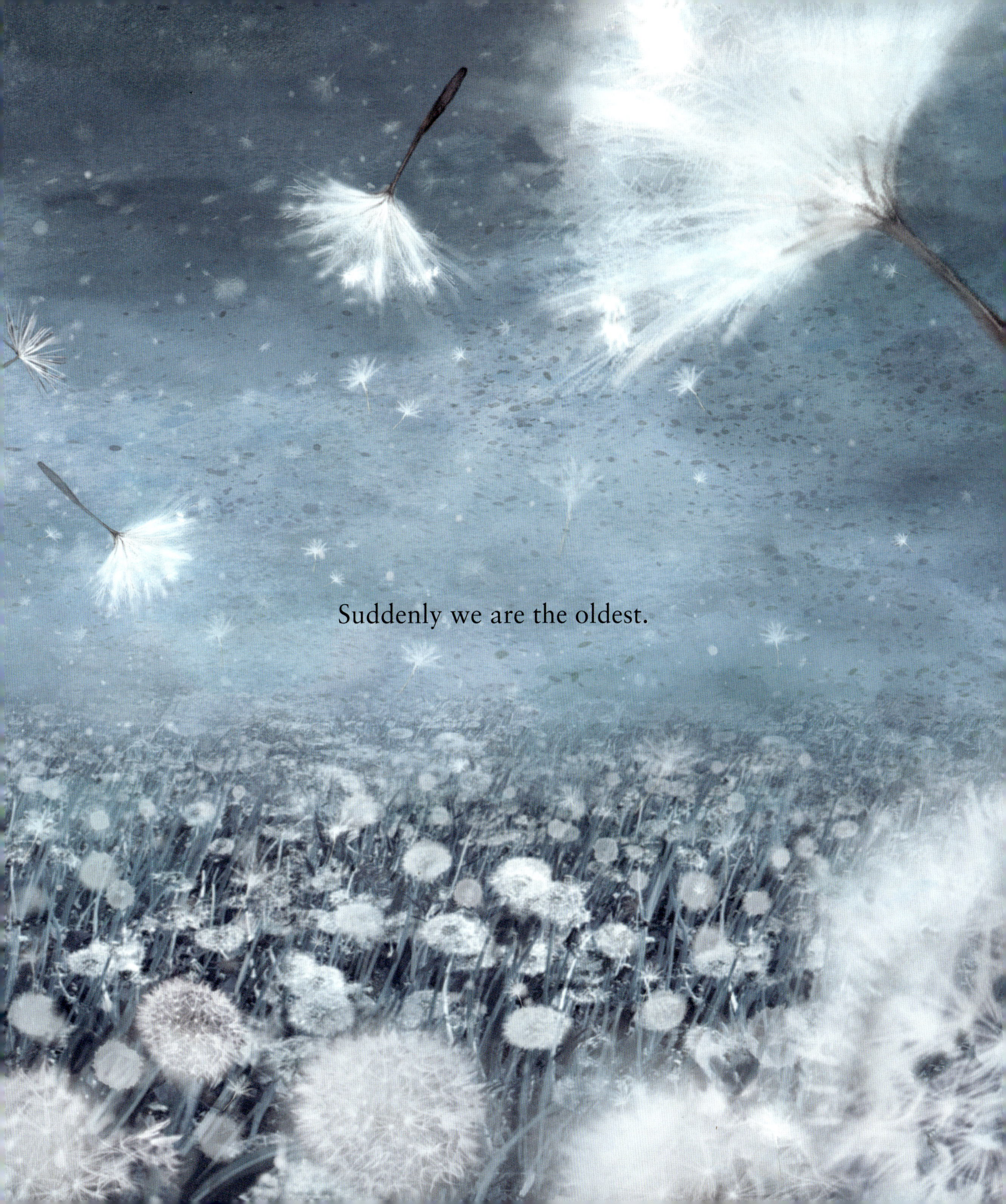
Suddenly we are the oldest.

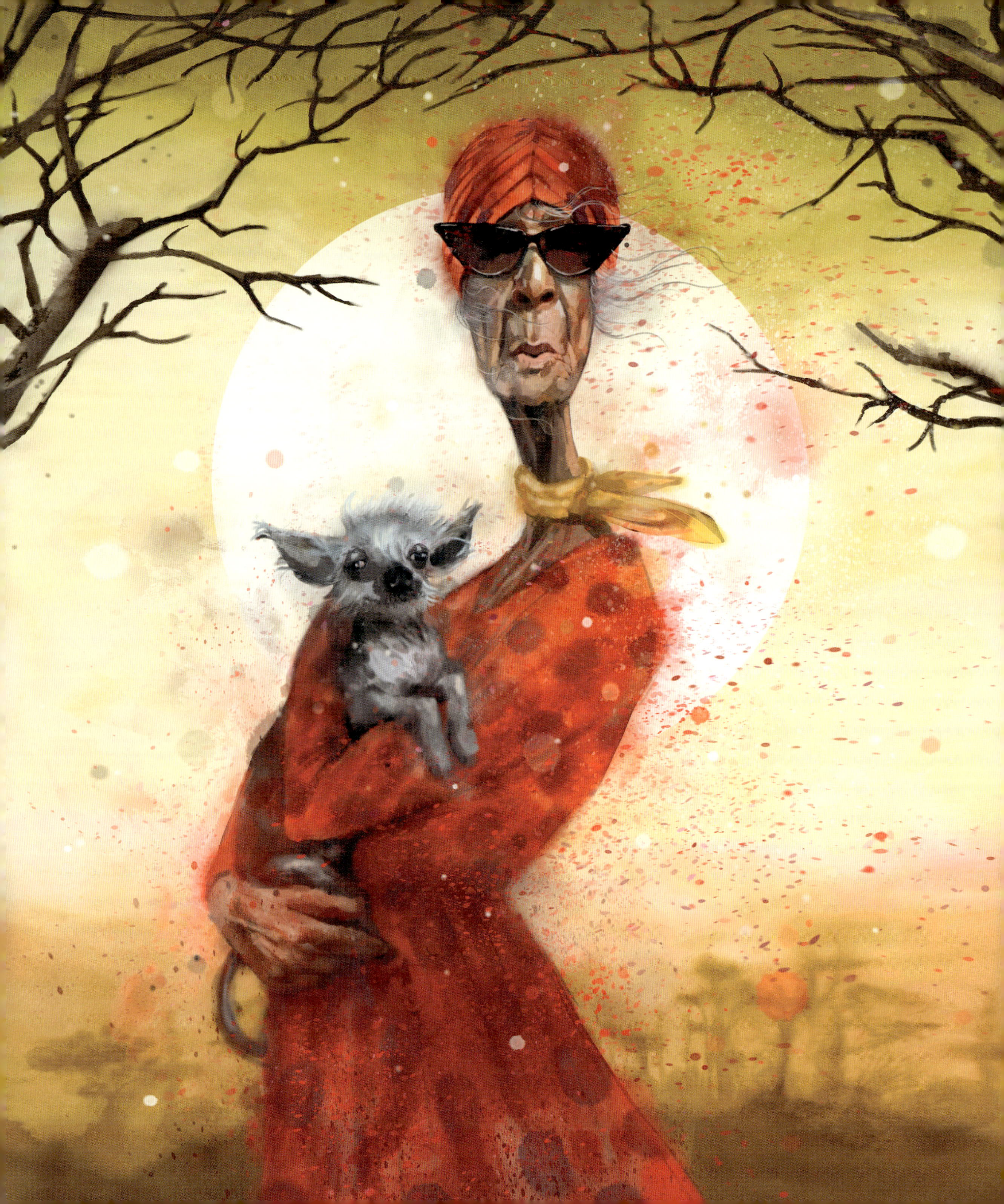

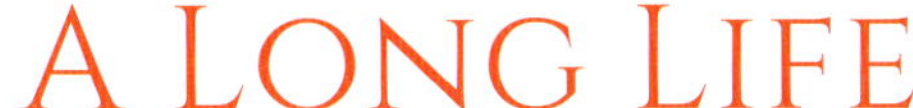

A Long Life

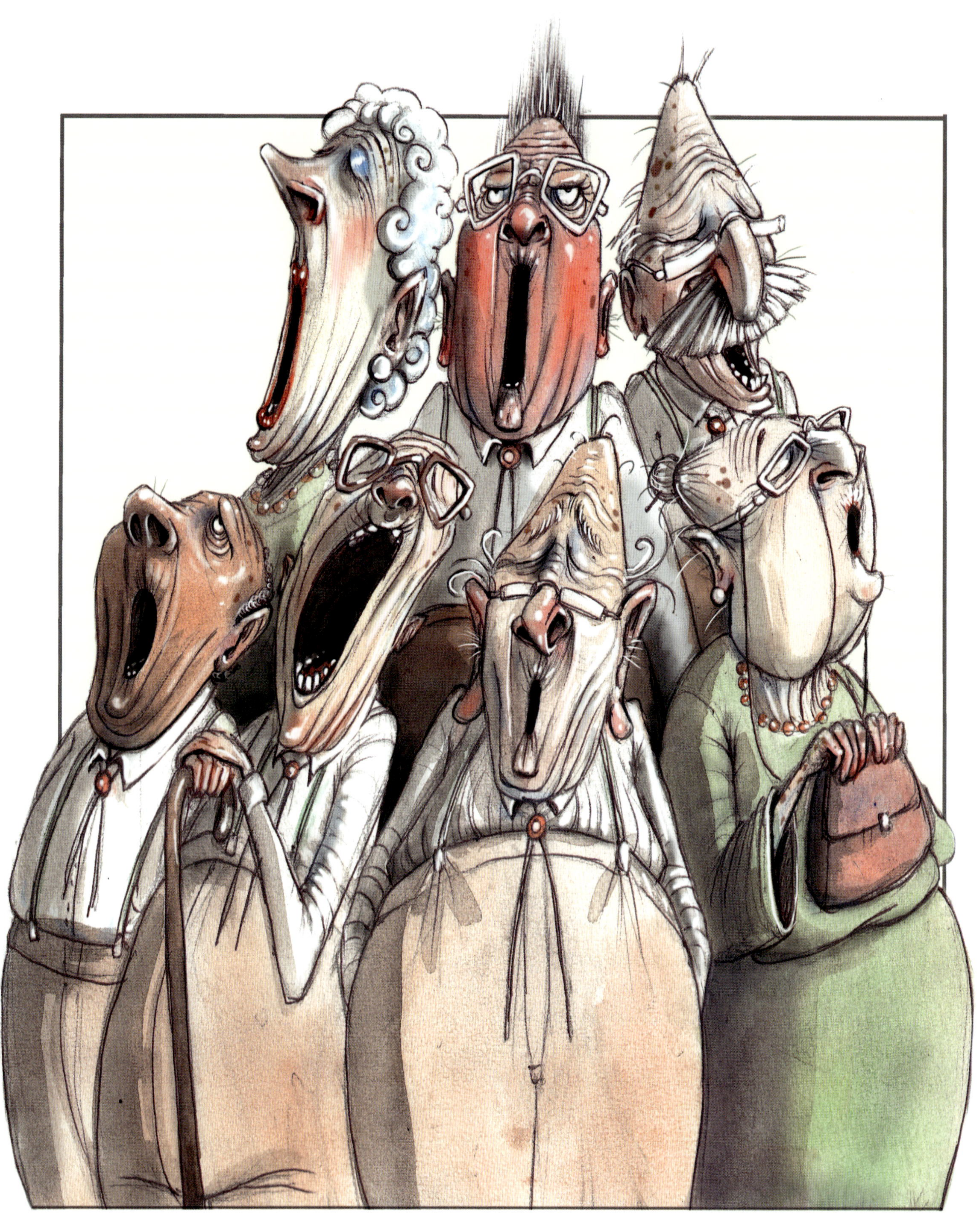

We have to start learning the song the retirees are singing.

But it's strange. On the inside you're twenty-two.

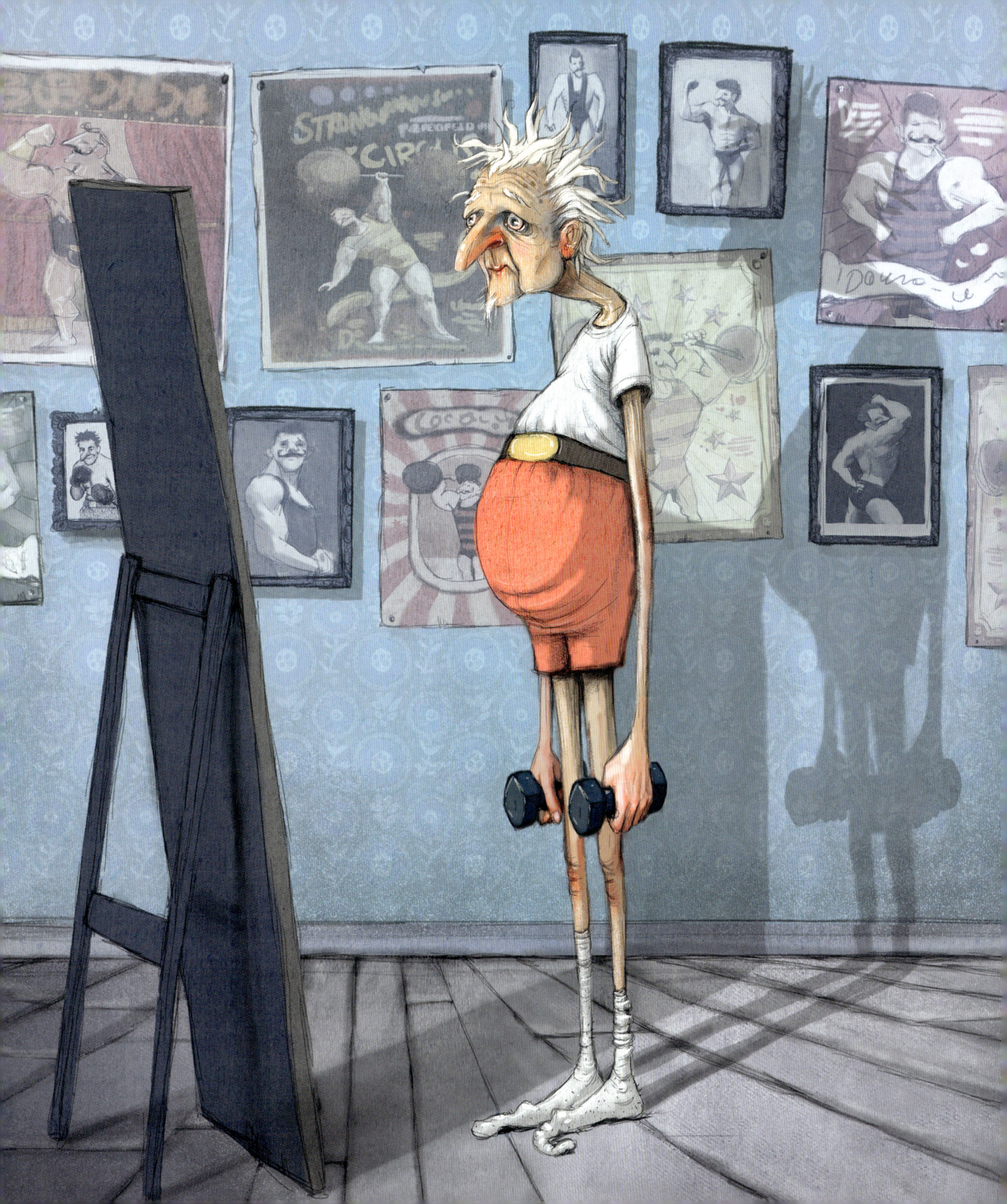

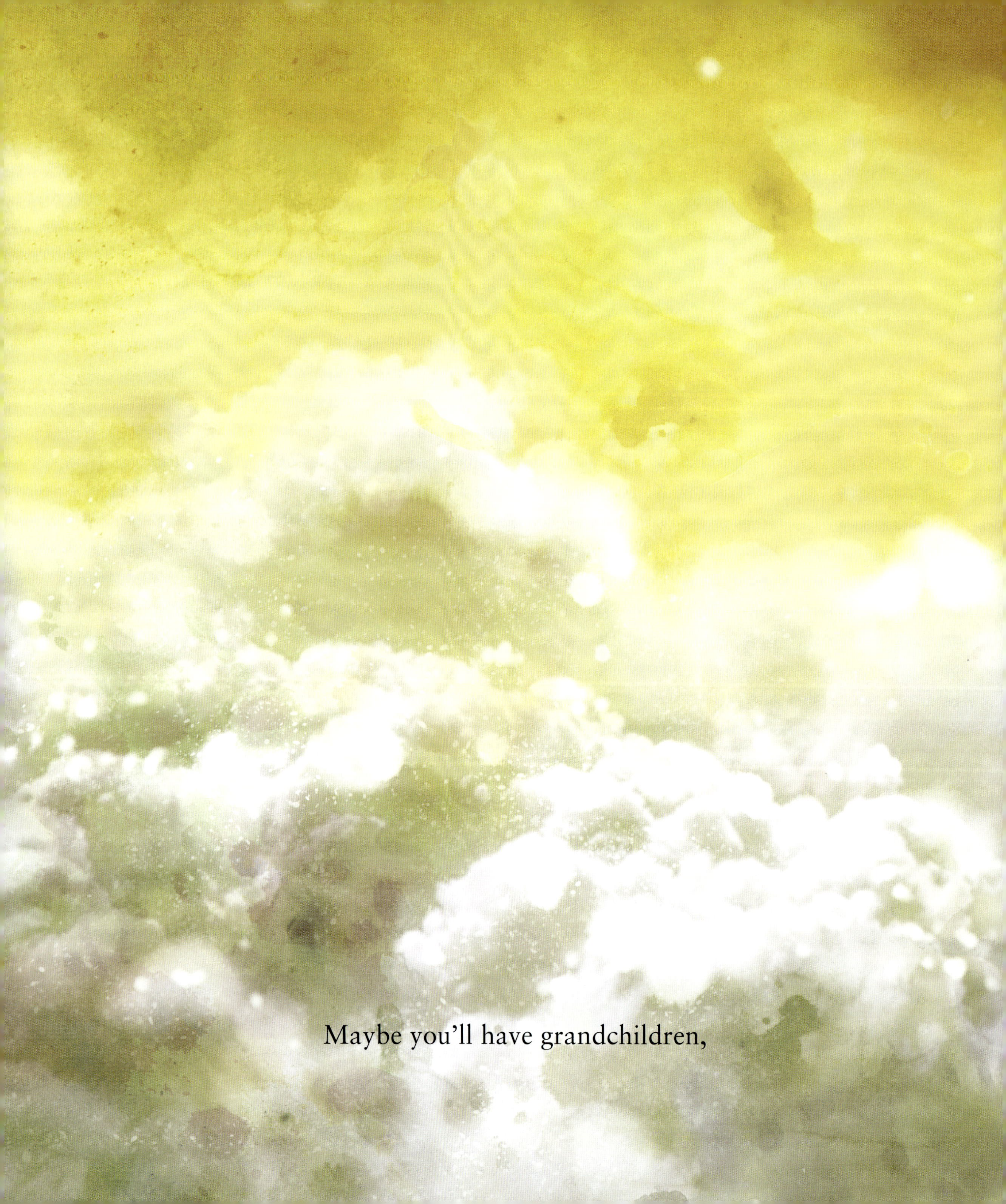

Maybe you'll have grandchildren,

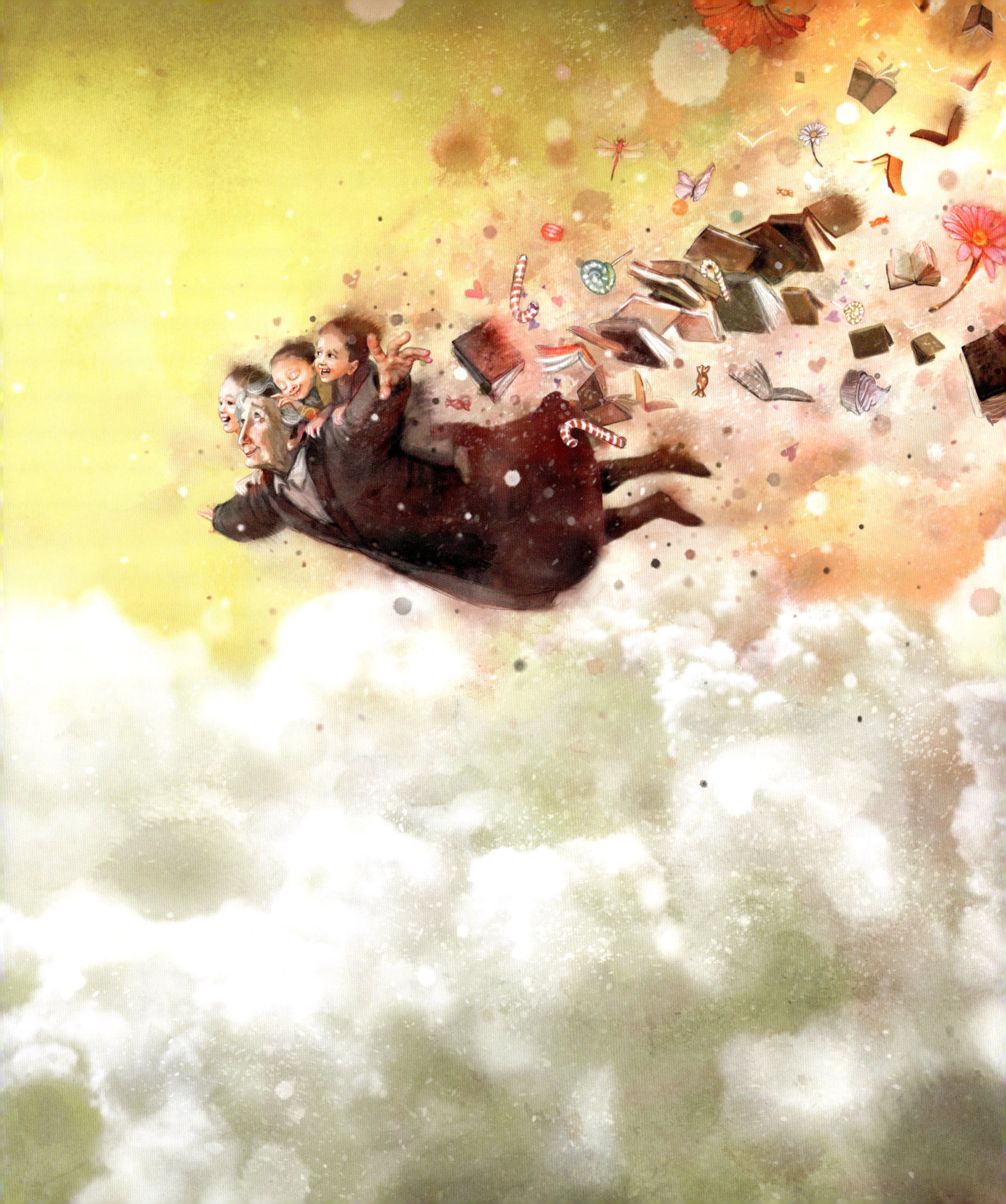

and Christmas will be magical once again.

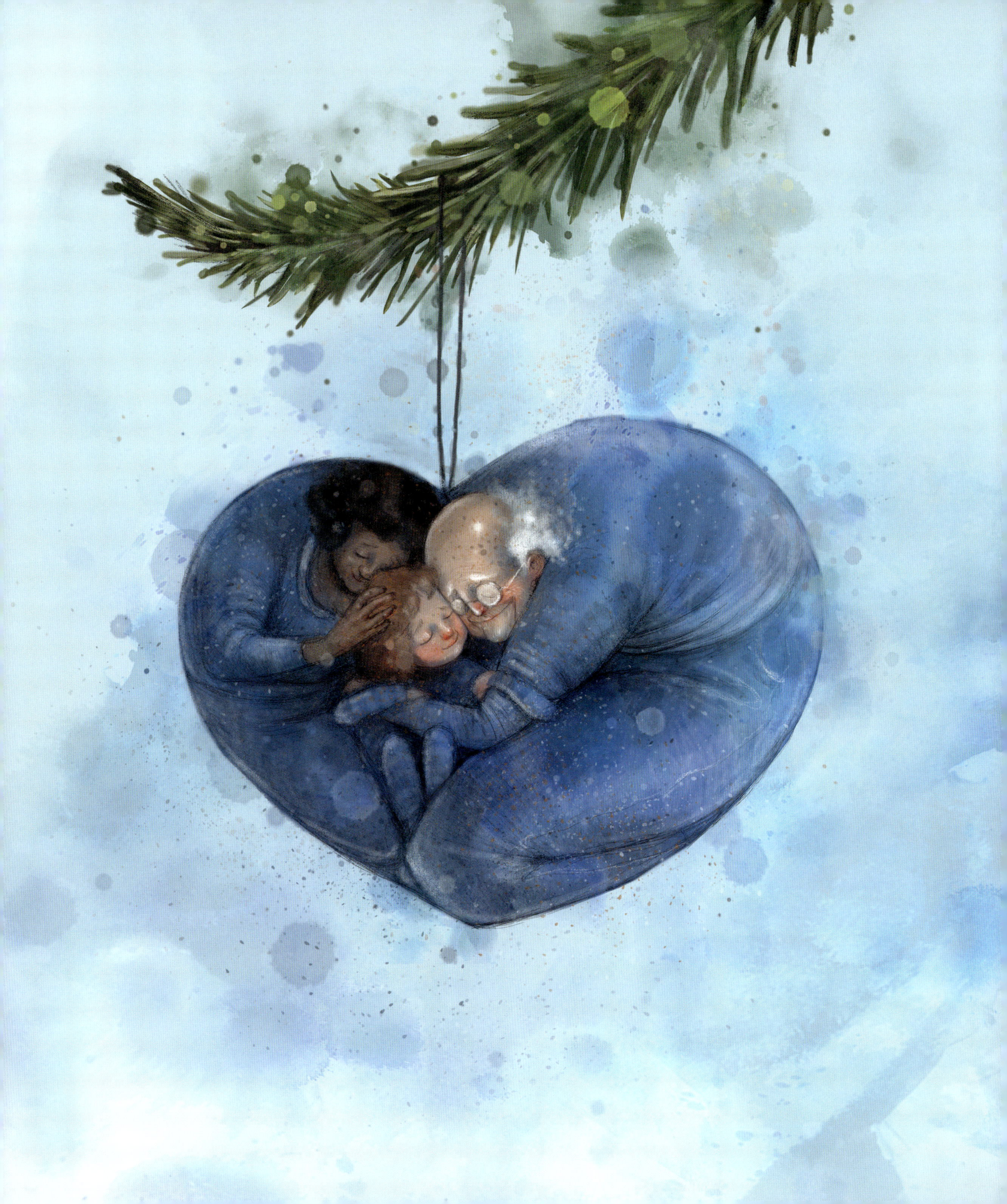

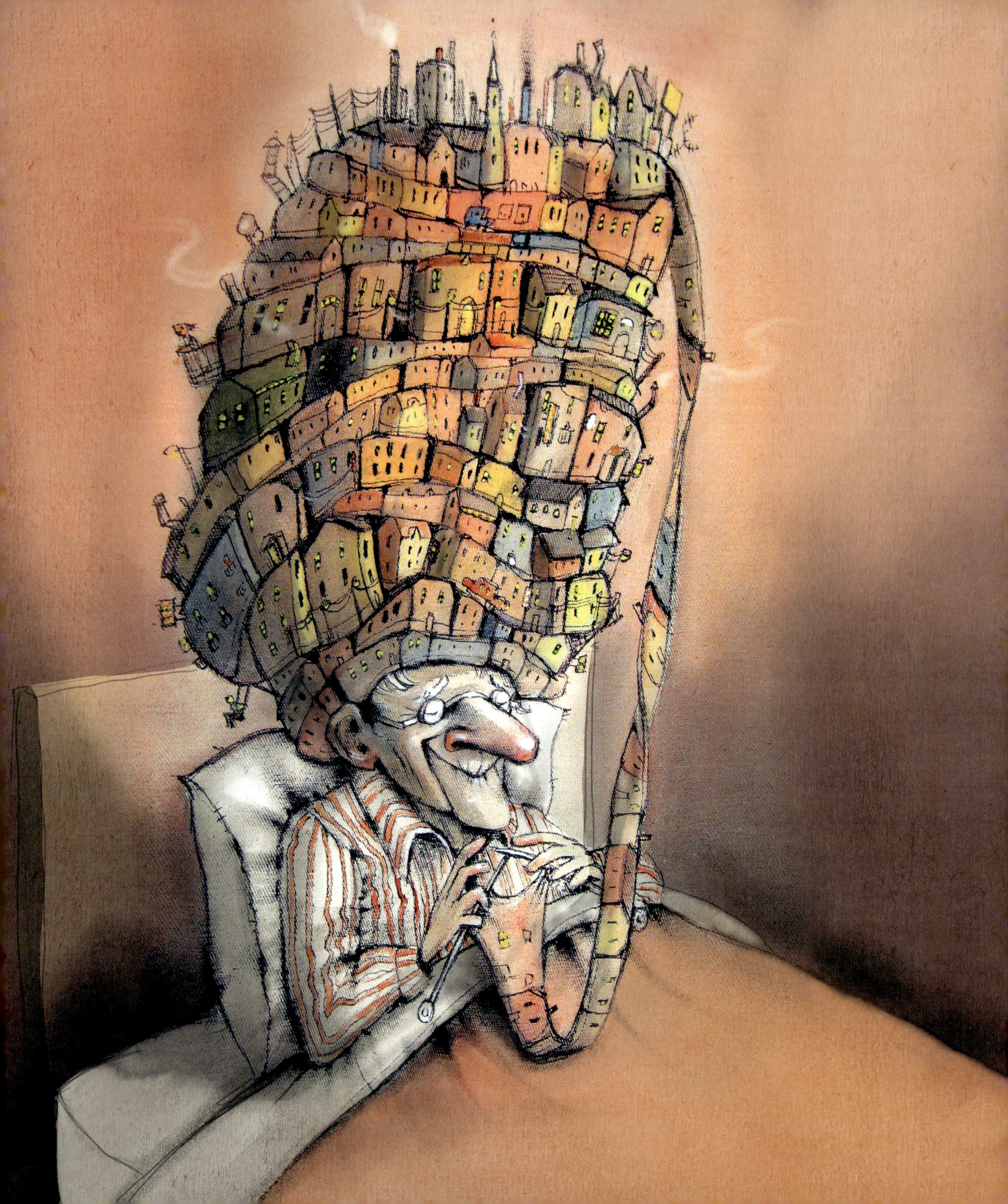

We finally have the time
to do what we want

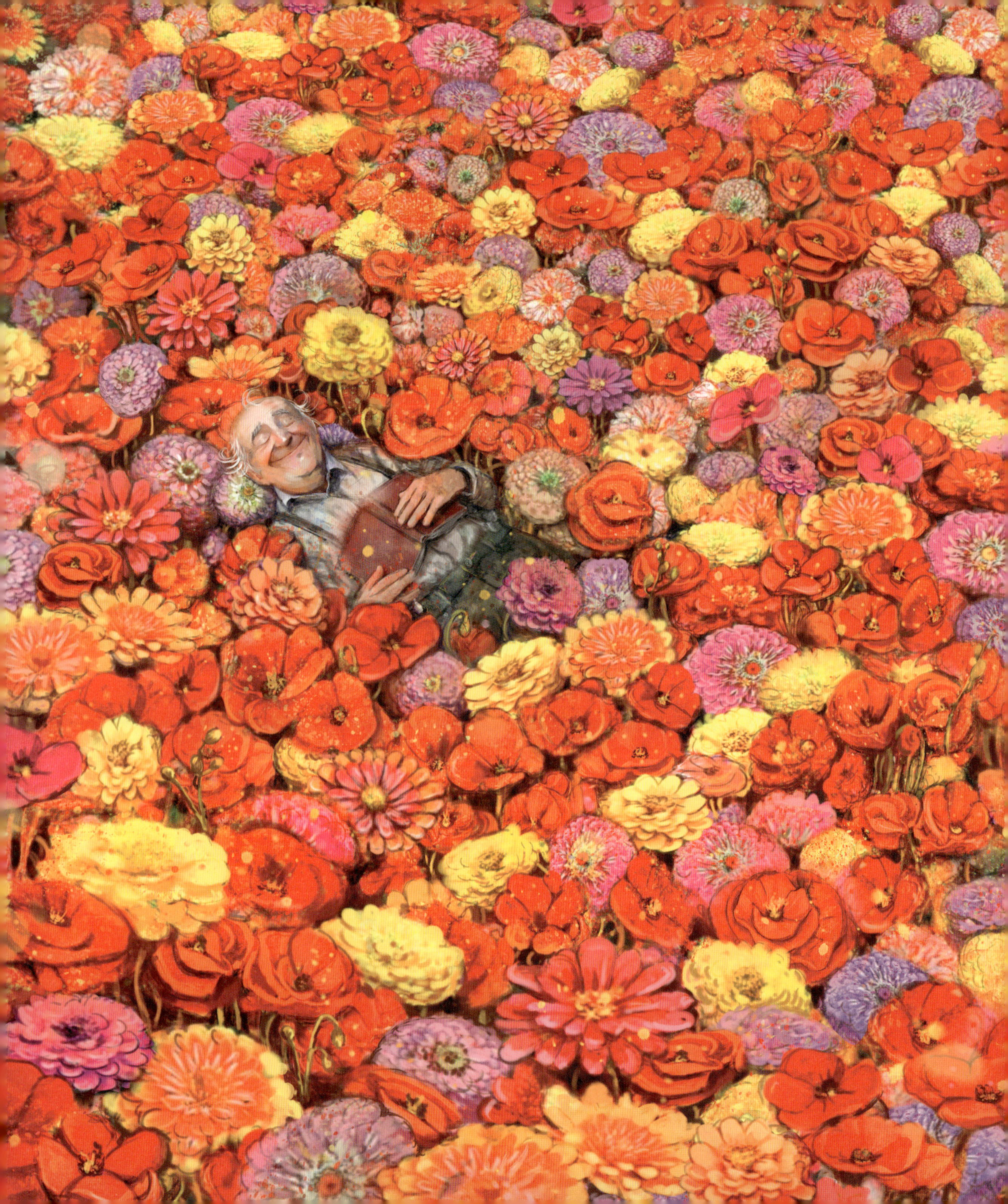

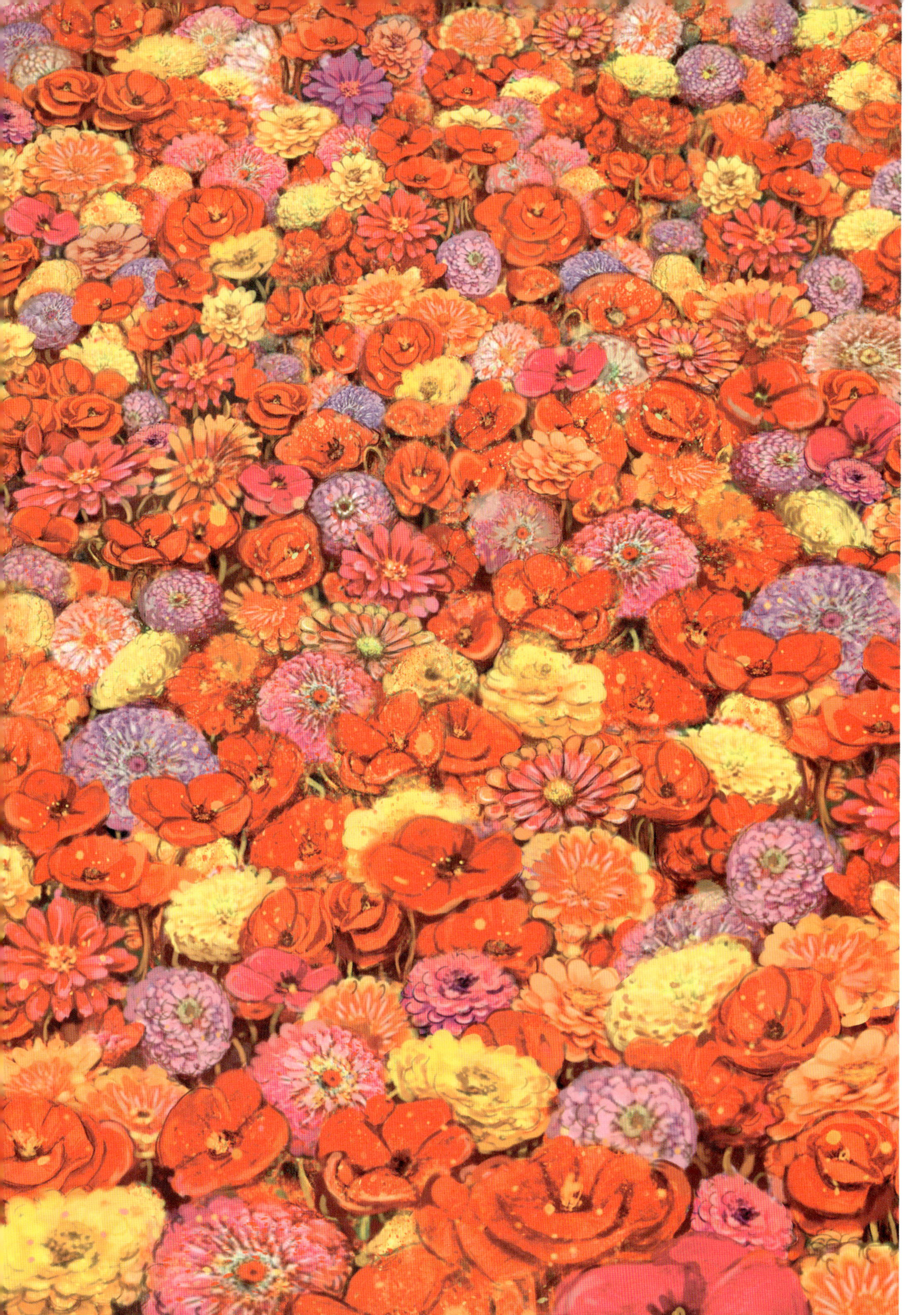

during
the day

and at night.

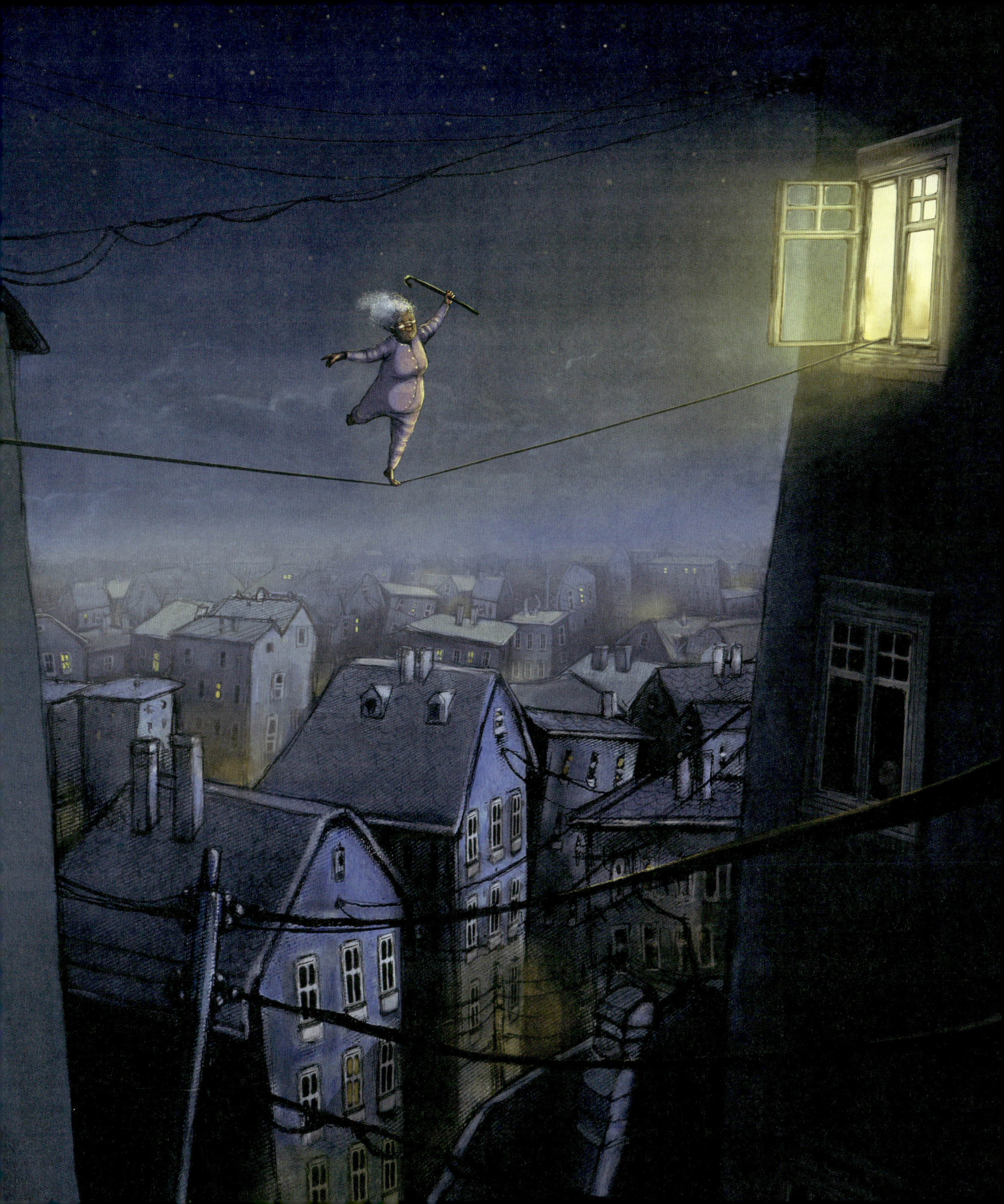

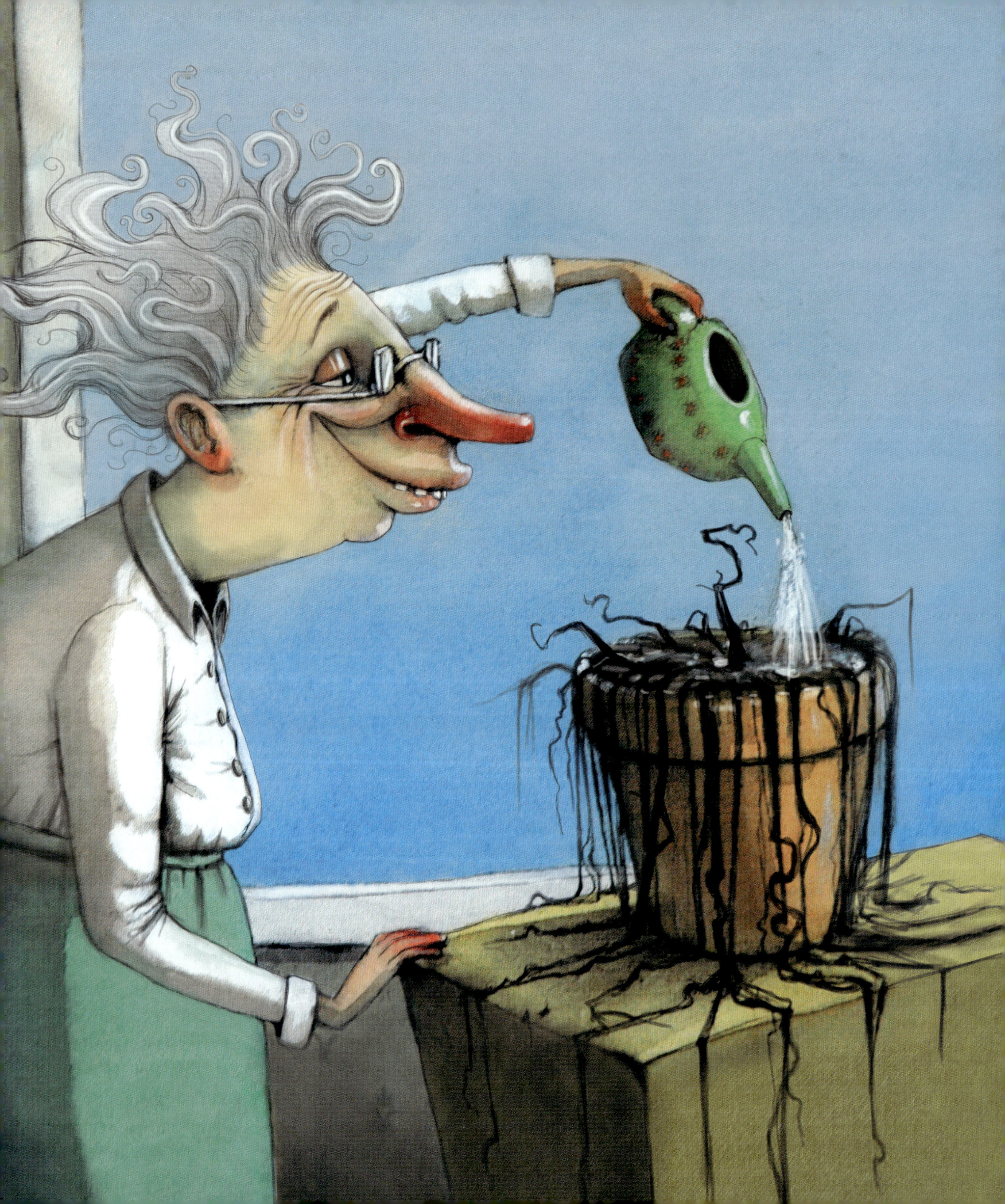

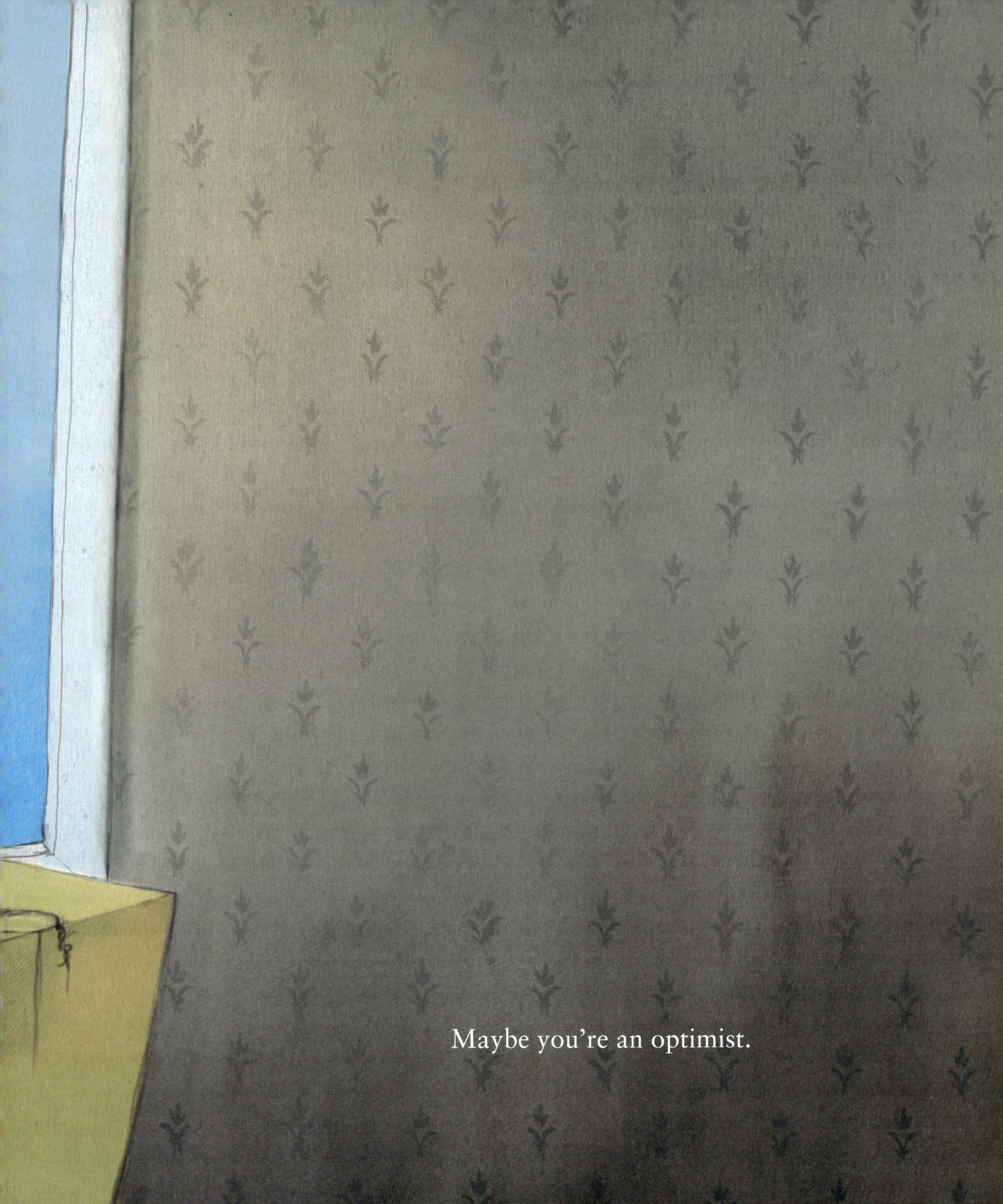
Maybe you're an optimist.

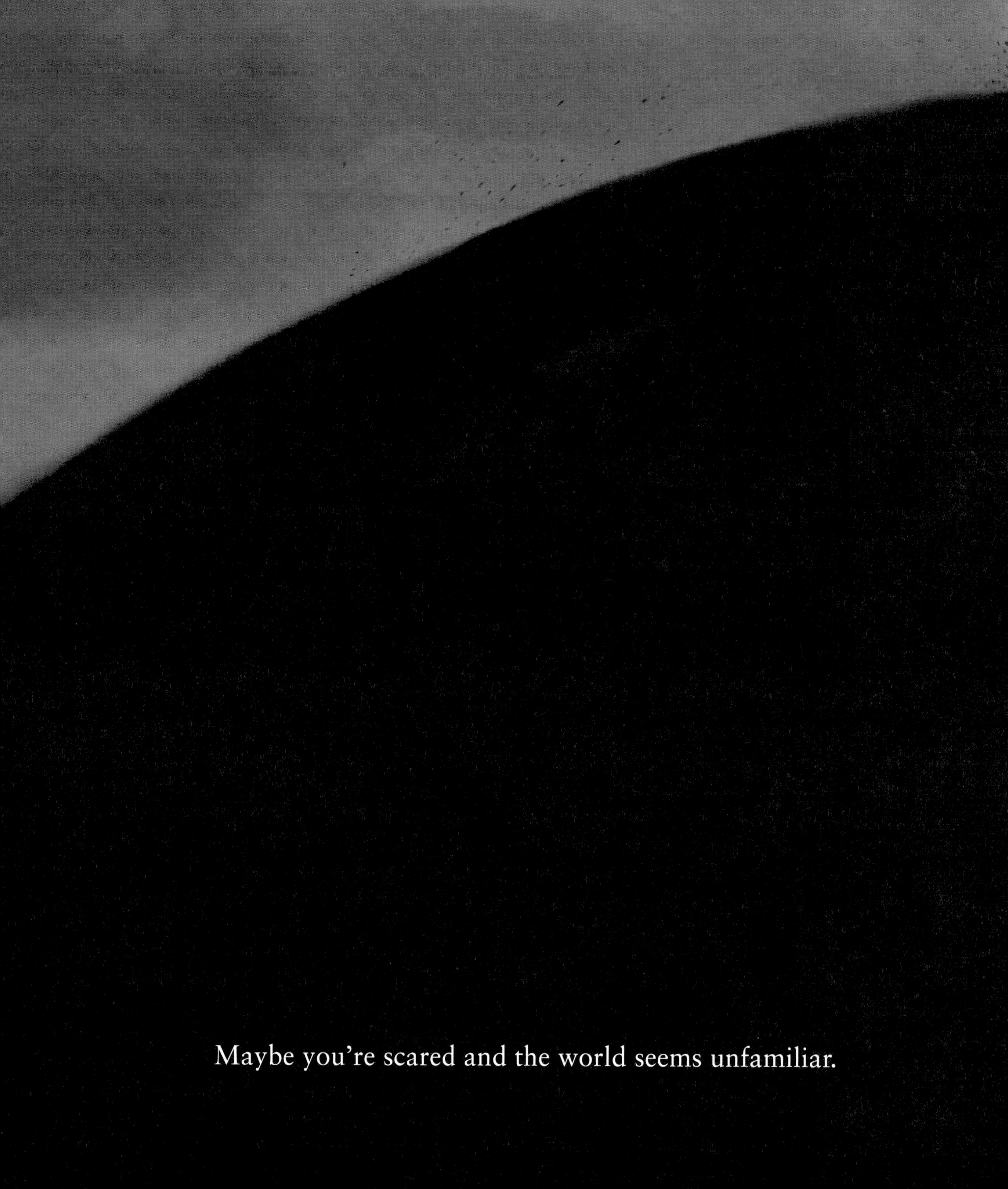

Maybe you're scared and the world seems unfamiliar.

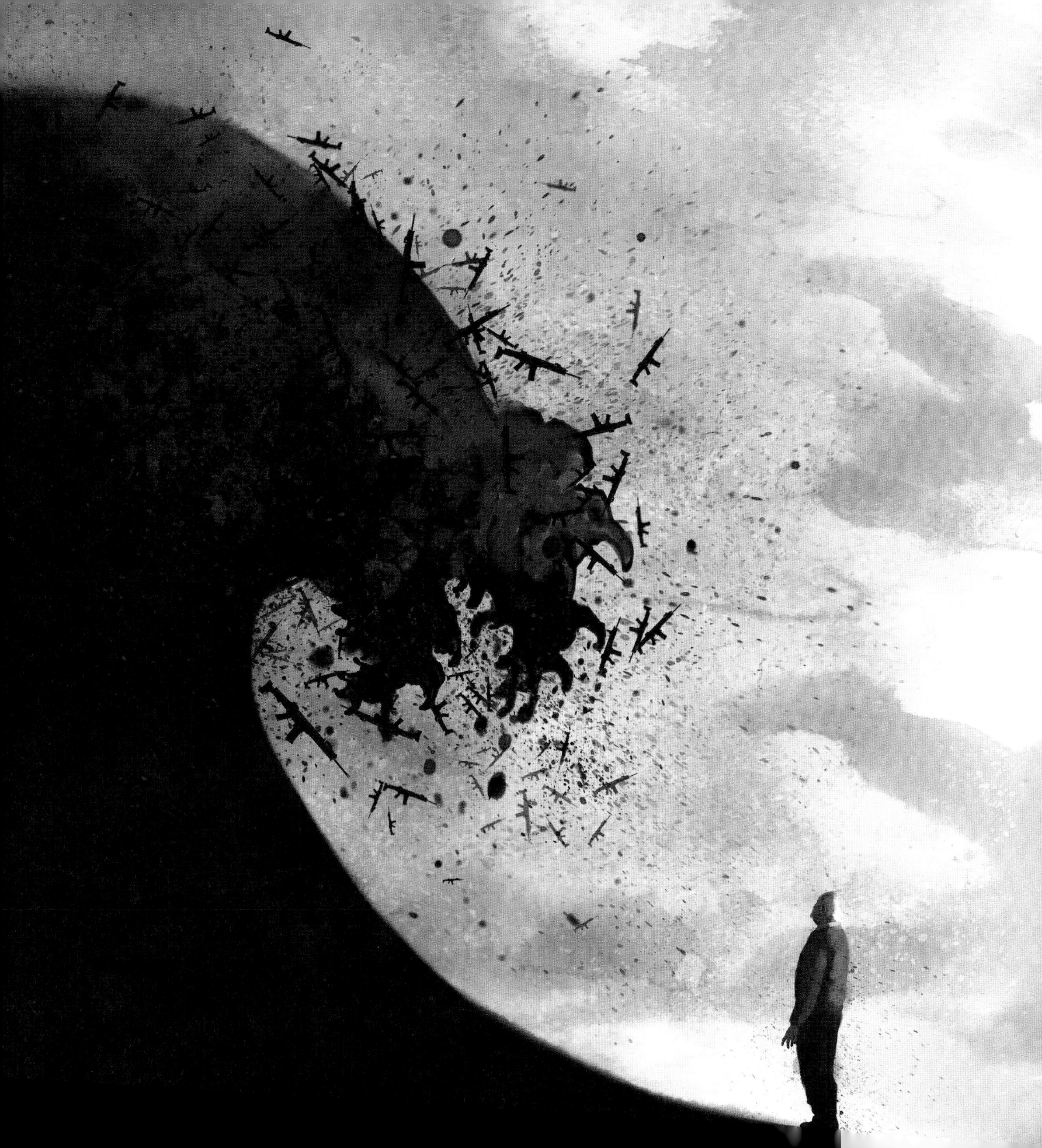

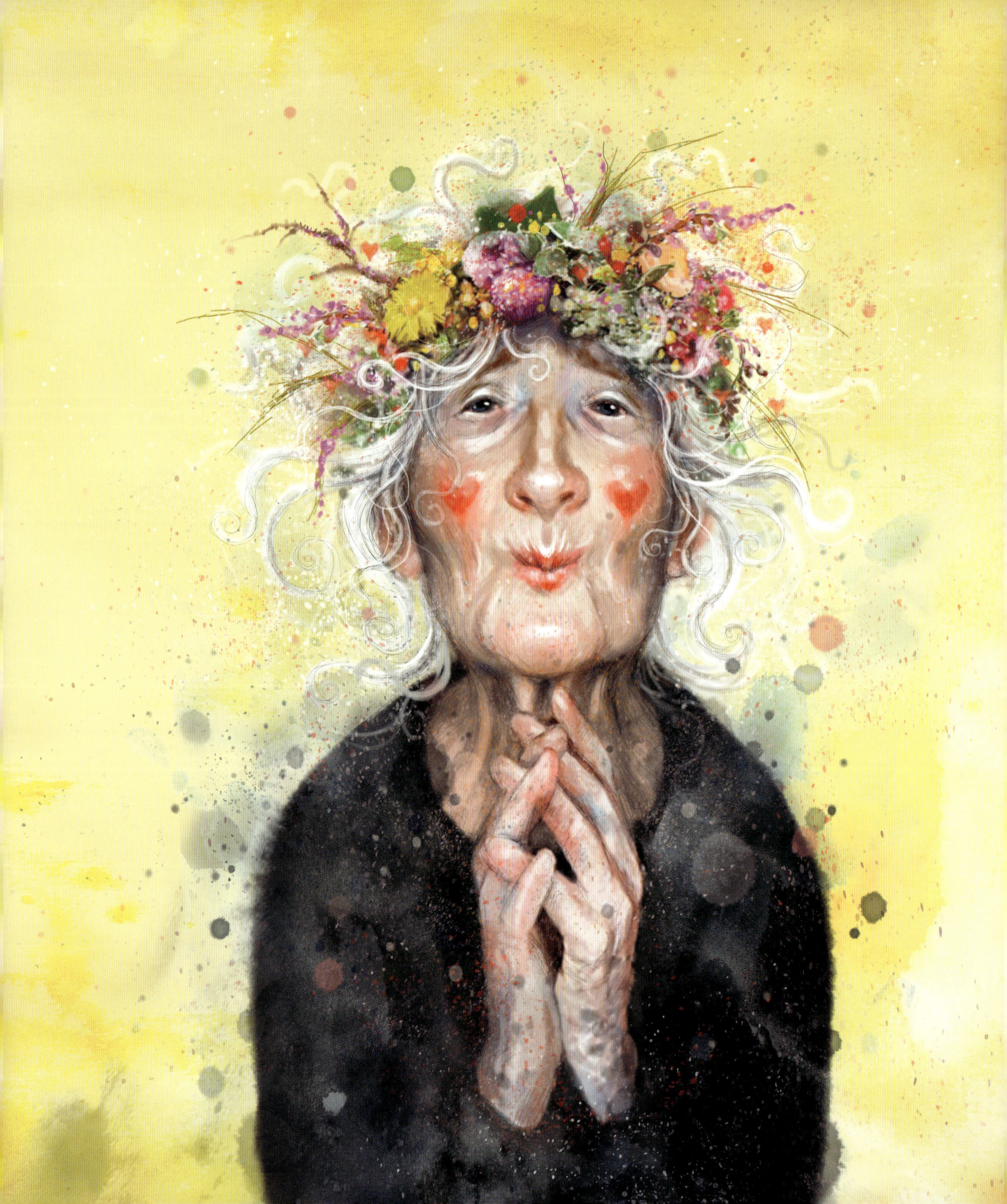

But I hope she still makes you feel safe.

I hope he still sees you.

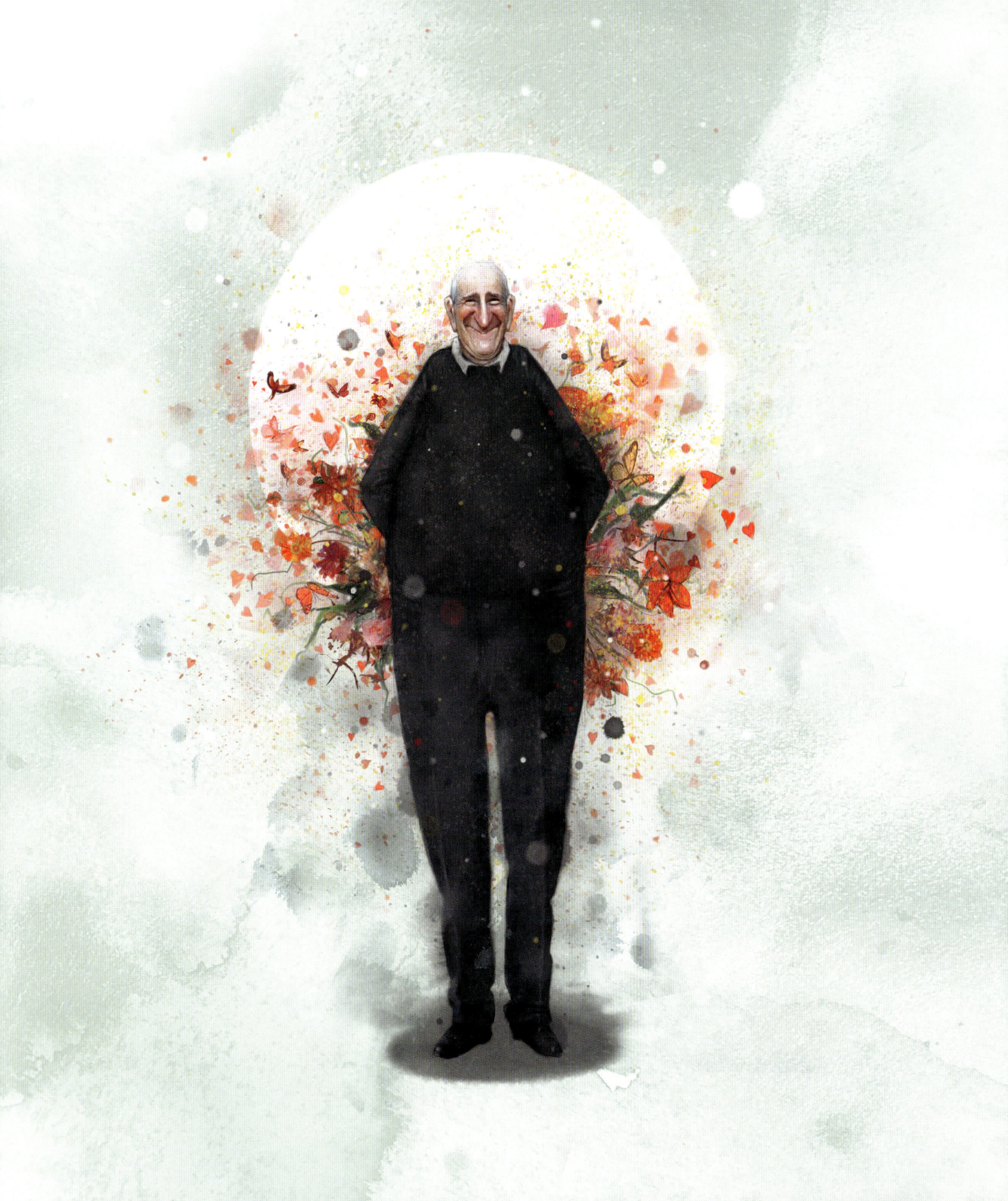

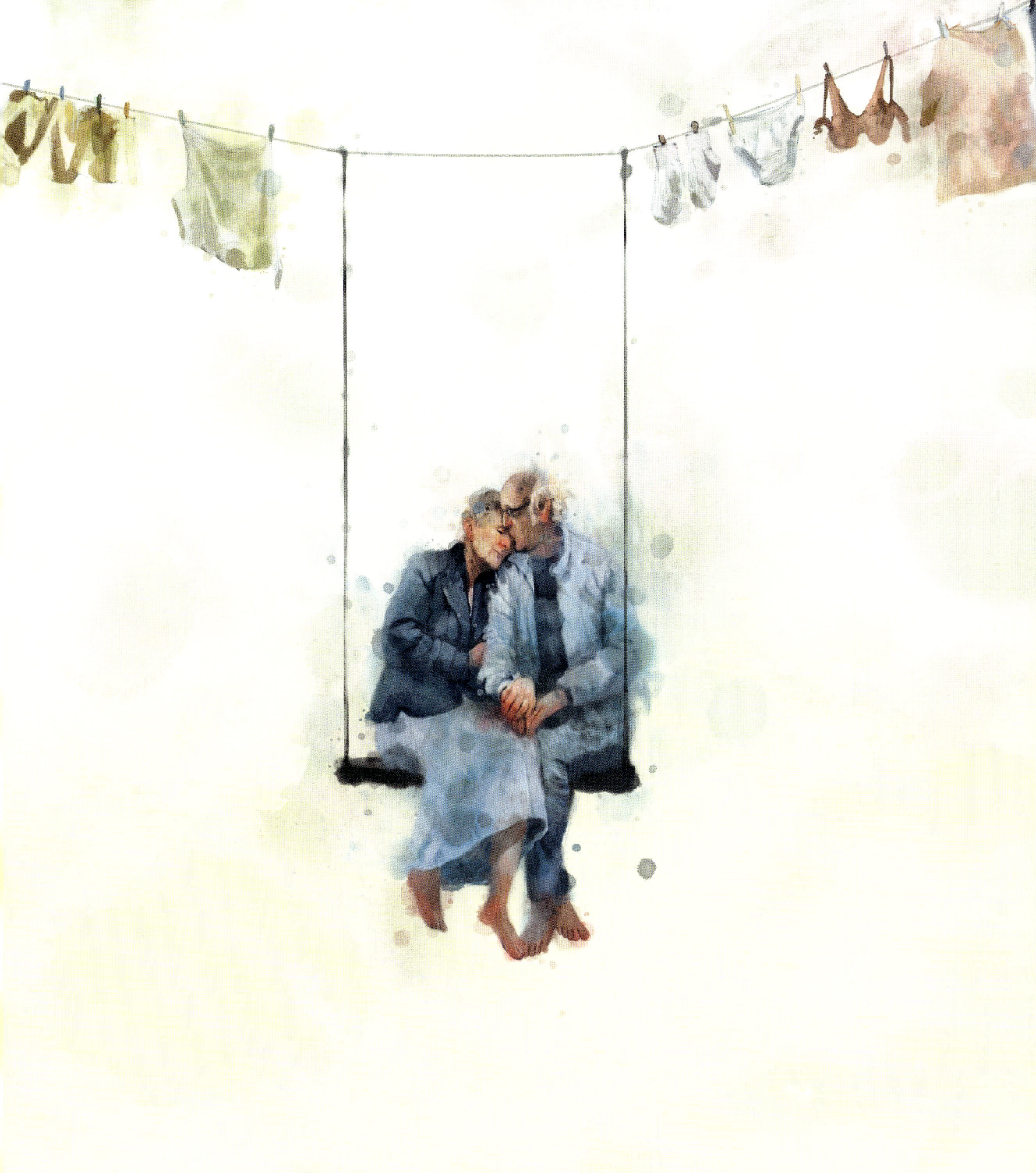

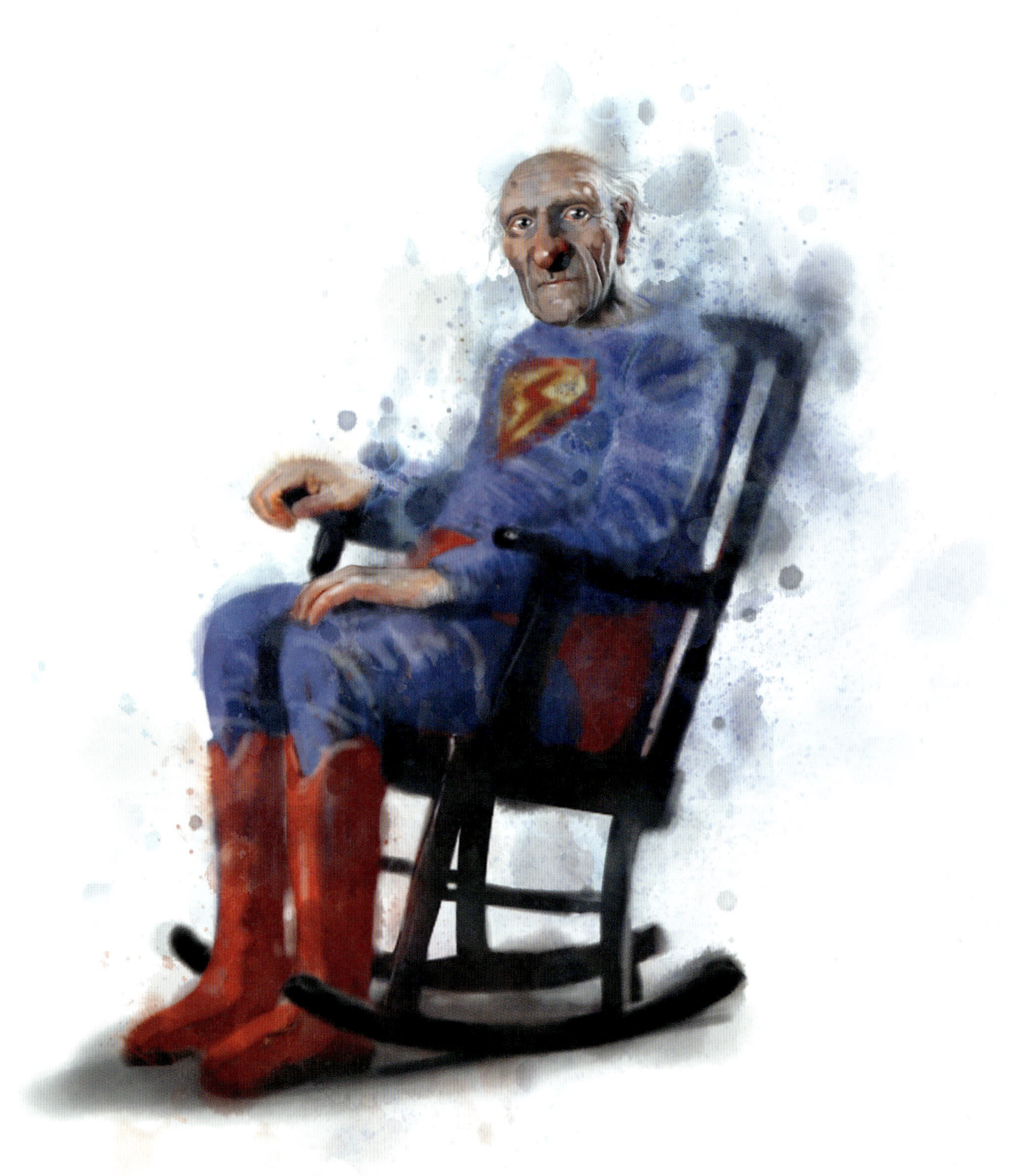

Then it's like your body is failing you.

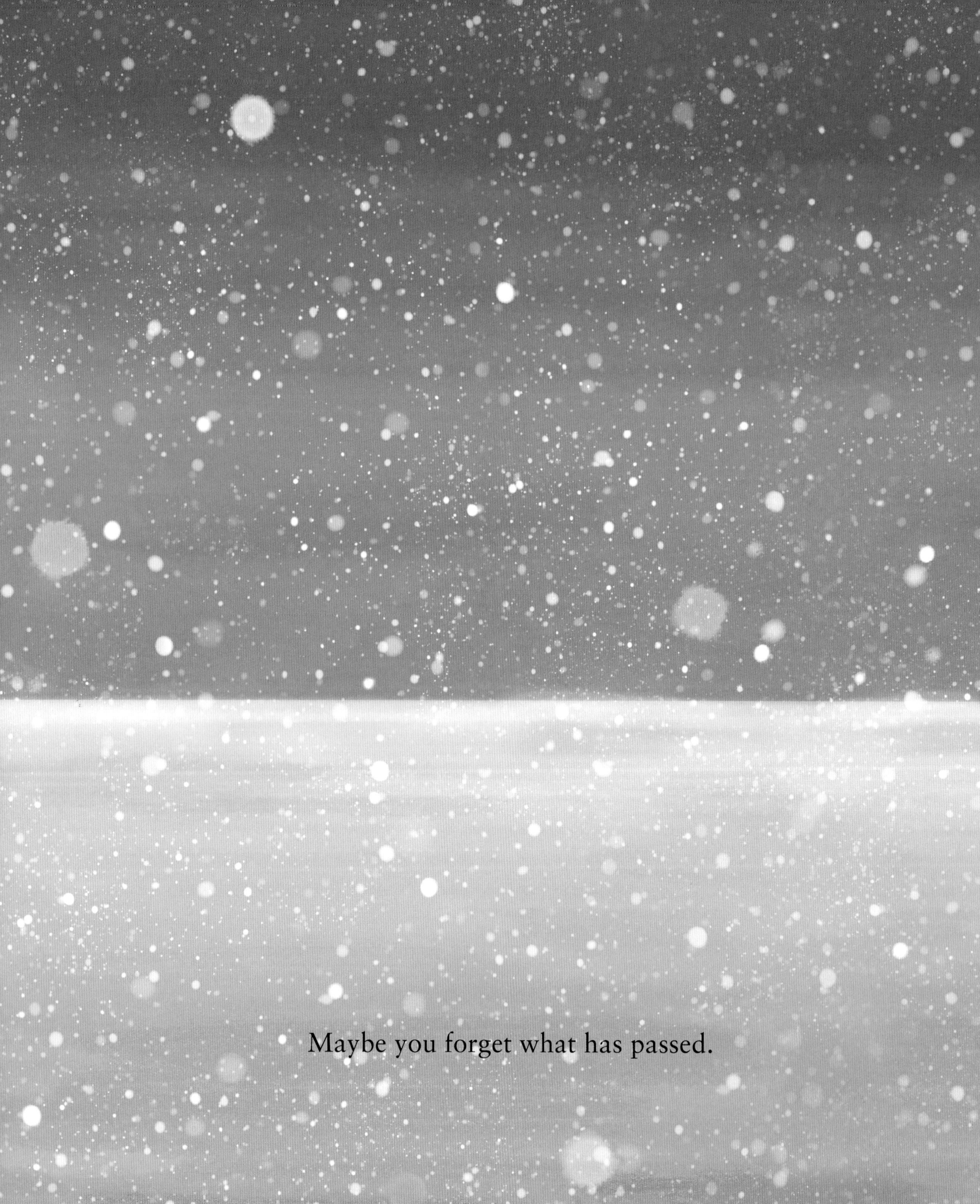
Maybe you forget what has passed.

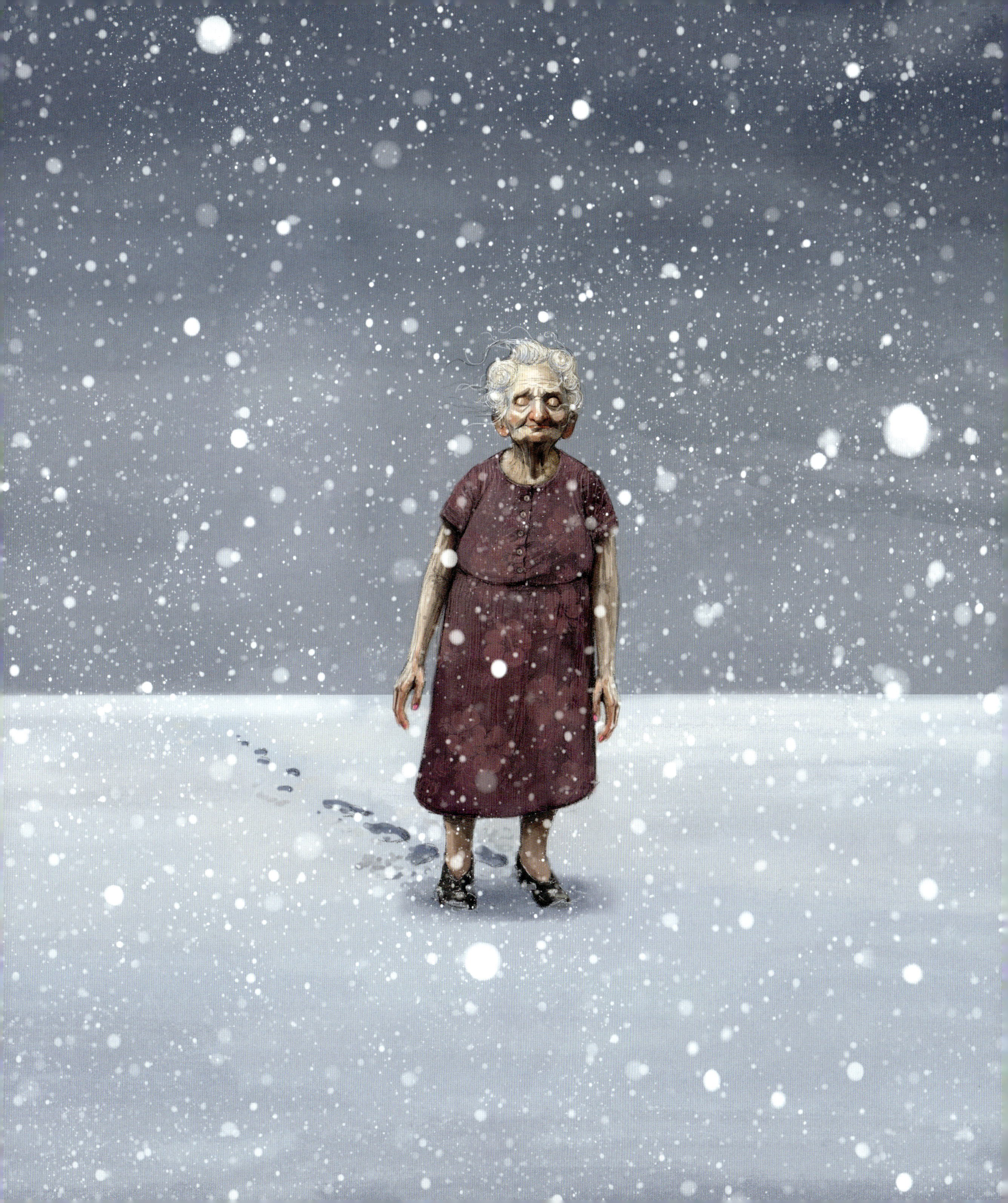

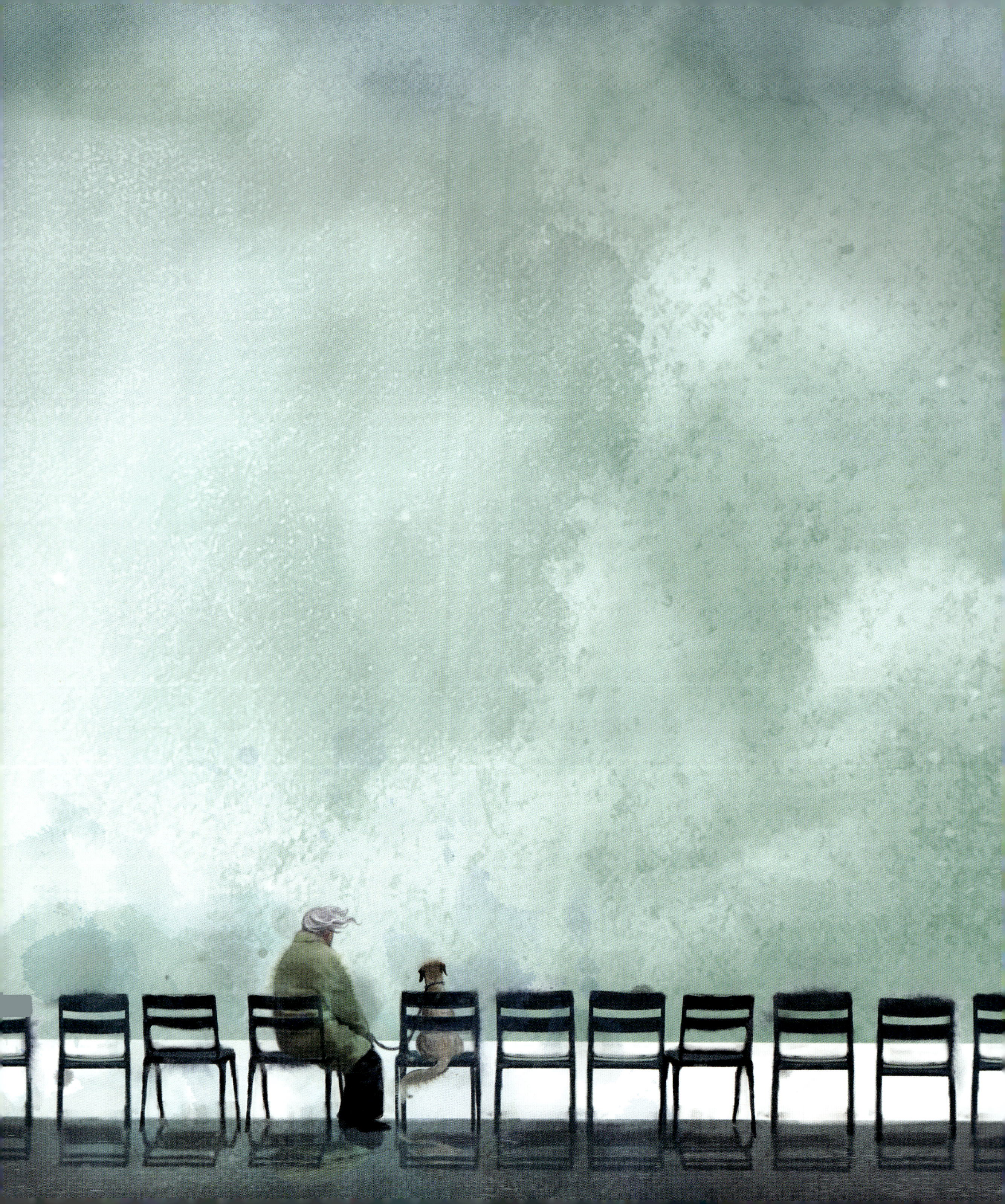

You *will* feel lonely,

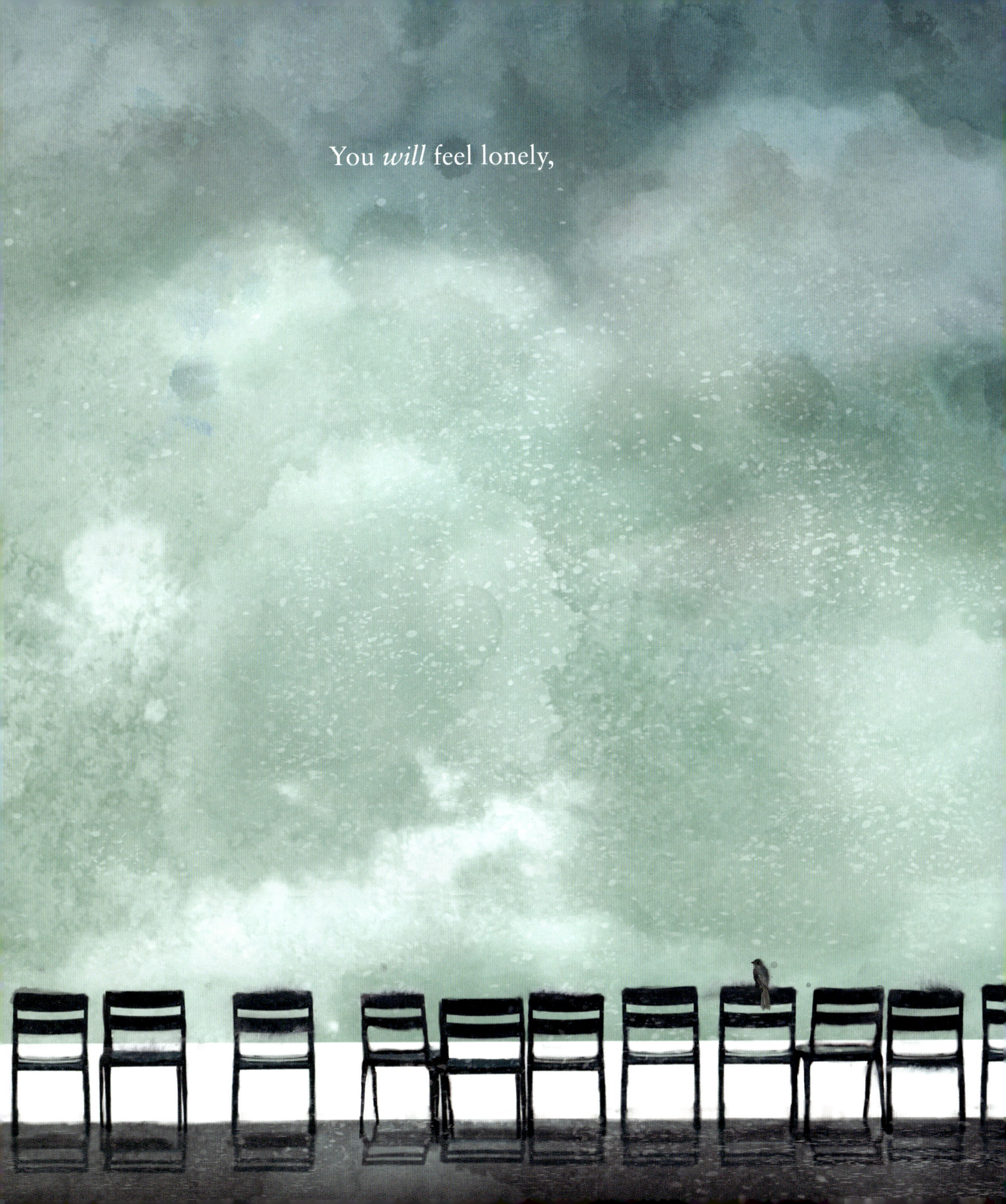

you *will* suffer loss,

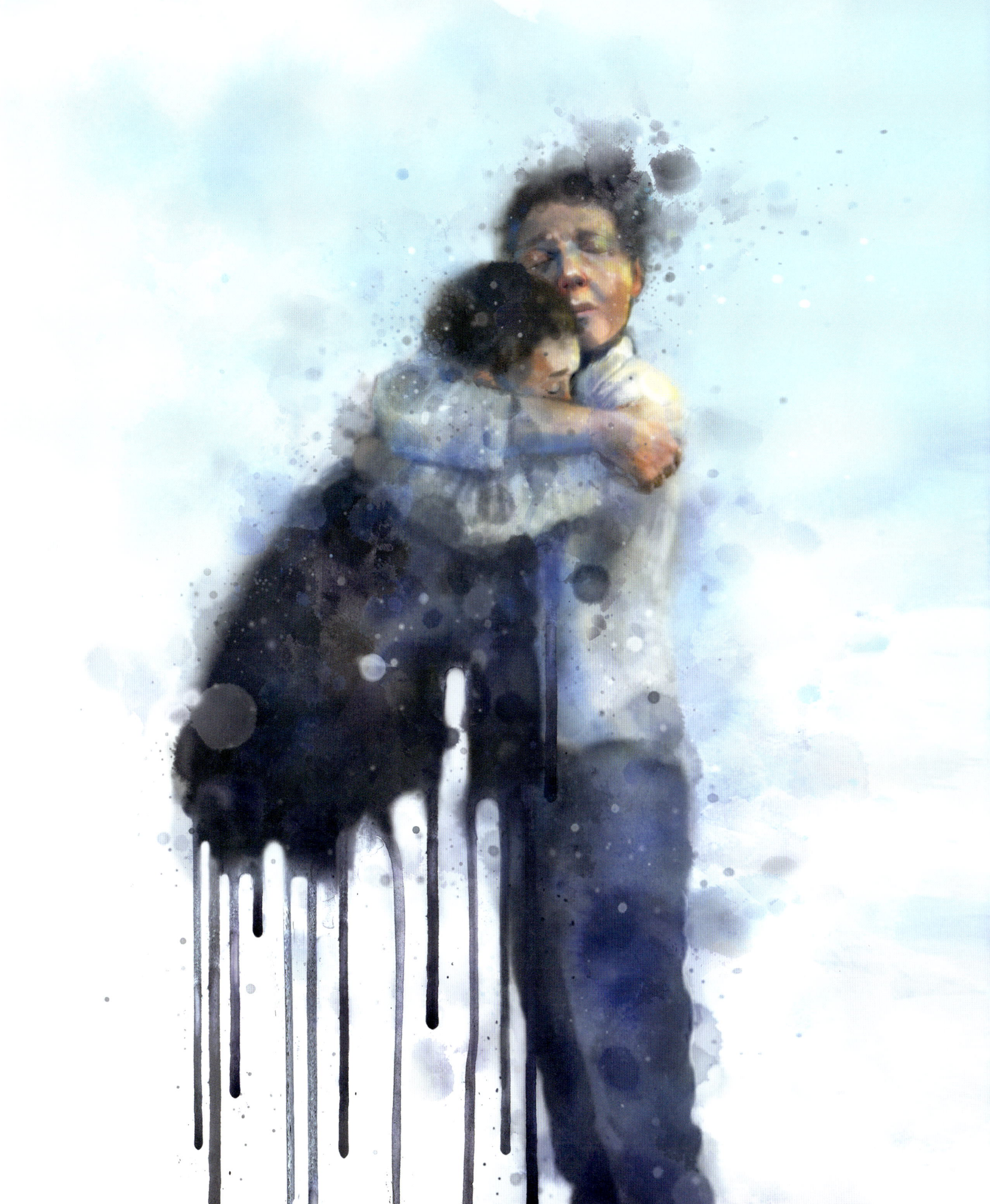

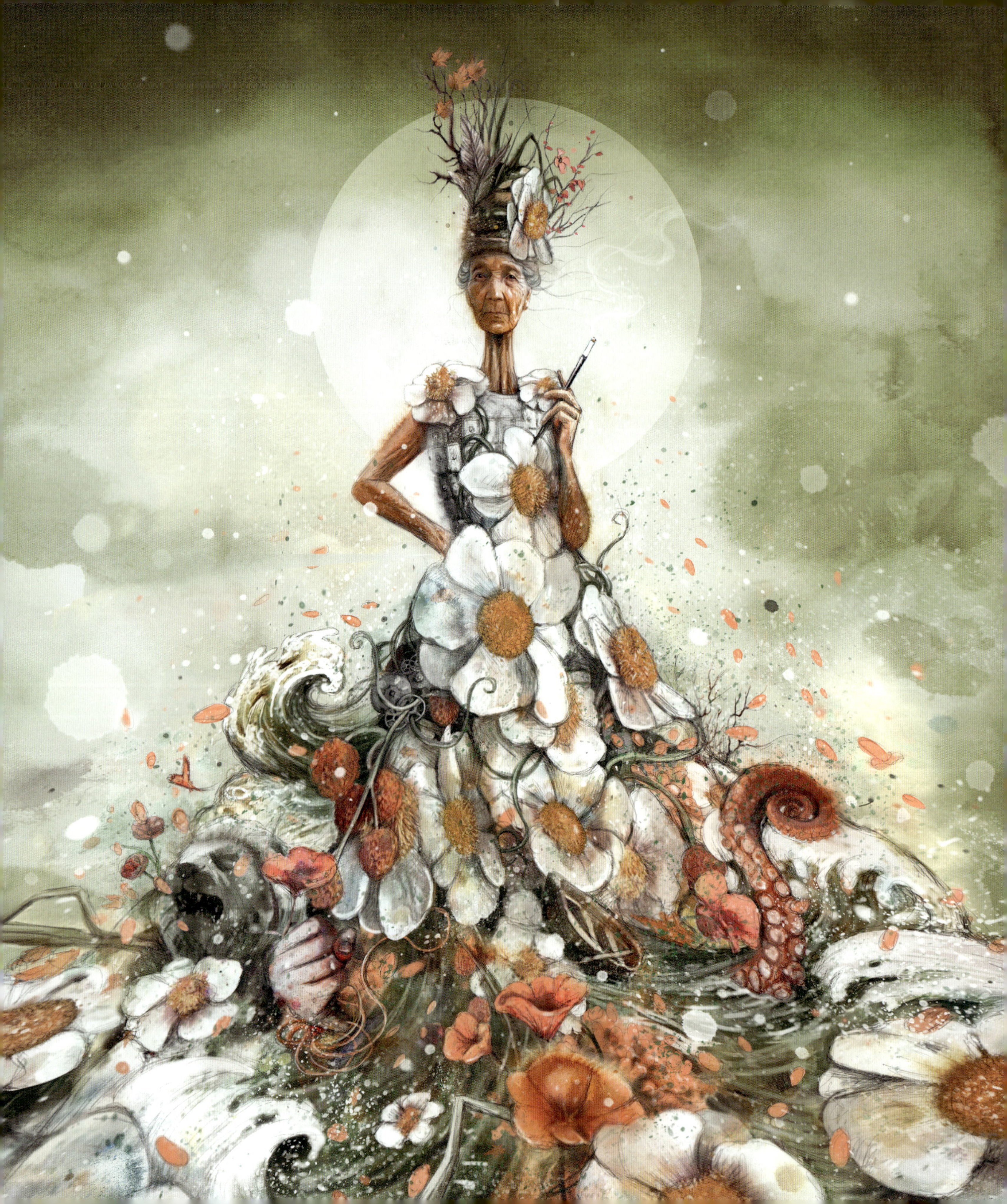

but you carry your whole life within you.

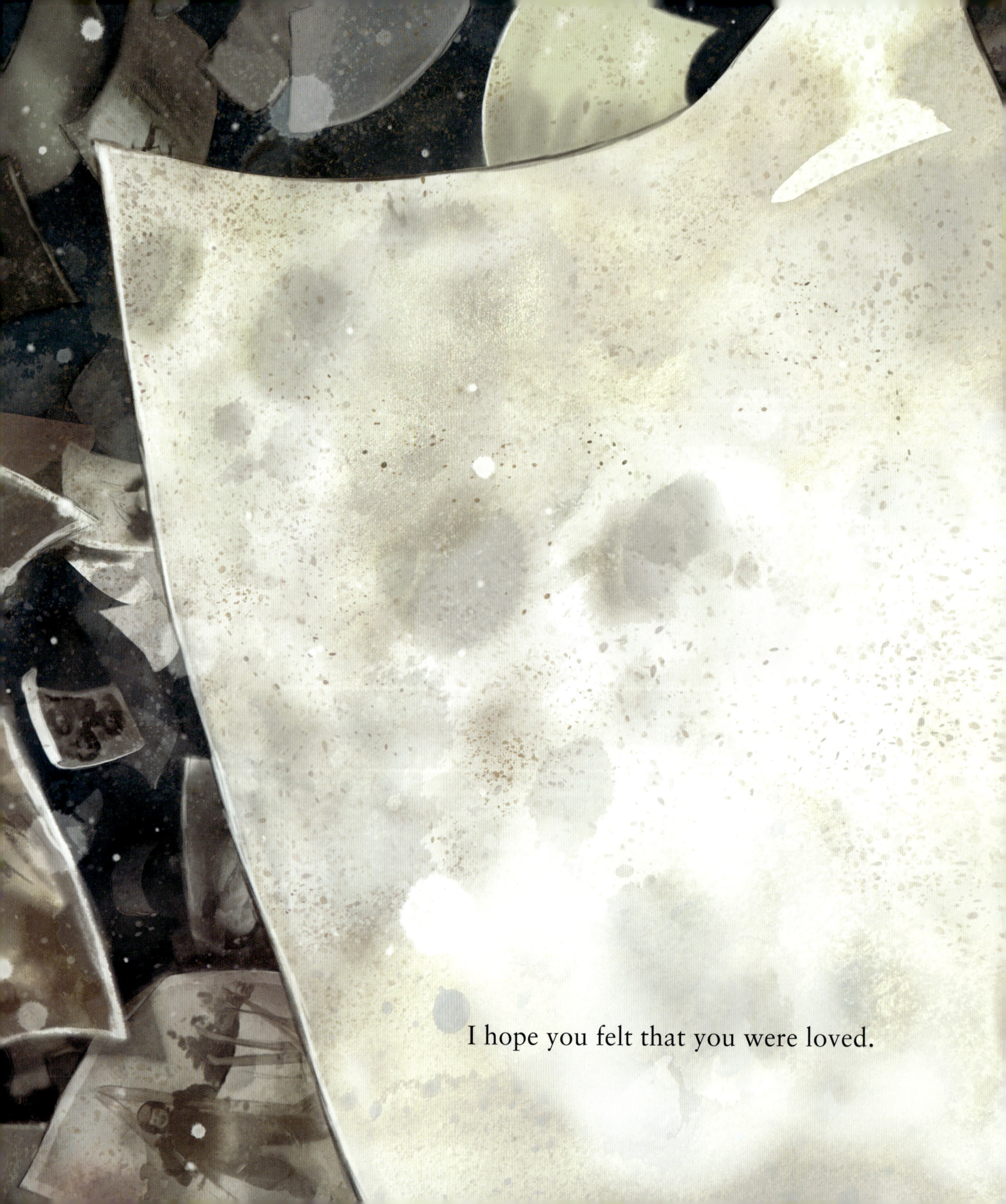

I hope you felt that you were loved.

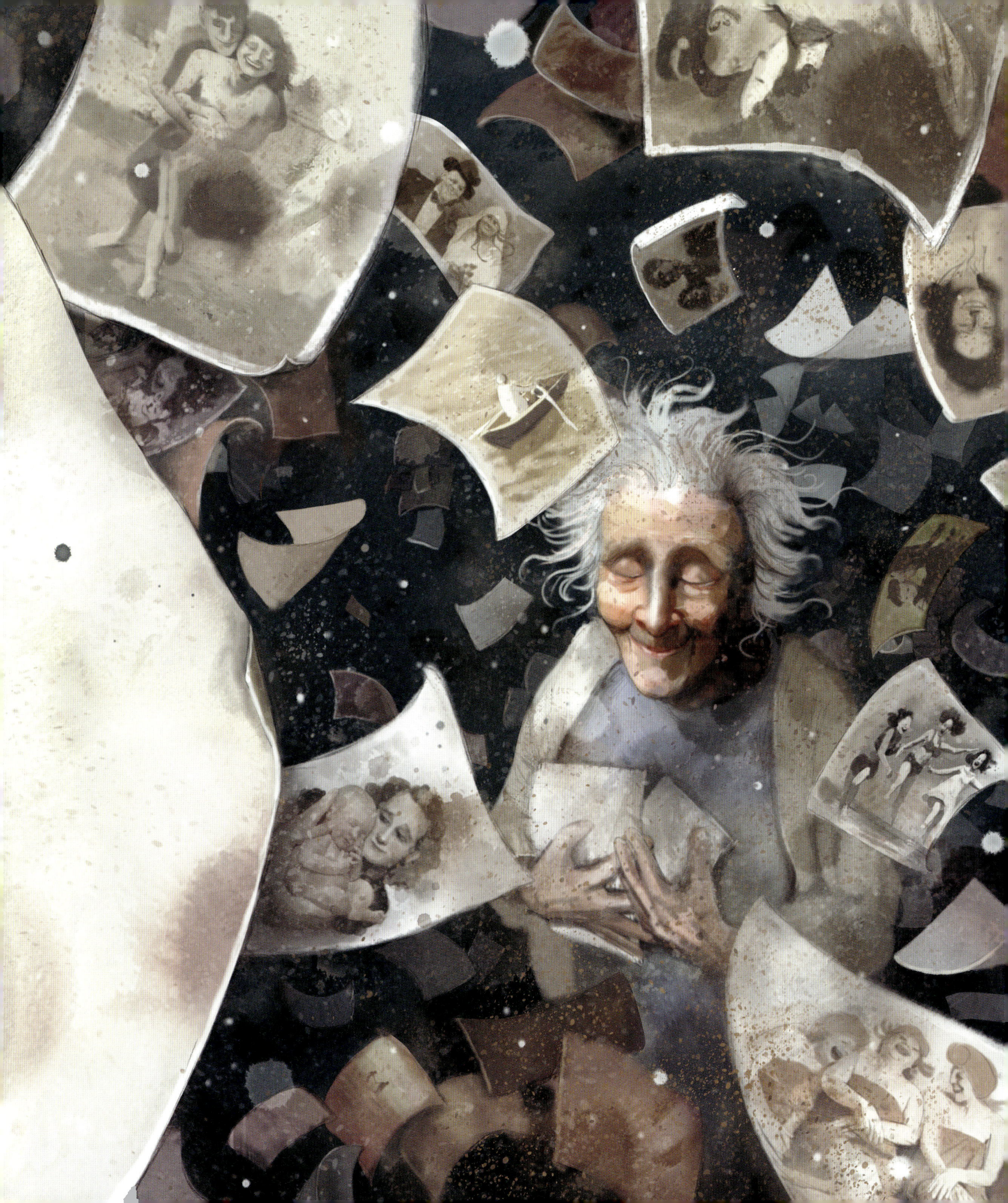

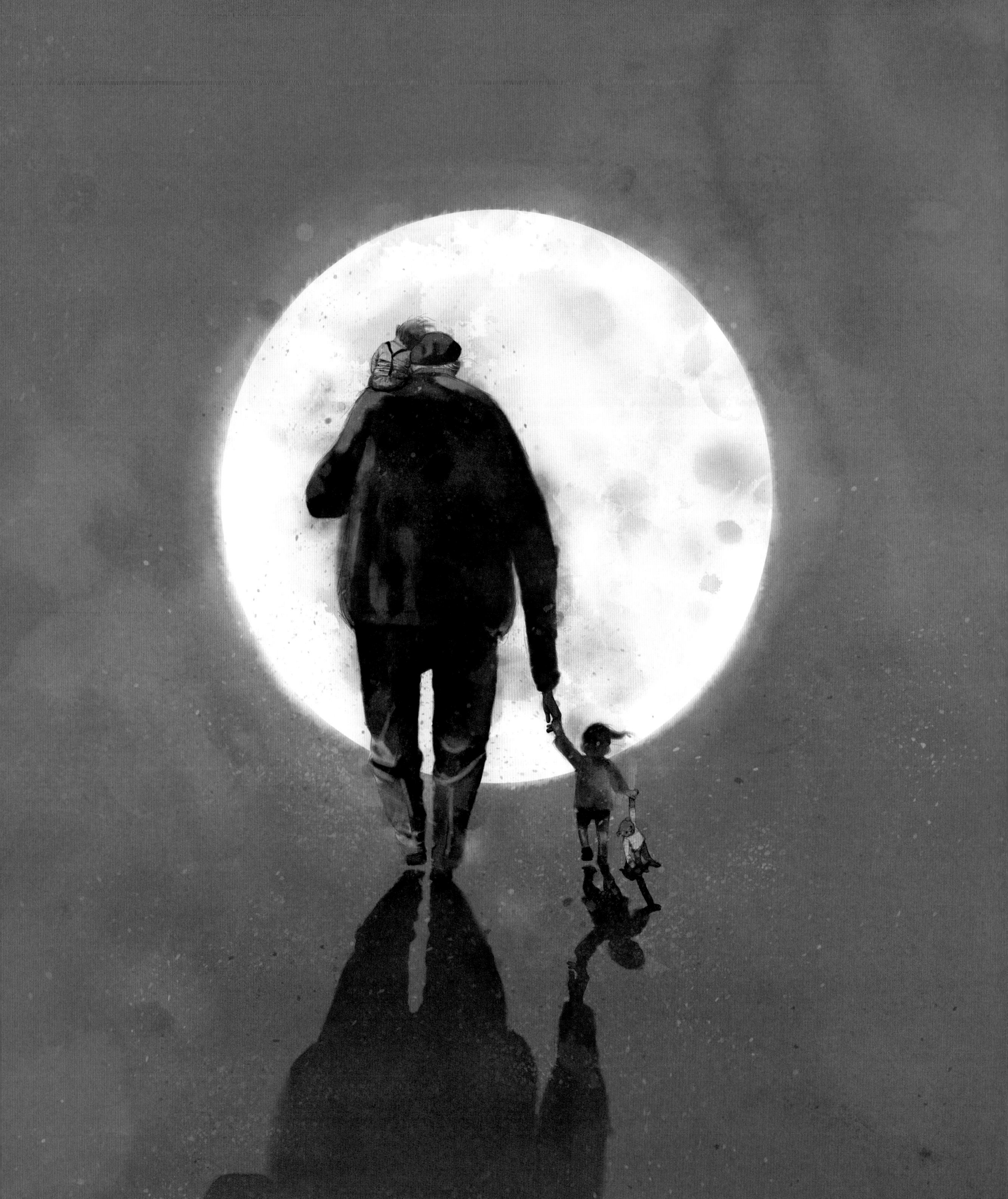

Overview of illustrations in order of appearance

Hope Your Wings Will Carry—2019

Dive—2007

Choir—2018

Daydream—2017

Student—from *Dagbladet Magasinet*, May 25, 2013

Praise—from *Dagbladet Magasinet*, March 29, 2014

Prince—from *Dagbladet Magasinet*, March 19, 2016

Winter Warm—from *Dagbladet Magasinet*, December 30, 2017

Glow—from *Dagbladet Magasinet*, November 23, 2013

Nuzzle Kiss—from *Dagbladet Magasinet*, February 13, 2016

Nuzzle Kiss 2—2018

Nuzzle Kiss 3—2018

Shelter—from *Dagbladet Magasinet*, July 8, 2017

Antisocial Media—from *Dagbladet Magasinet*, July 4, 2015

Bed of Roses—from *Dagbladet Magasinet*, February 1, 2014

Tacking—from *Dagbladet Magasinet*, July 27, 2019

Close—from *Dagbladet Magasinet*, March 15, 2014

Baby—from *Dagbladet Magasinet*, April 2, 2011

Baby Bubble—from *Dagbladet Magasinet*, March 2, 2019

Morning Mood—from *Foreldre & Barn* [Parents & Children], 2014

Home Office—2018

158, 159 …—from *Dagbladet Magasinet*, July 13, 2013

Morning Coffee—2004

Troll—from *Dagbladet Magasinet*, May 10, 2014

Time Crunch—from *Dagbladet Magasinet*, February 22, 2014

Rainfall"—from *Dagbladet Magasinet*, July 17, 2010

Everyday Love—from *Dagbladet Magasinet*, September 20, 2014

Summer Soar—from *Snart sover du* [Soon You'll Be Sleeping] by Haddy Njie,
    Cappelen Damm, 2016

Nourish—from *Vier Werte, die Kinder ein Leben lang tragen* [Four Values That Children
    Carry for a Lifetime], by Jesper Juul, Gräfe und Unzer Verlag, 2012

Young and Promising—2019

Summer Rain 2—2019

Cha-Cha-Cha—from *Snokeboka* [Snooping Around] by Lisa Aisato,
    Gyldendal Norsk Forlag, 2018

Search—from *Dagbladet Magasinet*, February 8, 2014

Summer Body—from *Dagbladet Magasinet*, June 18, 2016

Run Down—2019

Fly the Nest—2019

Quiet Night—2019

Grow—from *Dagbladet Magasinet*, October 29, 2016

Split—from *Dagbladet Magasinet*, June 23, 2018

Traces—2019

Tranquility—from *Dagbladet Magasinet*, April 20, 2019

A Helping Hand—from *Dagbladet Magasinet*, May 12, 2018

Silver Meadow—2019

Sunglasses—2019

Sprouts Youth Choir (60 Years Later)—from *Se Norges blomsterdal* [See Norway's Flower Valleys] by Ingrid Bjørnov, Vega Forlag, 2012

The Mirror Image—from *Snokeboka* [Snooping Around] by Lisa Aisato, Gyldendal Norsk Forlag, 2018

Grandma—2019

Snug—from *Dagbladet Magasinet*, December 24, 2016

Knitwear—2010

Senior Bed—2019

Queen of the Night—from *Snokeboka* [Snooping Around] by Lisa Aisato, Gyldendal Norsk Forlag, 2018

The Optimist—2008

Breaking Wave—from *Dagbladet Magasinet*, May 5, 2018

Gray-Haired Glow—from *Dagbladet Magasinet*, May 26, 2018

Surprise—from *Dagbladet Magasinet*, November 24, 2018

Stainless—from *Dagbladet Magasinet*, June 4, 2016

Super Grandpa—from *Dagbladet Magasinet*, September 12, 2015

Winter Path—from *Juleroser for barn* [Children's Christmas Roses], 2017

Unoccupied—2019

Loss—from *Dagbladet Magasinet*, August 27, 2016

Mother—2019

Timeless—from *Dagbladet Magasinet*, January 5, 2019

Grandpa—from *Dagbladet Magasinet*, February 10, 2018

Thank you to Linn Skåber, Thorvald Stoltenberg, Ingrid Bjørnov, Klaus Hagerup, Håvard Tjora, Bente Træen, Bjørk Matheasdatter, Jesper Juul, Agnes-Margrethe Bjorvand, Cathrine Moestue, Pål Johan Karlsen, Erik Bertrand Larssen, Marianne Kaurin, Thomas Marco Blatt, Einar Øverenget, and my dear sister Haddy for inspiring me with your texts over the years.

A special thanks to Gerd Børresen, Klaus Hagerud, and Mom, who told me about all of life's milestones after forty. And to my Einar. What a blessing to find the one to love.

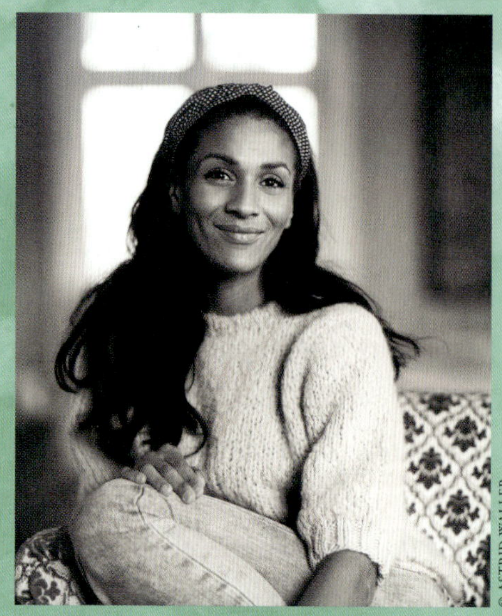

LISA AISATO has established herself as one of Norway's most celebrated illustrators. Throughout her career, she has been a magazine illustrator and written and illustrated six of her own children's books, including *Odd Is an Egg*, which was turned into an award-winning film. She has also illustrated more than thirty books for other authors, including *The Snow Sister* by Maja Lunde, which was a record-breaking success in Norway and was made into a feature film. Lisa's books have been translated into forty languages, and her artwork can be found in homes all over the world. She runs her own gallery at Hvaler islands on the Norwegian Southeast coast where she lives.

OLIVIA LASKY is an Oslo-based translator who focuses on Norwegian to English literary translations. She also translates from North Sámi, Swedish, and Danish. She received an M.A. in Scandinavian Studies from the University of Wisconsin-Madison and B.A.s in Scandinavian Studies and English Literature from the University of California-Berkeley. The winner of multiple awards, her literary translations include work by Laila Stien, Sigbjørn Skåden, and Tor Åge Bringsværd. For Arctis Books, she has translated Lisa Aisato's *All the Colors of Life*, and Marianne Kaurin's *Our Own Little Paradise*.